PRAISE FOR *MITZVAHCHIC*

"Anyone who wants to take the guesswork out of planning an upcoming bar or bat mitzvah and have a hoot doing so, must read this definitive and lively primer on the subject."

—CLEVELAND JEWISH NEWS

"With rich and colorful photographs, this is the Martha Stewart guide to bar mitzvahs."

—JEWSWEEK.COM

"Full and rich . . . I'm inspired by Greenberg's abundant creativity."

—THE WISCONSIN JEWISH CHRONICLE

"*MitzvahChic* ushers in a new style of celebration."

—THE METROWEST JEWISH REPORTER

"For parents who want to say 'This child is ours! And isn't he/she simply incredible?' *MitzvahChic* gives the road map."

—BALTIMORE JEWISH TIMES

"What distinguishes this terrific book—and its companion website—is that the emphasis is as much on the party planning as it is on the Torah portion."

—PHILADELPHIA *JEWISH EXPONENT*

"I was absolutely dreading my daughters' bat mitzvahs and the meaningless affair that would follow. Now I have so many meaningful ideas, I don't know how we'll choose and I'm utterly confident it will be a beautiful party. Words just can't express my gratitude. Thank you."

—SUSAN KLEIN

"A *huge* thank-you! We just had our son's bar mitzvah this weekend and everyone was so impressed. We did the coffee talk cards and so many people commented on the care and thoughtfulness we put into the party. Everyone had such a good time, including us. I'm sure *MitzvahChic* will be standard fare for bar/bat mitzvah parents from now on. Thank you so much!"

—SUE LASSER

"I made your spray-painted gold candle holders with 'shalom' on them. They looked gorgeous on everyone's plates and they were our party favors. I got lots and lots of jaw-dropping compliments. Thanks for the fabulous idea!"

—AMY WEBBERMAN

"If I had gotten just one idea from your book, I would have been happy. But your book was *filled* with amazing ideas. Lauren's bat mitzvah will be so meaningful and you have played a large role in that."

—STACY PELLERITO

"I don't know what people would do without a guru like you."

—NANCEE SAMLOFF

"This book does for bar and bat mitzvahs what *What to Expect When You're Expecting* does for pregnant mothers. Original party concepts and tips, what's hot and what's not, traditional vs. modern, it has it all. Whether you are having a small celebration or an over-the-top affair, this book is a must-have."

—KIM, A MOTHER OF THREE DAUGHTERS

mitzvah*chic*

How to Host a Meaningful, Fun, and Drop-dead Gorgeous
Bar or Bat Mitzvah

Gail Anthony Greenberg

A Fireside Book

Published by Simon & Schuster

New York   London   Toronto   Sydney

FIRESIDE
Rockefeller Center
1230 Avenue of the Americas
New York, NY 10020

First Fireside Edition 2006

FIRESIDE and colophon are registered trademarks
of Simon & Schuster, Inc.

For information regarding special discounts for bulk purchases,
please contact Simon & Schuster Special Sales at 1-800-456-6798
or business@simonandschuster.com.

Designed by Ruth Lee-Mui

Manufactured in the United States of America

10   9   8   7   6   5   4   3   2   1

ISBN-13: 978-0-7432-8492-9
ISBN-10:   0-7432-8492-5

*To Neil, the most loving husband a girl could have
and a great "rabbi" in his own right.*

*And to Gabriel, Griffin, and Julia, who made me first a mother
and then a believer in how precious it all is.*

Acknowledgments

A book starts as a solitary idea in the quiet room of one person's mind and finishes as a circus come to town. Through daily encounters with interested bystanders, books naturally evolve into a showcase of many people's insights and talent. An embarrassment of riches. Many chapters in this book were suggested or shaped by friends; other ideas dropped like pearls from the steam let off by frustrated parents I barely knew. I am grateful to all of them. In particular, I want to thank

My partner, Steve Kirschner, and all the people who "loaned" him to me

Robin Warshaw for telling me to write this book and coaching me through it

Belinda Hulin and Craig McCoy for copyediting it

Rabbi Lance Sussman for verifying all Jewish material

My original designer, Jacqueline Bofinger

Photographer Weaver Lilley and stylist Sherry Vitale

Printer Mark Bofinger of Colorlith Corporation

Contributors Benjamin Barnett and Tina Viletto

Graphic designers Liz West and Bill Bosler

Web guru Eli Garcia plus Matt Kapusta, Denise Vone, and the Membex team

And especially Caroline Bachman, for giving me wings.

Thanks also to the many people who generously shared their help and encouragement and—some without knowing—inspired me: Debbie and John Anthony, John Anthony Sr., Rosemary and Mark Anthony, Dina Baker, Barbra Berley-Mellits, Joan Blumberg, Maya Chayot, Joan Chevalier, Carol Chodak, Georgeanne Delgado, Rhea Dennis, Bill Ferstenfeld, Ron Gornstein, David and Lori Kaplan, Pamela and Heather Kates, Shari and Jodi Lazarus, Sally Leifer, Tiffany Lenherr, Ricki and Tony Lent, Linda and Paul Macht, Jennifer Miller-Davis, Ronnie Moomjian, Alene Nachsin, Linda Podietz, Nancy and David Rackow, Nancy and Carly Schaer, Carole Sheffield, Liz Alperin Solms, Emily Sullivan, and Janis Wilkoff.

Thank you to my family and friends, some of whom are named above. What a gift you have been to me. I love you all.

Finally, Samuel Johnson said, "The true measure of a man is how he treats someone who can do him absolutely no good." My deepest gratitude to Sam Raimi and Rabbi Harold Kushner, who supported me even though I could do them absolutely no good. You are princes among men.

Contents

A wacky, eclectic grab bag of information you'll need to create some of the projects or moments in this book. Includes prayers, a recipe for manna, and a suggested playlist for a CD of freedom songs.

Why You Need This Book

In the spirit of full disclosure, there are a handful of other bar/bat mitzvah planning books out there. Most are written by Jewish clergy or at least very observant Jewish people who know a lot about the ritual and want to explain it all to you. Although these are very important reference books, I found when I was a first-time planner that most gave too much information and too little real guidance on all the practical matters that parents struggle with. They went into great detail about how rituals vary at different synagogues but didn't answer some of the most basic questions of all:

> How can I—a normal nonscholarly person—get interested in what my child is studying?

> How can I better connect with my feelings of "Jewishness" at this most Jewish time in life?

> Or, presuming I know Torah and feel Jewish, how do I use it in the party . . . and keep it fun and engaging? How do I do justice, *partywise,* to this very powerful Jewish experience?

At best, the books paid little attention to the party; at worst, they implied that it's unseemly to care about the party at all. I understand where they're coming from. It's frustrating to devout people to see the attention lavished on bar/bat mitzvah parties, particularly when the parents cannot even say what their child's Torah portion is about. But the people who criticize those over-the-top parents have also missed some important points: First, parents of a child becoming a bar/bat mitzvah need *big* ways to express the overwhelming pride and happiness they feel; and second, no one has shown them a good alternative. A bar/bat mitzvah is an emotional high point in the life of a family—we all feel this potential and don't want to shortchange ourselves in any way.

This book is written by a parent for other parents planning a bar or bat mitzvah for their child. Parents who may know a lot about Judaism but not about how to throw a soulful and captivating party. Parents who can give an okay party but aren't really connected with what we're celebrating because the deeply philosophical "Jewish part" just seems too difficult to understand and use. Parents who lack confidence in both areas. Parents who, for whatever reason, are *not* loving every minute of this!

When you pick up a bar/bat mitzvah planning book, you should feel like you're "home," that you now have all the answers you need. The book should sing to you, "Rejoice! This will be such a special day . . . let me show you how!"

I set out to write such a book because I was once a parent with a date and a sense of utter bewilderment. Where to begin? I had resources—I was a professional writer and craft artist, meaning I had the ability to research what I needed to know and mold it into something attractive to put on a table. But even I was overwhelmed. Neither the serious bar/bat mitzvah books nor the frivolous party-planning books seemed to cover all the bases, and how could they? To really hit a home run when planning a bar or bat mitzvah, you need a command of the serious *and* frivolous. It may look similar to any big party, but it's not nearly as simple as, say, planning a sweet 16 party, because it's an event that's about ideas—first, the idea that your child is embracing the Torah, and finally the great ideas of the Torah itself.

In the process of writing this book, I went from having zero knowledge of the Torah to being in awe of it. I found a trail to take you inside the scroll that is the heart of the bar/bat mitzvah and the Jewish experience. That's how I can promise that, with surprisingly little additional effort, you too can experience the wonder, whether you consider yourself religious or not. And, having experienced wonder, you will inevitably host an event more moving and evocative than most people will ever achieve. And who knows where that will lead you . . . as a Jew and as a human being?

Parents lose a lot of precious time stressing over the "hows." How to figure it all out successfully, meet their own high expectations, and get the most out of the lavish financial and emotional sums required for even modest events. The demands keep many of us from really experiencing this magical time with our child. I wanted to write a book that would vastly simplify the process of planning an incredible event so that parents would be free to think, dream . . . and take the journey.

There is a whole world of wonderful ideas and resources out there that can make your mitzvah experience transcendent. They've never been compiled into one simple-to-use resource until now. *MitzvahChic* is a celebration of taste and style that also has soul, passion, and intellect. It's the thinking person's guide to expressing compelling ideas with style and élan.

No book, though, can answer everyone's questions, and that's why this book has been developed in concert with a website—www.MitzvahChic .com. Go there to talk to me and your fellow planners, to get ideas, and to find the links for products and organizations described in *MitzvahChic*. One of the most exciting features you'll find is a calendar where you can post your child's party date and time—and see the dates and times of others from your town—to avoid conflicts with your child's friends. Encourage every mitzvah-planning family you know to sign on here so that this becomes a really useful tool for everyone.

Once you're on the calendar, you will have a custom planning time line created for you on the site and you will receive planning reminders via email. This will let you relax with full confidence that, when it's time to handle another planning detail, we'll give you a prompt wake-up call and a handy checklist!

How to Use the Book

Use the time line in the back of *MitzvahChic* to get a rough idea now of the sequence of steps in planning your event. It will also help you understand how to use this book and the website. Then go forth with confidence. You will astound yourself with what you can achieve. May this special day you're planning be not just the thrilling end to one chapter but also the beginning of a life of renewed interest and pride in the enormous gift that Judaism has been to the world and to all of us who embrace it.

Introduction

One Bar Mitzvah, Hold the Camels

We've all attended, or chuckled at the mention of, bar and bat mitzvahs that the hosts considered ultimate achievements in event design. Hollywood dramas where the bat mitzvah was dressed as Cleopatra and carried to the banquet on a litter borne by slaves; '80s-era megaproductions where the bar mitzvah, dressed as Luke Skywalker, fights a choreographed battle with Darth Vader complete with special lighting and sound effects; or the relatively low-key affairs where the theme is simply "football" . . . but the entertainment is the Dallas Cowboys cheerleaders.

In the quest to create a memorable event, bat mitzvah parents have hosted medieval jousts, roller derbys, and space launches. They've re-created Vesuvius erupting over Pompeii, Studio 54, and the Hanging Gardens of Babylon. They've hired troupes of Polynesian fire dancers, Chinese acrobats, robot dogs, Tony Bennett, and the entire touring company of *Grease*.

It would be easy to be cruel about all this—the misspent fortunes and misdirected energy. But at the heart of all the excess is a very natural, human, *parental* desire to make the appropriate fuss, to express what words alone cannot seem to convey. To say, via camels, flaming headdresses, and light sabers, *This child is ours! And isn't he simply incredible?*

And rightly so. There are few enough occasions when you can get up and unabashedly declare how proud you are of your kids. Once they're in the teen years, even fewer occasions, frankly, when you will even *feel* like it. This is their moment to shine . . . and yours to gaze in wonder.

How do you make the most of it and capture all the magic and majesty of this once-in-a-lifetime experience? In the past, there were two schools of thought: Keep it simple, meaningful, and sincere . . . and risk having an event that feels drab, skimpy, and underwhelming. Or—bring on the camels!—adopt an outrageous theme and go to town with the decorating and entertainment. That approach fails in its own way by producing events that are dazzling while you're there but digest emotionally like fine pastry. Delicious on the lips, but almost totally lacking in substance, spiritual nourishment, and stick-to-your-ribs memorability.

People who consider themselves religious have shunned glamour because they think big bashes with themes trivialize and overshadow the bar mitzvah experience. The glamorous folk have shied away from being too religious because they fear it will suck the life out of an otherwise fabulous party!

How happy they will all be to discover there's a new, integrated way to go: *MitzvahChic,* the notion that the mitzvah—the good works and the meaning—can be fused with high style. More than just fused. *MitzvahChic* holds that the meaning and the joy, artfully expressed, are what make the celebration magical. *MitzvahChic* is a blueprint for how a family can have an amazing bar mitzvah experience and use their emotion to electrify their party.

Anyone can hire a decorator to create some mind-altering backdrop; what makes a bar mitzvah truly wonderful is the way it expresses who you are as a family and how this very special event—already experienced by millions before you—is still somehow uniquely your own. Have an experience that is soul satisfying and that works on every level by being fun, poignant, cool, moving, exciting, and completely unforgettable. Enter the *MitzvahChic* zone and have an absolutely perfect bar or bat mitzvah.

one Why Is This Party Duller Than All Others?

The party is not the most important part of a bar mitzvah, but it's a good place to start explaining why *MitzvahChic* thinking is so needed in the world. The party's the thing we parents tend to obsess over. When you receive your child's bar mitzvah date one to two or more years ahead of time, be honest: Your first thought generally isn't "How am I going to make sure he knows the Hebrew by then?" It's "Ohmigosh, where should we have the party?" This is not a failure of priorities; it's only natural. The rabbis, cantors, and tutors work on the service; we plan the celebration, right? Well, not exactly, and I'll take a look soon at how to get more involved in the service. But meanwhile, let's talk about that party.

It's not hard to throw a party, but it is hard to throw a good one. There are lots of things that can ruin a party; these same things, well handled, can also make a party wonderful. The trick is knowing how. Every bat mitzvah is planned to be wonderful and the family always has fun. The relief they feel plus the emotional high is enough to produce euphoria for them. So we needn't be concerned about them having a good time. This chapter is really about how to make the experience feel that good to everyone else. Then, of course, the love and gratitude that come pouring back and the knowledge that they have made the day wonderful for their guests will give the family still more lasting satisfaction.

Groundhog Day Syndrome

Since you're in a Jewish family, you've probably been to several bar mitzvahs, and probably a lot of them seemed the same. The decorating and, of course, the guest of honor change, but little else seems to. If you live in a midsize to small town where there are few choices of banquet halls, DJs, etc., it can feel like a Jewish version of the movie *Groundhog Day*—you just keep waking up and going to the same bar mitzvah over and over again.

I live on the edge of a big city where the choices are truly endless. Yet the Groundhog Day scenario happens here too. It's simply because we all go to each other's events, we like the band or the restaurant, and we decide to use it as well.

But is it that simple? There's a subtle psychology working here. Sometimes we duplicate each other's bat mitzvahs because we do truly like what other people have done or because we don't have the time to go out and reinvent the wheel. But there can be another, more powerful reason: We unconsciously copy our friends because we're afraid to stray from the formula. We're afraid if we do something new or different—something truly *us*—and it's not as good as the old standby, we will be judged harshly by our peers and (gulp!) our mothers-in-law. We'll go down in local history as having thrown a bad party, we'll have ruined our child's big day, and we'll feel personally rejected as well because, after all, in the chilly light of day, whose taste and ideas did the guests find lacking?

The Hazards of Being Yourself

If you really put yourself into the plans, really make the event your own, and it's a flop, are you going to feel, "Well, so I'm not a great bar mitzvah planner. Big deal"? Or is your inner voice going to sound more like your mother's and say something like, "You did your own thing and it was a disaster. You're not creative; you never were. You should have just done everything the way cousin Debbie did it for Josh's party!"?

For most of us, there's a lot on the line when we plan a bat mitzvah. It's no wonder you get nervous and your head and stomach ache every time you think about it. Apart from your concerns for your child and how all the pressure may affect her, plus the big money involved, consider this: The bat mitzvah may actually be the first big event that we plan *all by ourselves*. That's a lot of pressure.

If you married in your twenties and your parents paid for the wedding, it's likely they had a lot to say about the arrangements. We all complain about how our mothers made us invite so-and-so and hire an orchestra instead of a DJ because it was more elegant and so on. But the bottom line is that having someone bossing you around, setting parameters, and voting on all your decisions actually made things easier! There was less to think about. Fewer decisions to make . . . or to get wrong. A more experienced person to guide you. And someone to share the responsibility for anything that didn't go well.

At the time of your first child's bar mitzvah, you stand alone for the first time before a blank canvas. And you contemplate—in party terms— who you are and what you want to say with this piece: Do I want my event to be modern or traditional, splashy or subtle, big or intimate?

Most artists and writers will tell you that the moment they confront the vast emptiness of a blank canvas or page is always very powerful and daunting, even when you have a lot of experience doing it. Which you don't. Even many seasoned veterans report that their minds initially go blank and they feel a fleeting sense of panic.

Being Judged on Your "Bar Mitzvability"

With this first bat mitzvah, you make your debut as someone who's either "good at these things" or not. Worse yet, you may live in a community where the fashionable moms before you have set an incredibly high standard for how creative and fabulous a party must be before it's considered even minimally acceptable. The blank-canvas analogy is dead-on: The bat mitzvah is like a big art project being judged on creativity, content, and overall brilliance.

No wonder all but the most confident bar mitzvah parents run for help to party planners, the surrogate mothers and fathers of event hosting. These people, like your parents at your wedding, will narrow your choices, guide you, and tell you in a nice way when you're wrong. In short, they will make things much easier for you.

Why So Many Events Feel Generic

Party planners and other event professionals—the decorators, the DJs, the florists—are hugely helpful when you're planning an event of this complexity because they know from experience what works and they can keep you from making mistakes. Be aware, though, that doing things the way "everyone does them" is also what threatens to make your event feel a bit stale. You need to find that middle ground where you're accepting good advice from your vendors on routine matters but also challenging them to help you present yourself and your experience in a unique way. You may be their thousandth bat mitzvah client, but your planning should still begin with a contemplation of who you and your child are and what makes your experience one of a kind.

Many parties fail to excite because they are generic; you could plug any bar or bat mitzvah child into almost any one and he or she would fit, more or less. A party like that presents your bar mitzvah experience as just one more rolling off an assembly line. It's the antithesis of *MitzvahChic*, which focuses on how every child and family is different, not on what they may have in common.

We are all in a bit of a rut, we party givers. There are always new products and technologies to make parties more visually dazzling, but when you talk about bar or bat mitzvahs particularly, the content of them hasn't changed at all in decades! I recently flipped through my husband's bar mitzvah album from the 1950s. In terms of the content—what happened—it was the same party I attended a week ago. You could go down a checklist: There's the hora, there's the candlelighting. All that had changed were the clothes and hairstyles! You may say, What else is there? Well, I'm glad you asked! There are three necessary ingredients in cooking up a transformative party experience.

Fun People

What could feel better than a room full of happy, engaging, charismatic people? They infect everyone with their adorable energy. If your friends and family are not fun, don't despair. You can put them into fun mode by pampering them, flattering them, and giving them whimsical things to see and do.

Magical Moments

These are the heart-stopping speeches and ceremonies that, when done correctly, produce that experience-of-a-lifetime feeling. Like watching a bride dance with her father and feeling all the excitement and loss contained in that moment, these stir our deepest emotions. At bar/bat mitzvahs, we've had nothing but the candlelighting ceremony to be the heart and soul of the event. It was never adequate and now it's a worn-out idea. I'll talk about alternatives and how to infuse the whole party experience with layers of meaning and mystery.

Delightful Surprises

A great dessert, a particularly beautiful decoration on the table. Like a simple outfit with an amazing pair of shoes, a few grace notes—a few well-placed sensuous delights—have the power to bowl guests over.

My goal with this book is to help you use these ingredients to make your event not only richly satisfying for everyone there but also the experience that no one will be able to stop talking about for years. The do-it-yourselfers may want to do a lot of the work themselves, but you certainly don't need to. For every suggestion I make in this book, there is a professional ready to perform the actual labor. The book will help you figure out what you want and whom you need. Once you do, you will be able to give good specific direction to your contractors. If you use event planners, this book will make their job easier and help you get their best work.

two Where Party Excitement Comes From

So now we've analyzed why so many bar mitzvahs look and feel generic and interchangeable. And why so many parents don't like to tinker with the "formula" for success. If tired, overused ideas and dreary sameness make parties dull, what on the flip side makes them wonderful? Doing something different, obviously, but it's trickier than that. Every bar mitzvah parent who has turned a banquet room into medieval Venice or hired a trained monkey or a robot dog was trying to do something different, something he or she hadn't seen before.

But eye-catching decorations and amusing entertainment alone aren't the answer. They make a beautiful wrapper, but what's inside the package? To return to my earlier analogy, dazzling decor is pastry. Guests at a real party want a meal, sustenance. It's not enough to handle the superficial details—the production values—in an original way; you need to provide real excitement. You need to infuse your party with life and a special energy.

So how do you make a party exciting? Well, I would ask you, what makes anything exciting? You probably instinctively know the answer I have in mind but have never put it into words and certainly haven't dreamed of applying it to a party.

For the sake of the people who like guessing, let's sneak up on the answer in a roundabout way. What are some of the most popular categories of television show? Reality shows and talk shows, right? And what kind of talk shows do we find most compelling?

Not the author visits or the famous person interviews. Human dramas—ordinary people living through extraordinary events. Like a book you can't put down, there are shows we cannot look away from: reunions of parents and children separated at birth, people growing from tragedy and triumphing over grim circumstances.

We love to see the heroes of the world recognized and rewarded. We love the cops and the firefighters, but also the unintentional heroes. Teachers who inspire, grandmothers who selflessly raise their children's children, and regular people who find courage in a moment of crisis. Television guests share their feelings and experiences more openly than all but our closest friends, and we can't get enough. Unless, of course, they're *Jerry Springer* guests.

Let's Get Emotional

We love celebrating things that are uniquely human. We feel proud and inspired by the example of someone's decency; we think, "Maybe I have that in me too." We are deeply moved to witness great humanity in all its forms.

People learn and experience things through each other. We are all students of life, and the world is our classroom. It is also our roller coaster—we reach great highs and lows by watching other people go through their own agonies and ecstasies. The ancient Greeks understood how compelling and satisfying it is to "join in" emotionally while watching other people. The characters and situations in their stage dramas were specifically designed to trigger catharsis, huge outpourings of emotion in the audience. Thus, in the pretherapy era, theatergoers of old could count on releasing their pent-up sadness or kicking up their mood just by going to watch a simple entertainment.

Few of us, thankfully, have lives of huge ups and downs. Mostly, life is routine and predictable. It hums along, only occasionally punctuated with moments of great joy or sorrow. Getting in on other people's joyous moments, then, is a way of adding to our own lifetime supply of emotional highs.

It's also the truest kind of thrill. When virtual reality technology first came on the scene, everyone was excited about the prospect of being able to clamp on a helmet and know, from the safety of an armchair, what it was like to jump out of an airplane, climb Mt. Everest, or raft down the world's wildest rivers. But I always thought the ultimate adventure would be found not in the outside world but inside the heart and head of another person at some incredible moment of his or her life.

Imagine if you could be inside the mind of an Olympic athlete at the moment she realizes she's won the gold. Or inside the heart of an ordinary man gazing for the first time at his newborn baby. Personally, if virtual reality ever becomes a practical reality and you can customize the experience, one of the things I would most like to experience again is how it felt to have my toddler daughter's soft little hand in mine when we walked together on a beautiful spring day. How much I would love to revisit the overwhelming feelings of peace and contentment.

Making It Special

There, see? We just shared a moment, and it was rather special, wasn't it? Now what does this have to do with throwing a party? Just this: Your guests will be delighted by good food, beautiful decorating, and wonderful music—you should definitely give them that. But the most magical thing—the only unique thing—you can give them is yourself, access to the world inside of you on this amazing day. You can, through your words and deeds, give them some affecting, magical moments in the course of a party. Moments where they make a connection with you, with Judaism, and with the compelling symbolism of the day and feel the enormity of it. "Eight Complete Parties That Will Leave You *Farklempt!*" and "Party Ideas for Each Torah Portion" later in this book give dozens of specific ways to do this. And "The Major Party Decisions You Have to Make First" and "The Little Party Details That Really Matter," as well as the speechwriting chapter, will help you get the maximum impact from everything you plan and do.

Delivering affecting moments isn't hard to do, and it's extremely worthwhile because it elevates your event from mere celebration to compelling human experience. It will also make this bar mitzvah passage even more special for you because, on top of the religious significance, you will feel that you have made a real connection simultaneously with all the people who are important in your life.

The *MitzvahChic* plan, in essence, is to first help the family have a big, meaningful, and exciting bat mitzvah experience for themselves. And then to help the family express the power and thrill in a way that lets the celebrants feel it too.

This doesn't require reinventing the bar mitzvah wheel. You don't need to throw away all the elements of the traditional celebration in order to achieve *MitzvahChic*. You do need, though, to rethink some traditions and to add some new ideas. And let's not forget the "chic." You need to make sure your celebration, rich now in feeling and excitement, is also an absolutely glorious-looking party. Where every detail is considered and beautifully executed.

three Ordinary vs. *MitzvahChic:* Which One Is for You?

We could go back and forth forever tossing out one-liners about what is and is not *MitzvahChic*. But you've got an event to plan, so let's crack open the playbook. Here are the fundamental differences between what old-style and *MitzvahChic* celebrations seek to accomplish.

Goals for an ordinary event

- To honor the bar/bat mitzvah child and family
- To host a dazzling party

Goals for a *MitzvahChic* event

- To honor the bar/bat mitzvah child and family
- To give everyone entrée into the family's euphoria
- To make guests feel treasured
- To have the party be dazzling . . . but then take it to a new level
  - To pursue a higher order of meaning and relevance by keeping the celebration focused on the child and the message of mitzvah
  - To pursue a higher order of chic by avoiding the ordinary and employing only fabulous solutions to the classic dilemmas

Catch the Euphoria

If you started this book at the beginning and read continuously to this point, you already understand the part about the joys of getting emotional. If not, see "Where Party Excitement Comes From."

Let it suffice to say, your guests want to plug into your emotional energy on such an important day. Both because of the excitement and buzz it will give them and because being with you and sharing a big experience affirms their connection with you.

Make Guests Feel Treasured

Moving down the lists of party models, one of the first things you'll probably notice is that in a *MitzvahChic* celebration, there is a greater-than-customary emphasis on the guests: their feelings, their experience of your bat mitzvah. Traditionally, guests have been treated as the audience. They sit attentively—initially for the child's Torah reading but also later at the party. We count on our guests—our family and closest friends—to support us through our pre–bat mitzvah frazzles and to praise our child and us lavishly on the big day, but we frankly don't give much back to them in terms of a role and a sense of importance.

In the traditional model, guests have been relegated to the sidelines, allowed only to dance or make the occasional toast. They've been forced to sit through interminable candlelightings that don't include them and speeches that don't even fleetingly recognize their fundamental importance in your life. And then we expect them to clap appreciatively afterward.

These are the most important people in our world; in social terms, they *are* our world. So why don't we treasure them more? Frankly, I have no clue. It would never happen this way in, say, Italy. Virtually every movie made that shows Italians at a wedding includes someone getting drunk and getting up and telling everyone how much he or she loves them. We all laugh but, really, isn't that the way it should be—not the getting drunk part, just the part about cherishing your friends? And making it clear that you do?

So this is something qualitatively different in *MitzvahChic:* the guest as participant, key player, and occasionally even focus of the celebration. If you can imagine such a thing! But wait, let's stop and imagine it for a second. What if a friend told you over lunch one day how important you are to her and how much she appreciates having you in her life? Or let's assume your friend is shy and could never actually speak those words but instead did lots of little thoughtful things—like remembering how you like your coffee and calling you on every major holiday for a whole year after you've lost a loved one just to make sure you're okay? It would be quite wonderful, *non*? Well, at this party you're going to do exactly that for all your friends. You're going to make it clear that you think about and treasure them—not necessarily using words alone, but by the way you consider them in every aspect of your planning.

This is not only the right thing to do; it also will energize your party because it will make your friends and family feel happy. People in a playful, happy mood are obviously a lot more fun than any other kind of guest, and they're capable of doing all kinds of spontaneous cool things that will make your party feel exuberant, more like a "happening" than a scripted affair.

Which raises another important point. It's a host's job to anticipate the needs of the guests. On the most basic level this means knowing if someone has special food needs (vegetarian, allergies), needs babysitting at the party in order to be at ease, etc. Beyond that, *MitzvahChic* requires you to take it up a notch and tend to your guests on a higher level by valuing them, recognizing their worth, and building a sense of connectedness with them. But whatever plans you make for your guests, you shouldn't confuse being a thoughtful host with being a micromanager.

You already understand that your guests are all different: Some are introverts; some are party animals. Some would dive under the table if you put a microphone in their face and asked them to say a few words; others will grab the mike and never give it back to you.

So it's important to recognize these differences and not put people on the spot by requiring them to say or do things that make them uncomfortable. Create opportunities for people to jump into the festivities, but don't require them to do it. The most successful hosts create an atmosphere where guests feel comfortable, excited, and inspired. Hence, the hosts create the conditions where exciting things can happen on their own. They don't try to control everything and make it happen.

Having successfully created such an atmosphere, you can be sure your guests will respond. You may not see grandiose displays of enthusiasm—people dancing for sheer joy on the tops of tables—but even their interactions with each other will be more animated and fun. And you will likely have a lot of guests tell you afterward how much they enjoyed the people they were sitting with.

Keep the Focus on Your Child
and the Message of Mitzvah

Bar mitzvah embraces two concepts: *bar* meaning "son" and *mitzvah* meaning "commandment." A bar mitzvah is literally "son of the commandment." On a boy's thirteenth birthday (it's age twelve for girls), he is automatically a bar mitzvah, even if he doesn't read Torah or have a party. It simply means that he has reached the age where he assumes the ritual obligations and receives the privileges accorded to adults under Jewish law. Becoming a full-fledged member of any religion is a very important milestone, so much so that every faith has its own way of marking the occasion.

It's important when planning a bat mitzvah to keep in mind that this is the true reason we gather: to celebrate a young woman's emergence from the tiny community of her family to the larger world of a faith-based community. In the case of Judaism, it is a community that has existed for millennia; it has a majestic and sweeping beauty and an astonishing history of both embracing blessings and handling tragedy with conviction and equanimity. This is a religion that gives things *to* you and asks things *of* you . . . even that you theoretically be willing to perish—as so many have—for its sake. It's an awesome thing to think about and for a thirteen-year-old child to do.

That is perhaps why I feel personally so depressed to go from an inspiring service in the sanctuary, with its contemplation of all the meaning and symbolism of the day, to a reception hall that's decorated with . . . hockey sticks. And has nothing else to say—not about the child, the family, or the day.

No doubt your children love to play, or watch, hockey. Or they love art. Or the beach. But is that really it, the best we can do? Is that *who* they are? And all that this event is going to be about?

Kids at this age are growing and changing very quickly. Even the people who have known them all their lives may feel, in some sense, that they're meeting them for the first time on bar mitzvah day. As a grown-up at a bar mitzvah, I know for sure that the guest of honor is not going to hang around and chat with me. No newly minted teenager has the slightest interest in indulging the adults a minute longer than he has to. Still, I want to leave at the end of that party knowing more about the bar mitzvah boy than I knew going in.

I want to catch up on who he is and trade observations with my fellow child-raising village members. We're here for him and his family, and I am totally with the program. I want to know him now because I knew him when he was smaller and I'm going to know him when he's bigger . . . and when he marries . . . and when he has kids of his own. His family and mine share a life together. And knowing him—and them—at every stage makes it a richer experience. We have history with each other.

To me, learning about the bat mitzvah girl means I want to see photos, quotations from her, or other personal effects. This is easy to do and it's fun. It also simplifies your decorating decisions by giving you a clear mission.

I also want to feel like the Torah and the idea of mitzvah got a nod somewhere along the line. *Mitzvah* means "commandment," but people use it more generically to mean a "good deed." The world, the Talmud says, stands on three things: worship, Torah, and good deeds. Performing charitable mitzvot before, during, and/or after the bar mitzvah is a great way to introduce a child transitioning to adulthood to the very grown-up responsibility of considering the plight of others and trying to do something about it. See "Making the Event More of a Mitzvah."

The Hebrew word that is used to mean "charity" is *tzedakah*. But tzedakah literally translates as "justice." This is a really inspiring idea. It says that when we give to someone who has less than we do, we're making an effort to restore justice to the world. Not every community recognizes an individual's obligation to create justice, but the Jewish community does. Even after suffering great injustice ourselves. This is a very life-affirming, inspiring vision, one that's well worth celebrating at your bar mitzvah.

Many synagogues require the bat mitzvah and her family to complete a "mitzvah project" prior to the service. Even without this requirement, though, some bat mitzvah parents and kids go to great lengths to make the celebration itself a mitzvah. Some request, for example, that everyone bring canned food to the service or donate to a charity in lieu of giving a gift. Others buy items from charitable organizations for use at the service or party. If you're interested in doing that, refer to "Making the Event More of a Mitzvah" or visit www.MitzvahChic.com to find suggestions and direct access to charitable organizations offering appropriate products.

The ultimate realization of the concept—and some people have done this—is to cancel the bar mitzvah party entirely and give the money instead to charity. But that seems rather extreme. Is it in fact a mitzvah to give your family and friends no chance to celebrate with you? Further, it is considered a mitzvah for a father to make a festive meal for dear ones on the day his son reaches the age of bar mitzvah. Whether or not you perform special charitable mitzvot on this occasion, remember that performing mitzvot and giving tzedakah are lifelong duties, not something to do just on special occasions. Focus on being a good Jew and raising your children to be good Jews, and every day you will be contributing something wonderful to the world.

Avoid the Ordinary—Use Only Fabulous Solutions

This is self-explanatory. Seek novel and beautiful ideas throughout. When confronted with a choice, go with the one your instinct tells you is the winner. Don't talk yourself into something because it's more practical or, heaven forbid, the one your mother would approve of.

This is *not*, however, permission to overspend. It's unseemly and undignified—and totally not *MitzvahChic*—to be someone you're not and try to come off as richer, grander, or . . . whatever. Your job is to be who you are and to reveal the essential fabulousness of it! There are great ideas for decorating, party favors, etc., at every price level. I constantly look for them so I can put them up on my website. See what's out there, set a realistic budget, and stick to it. And, within the affordable options, choose with the goal of surprising your guests and delighting yourself.

If your budget is modest, don't try to beat the big-bucks crowd at their own game. If a party favor at one big-budget event in your community is a very high-quality Kate Spade–type bag with the bat mitzvah's name replacing Kate's as the logo, for goodness sake, don't go out and try to find a lower-cost version of the same thing. Go in some completely other direction. Give out paint cans with a custom label (easily done at Kinko's) and filled with spa items and everything else your daughter's friends will need to have a wonderful sleepover together on some future evening. It will be innovative and refreshing, and none of the competitive scorekeeping parents will be able to peg you as a big spender or a hopeless miser. They won't even think about how much you spent—they'll just wish they knew how to be half as cool and creative! See "Crafts for Style and Therapy" for the particulars on making this project.

When planning a big multidimensional party, it's relatively easy to find out who are the good caterers, DJs, bands, etc. In fact, MitzvahChic .com has a huge directory of vendors who specifically want to serve bar/bat mitzvah families. It's much harder to find good ideas and sources for the smaller things like the party favors, place card holders, and room and tabletop decor. (Though—*ta-da!*—they are also in my online directory.) In addition, two chapters, "Party Ideas for Each Torah Portion" and "Eight Complete Parties That Will Leave You *Farklempt!*" are full of decorating and party ideas.

I hope this book will answer all your questions and solve all your problems—well, the ones related to your mitzvah planning, anyway. But if it doesn't, go to www.MitzvahChic.com to send me an email or ask a question on our message boards and get input from recent veterans or other parents still in planning mode.

four The Major Party Decisions You Have to Make First

Why, you may be thinking if you're the confident type, do you need help to plan a party? No doubt you've thrown a few birthday parties and, except for the fact that the clown you once hired was drunk and the purple dinosaur on another occasion never showed up, there were no *real* disasters! Well, first it's a matter of scale. Even modest catered affairs in hired halls today cost more than houses did when we were children and are similarly bursting with fine detail. And then, of course, you are reaching for a considerably higher standard than a party that simply has no disasters. You're spending big bucks and investing great emotional energy, and you want wonderful. Period.

Can you figure it all out by yourself? I think actor Mickey Rourke is perhaps best qualified to answer that question. In the movie *Body Heat*, Mickey plays a bomb expert who's on parole and trying to go straight. When good guy William Hurt comes to him for advice on how to blow something up, Mickey tries to dissuade him by saying, "Whenever you try to do something like this, there are fifty ways to [mess] up. And if you think of twenty-five of them, you're a genius."

Why, he could just as easily be talking about planning a big party! William Hurt, he points out, is no genius—and neither is the typical bat mitzvah–planning parent. You may be a genius as a doctor, or a baker, or a parent, but you're not a genius at this. Not yet. Someday, after you've planned several big parties, you may be a genius. But by then it will be too late—you'll be done already. This can make people bitter, or it can make them . . . write a book! Obviously, I've made my choice.

But even though you're not a bar mitzvah genius, don't worry. I've picked the brains of lots of bar mitzvah geniuses and synthesized their advice. By reading this book, you have zoomed ahead along the learning curve, like hitting one of the up-going slides in the Chutes and Ladders game. So here, without further ado, are the main things you need to consider in planning your party.

What Time of Day and Year Will You Have It?

Orthodox and some Conservative synagogues have Torah services three times per week: Monday, Thursday, and Saturday. Most Reform and Reconstructionist congregations have them only on Saturday morning or, rarely, Friday night. The overwhelming preference for b'nai mitzvah families is to have their child participate in a service on Shabbat. But even here, there may be a few options: Friday evening service, Saturday morning service, or a late-day Saturday service that includes the havdalah ceremony marking the end of Shabbat at sundown. Typically, the Torah is not read at the havdalah service, though special arrangements can often be made to include it. Because the demands on the child to read Hebrew are significantly less at a havdalah service, this is often the service preferred by families whose child has a reading disability or other issue that makes the bat mitzvah preparation particularly difficult.

The rules and customs vary from synagogue to synagogue, so you should check early on with your own congregation to see what your options are. What difference does it make participating in the morning or evening service? Well, Orthodox and Conservative Jews do not have celebrations on Shabbat that include alcohol or music. So a drinks-and-dancing party that follows a Saturday morning service cannot be held until after sundown on Saturday. If the bar mitzvah is happening at a time of year when sundown occurs rather late in the evening, this usually means the party can't happen until the next day. Even if you're from a more liberal congregation and you personally don't observe this rule, you need to consider if some or a substantial number of your guests might be observant and, hence, conflicted about attending a Saturday afternoon affair.

You also need to consider the age and traveling distance of your family and friends plus the time of year. My son's bar mitzvah was in December and we had a fair number of elderly relatives traveling about two hours by car to be there. Our synagogue is Reform and has no restrictions on the type of party you can have on Shabbat; our guests were similarly flexible about when they could attend. The fact that Philadelphia weather can be iffy in December and that it gets dark early made it vital to participate in the morning service and have a luncheon right afterward in the synagogue auditorium for those guests. That way the older folks who can't see very well at night but had all that driving to do could leave in plenty of time to get home before nightfall. Otherwise, they would have had to stay overnight. I don't know about your elderly relatives, but that would have been a very big deal for ours: a financial strain for some, a great physical discomfort for others, and reason enough for just about all of them to bail out of the celebration entirely.

Many synagogues in cold climates don't even schedule b'nai mitzvah in the dead of winter. This may seem inconvenient if your child has a January or February birthday and you are forced to wait until late March or April, but they may be doing you a favor. Who wants to do a year's worth of planning only to have the whole celebration shut down by a sudden blizzard? Even if bad weather doesn't materialize at the last minute, the mere prediction of it some days ahead will be enough for many out-of-town guests to cancel their flying or driving plans. You will also be on pins and needles yourself until the last moment watching the darkening skies, and no bat mitzvah parent needs any additional anxiety.

Similarly, many synagogues try to dissuade families from scheduling their events in midsummer, postulating that too many kids are away at camp and adults on vacation to have a proper showing. This is something you can decide for yourself—after all, you know your friends and your child's friends better than the synagogue does. If you live in an interesting place, coming there for your bar mitzvah could be the high point of someone's summer vacation. Or you could actually plan it that way: Pick a holiday weekend, declare it a combined bar mitzvah/family reunion, and segue right from the bar mitzvah into a giant BBQ and beach party. If it turns into a multifunction visit, just make sure your child gets proper attention before everyone moves on.

One final complication about picking a day and time is the plans that other people are making. In medium to large Jewish communities with several synagogues, you can count on there being at least one bar or bat mitzvah per synagogue per weekend and conceivably several (one or more on Friday evening, Saturday morning, or havdalah). Particularly since all those winter and summer kids get squeezed into the spring and fall along with the kids whose birthdays actually occur in those months. This leads, inevitably, to scheduling conflicts and then competition for guests, as you may find that your child's event coincides with that of another child who shares the same circle of friends.

There used to be no good way to track the plans that others are making, particularly since they can keep changing up until the invitations go out. I'm delighted to say again, though, that www.MitzvahChic.com has an Event Calendar where you can post the dates and times of your child's service and party. Encourage all the parents you know who are planning a bar or bat mitzvah to post their child's information on this calendar so that everyone in your community can check it and avoid scheduling conflicts.

One Family's Answer to the Day vs. Night Dilemma: Both!

I present the following case study for educational purposes and because I know everyone's always curious about how the so-called experts handle their own affairs: what kind of weddings wedding planners plan for themselves, what decorators' houses look like, etc. So this is my bar mitzvah story. You may have noticed that I said we had a luncheon for our son Griffin. But I have to confess we actually had two parties . . . or possibly three, depending on how you count them. I wanted to make the older folks comfortable and accommodate the other younger family members who came just for the day, so that meant a luncheon. But I much prefer evening parties. They are intrinsically more festive and glamorous. From the time you're too young to stay up late, the nighttime just means big fun, doesn't it? So we had both.

Our improbable plan evolved innocently. Then it became sort of an experiment to see if it was truly possible to make everyone happy: our friends, our family, our son, ourselves. We initially made the needs of the day-trippers our highest priority and planned to have a luncheon and leave it at that. Our son, however (like so many other Jewish children), is a genius who skipped a grade and so was a full year younger than his classmates.

This sounds like bragging for its own sake, but here comes the point: Griffin attended his first "friend" bar mitzvah when he was only eleven. And in the party-hearty year that followed, he attended enough blowouts to have formed a very clear idea about what he wanted by the time our planning began in earnest.

Griff was a modest and undemanding young man. In his entire life, he'd never so much as requested a particular brand of sneakers. But now he did make one request. He wanted what all kids fantasize about: a party that's just for them and makes not one concession to the needs, desires, and tastes of the grown-ups. Okay, I thought, it's his day after all and I was sure that through clever economies, I could pull off the two parties without major financial ruin.

Then my husband stated a desire to have "a few friends help us chaperone the kids." Plus some food and drinks. And entertainment.

Some of you already see where this is going. By the time we added into the evening plans our immediate family—the bar mitzvah boy's aunts, uncles, cousins, and grandparents—there were ninety-plus people coming to help us chaperone about sixty-five kids.

It was complicated (for the invitation alone there were four different enclosure cards inviting people to various parties), and it was certainly more expensive than a single party would have been. But let me go on the record right now by saying I don't regret a thing because it was a total blast! So much so that people I barely knew were coming up to me in the days that followed and congratulating me on what they'd heard was a tour de force in big fun terms.

Through careful shopping, some ingenuity, and handling the decorating myself, I managed to bring in the three parties (lunch, adult evening, and kid evening) for about the same total spent on just one very elegant bar mitzvah evening party held twelve years earlier for our first son—my stepson, Gabriel. To give you the big picture on our three celebrations: The daytime one consisted of a kosher dairy buffet plus omelet station, juice and wine bar, a cake, cocktail piano played by Griff's piano teacher, and a fellow leading a few sets of Israeli folk dance (RAK-DAN—find his contact information in the vendor directory of my website). So it wasn't just a kiddush—it had more of an entertainment component.

For the evening's revels, I had found a country club that was past its glory days but had great athletic facilities, a ballroom, and a good, very reasonably priced in-house catering operation. It didn't matter that the ballroom was threadbare, because I covered all the tables with copper metallic table-cloths, turned out the lights, and used hundreds of candles to supplement the only other light source—little twinkly white party lights draped over ficus trees all around the room. The effect was magical and I have never seen such flattering lighting. It was romantic and everyone looked gorgeous. They acted like they felt gorgeous too, they were so relaxed and happy.

How was it, you may be wondering, that the presence of sixty-five kids did not break the spell? Well, that was the best part of all. The club had a separate party room for the kids that was like a miniclub in itself. It had a dance floor and tables and, best of all for the shy kids, a side porch full of video game terminals, air hockey, and other amusements.

The kids had a cool, hip-hop DJ; the adults had a great dance band. The kids got pizza, soda, and cake; the adults had a prime rib buffet and an open bar. In short, everyone was very happy. All evening long, many of the twenty-somethings and hip adults drifted in and out of the kids' party. Some went and never returned. Back in the ballroom there were intermittent sets of communal Israeli folk dancing that gave even nondancers and non-Jews a chance to connect with each other and a beautiful musical heritage.

Near the end of their party, the kids got to throw their sweaty selves into an indoor swimming pool while the DJ played CDs. Some kids who didn't want to swim took turns rapping while the DJ played backup. While the kids swam, we said good-bye to our adult guests and came over to the pool in time to watch them. Then we fished them out and gave each one a souvenir towel as a party favor. (A line on their invitation had stated, "Just bring a bathing suit; a souvenir towel will be provided.") They all practically fell asleep in the locker room as they were getting dressed, but it was a good kind of tired, if you know what I mean.

So that was it. It wouldn't be everyone's dream event, but it was perfect for us. And for Griffin too. Every time he recalls it, he glows and says it was the best time he ever had. And isn't that what we all want to hear?

Picking the Place

There is really only one big mistake you can make in picking the place for your party: choosing a venue that's uncomfortable or unsuitable in some way just because *you* find it captivating. Remember, *MitzvahChic* requires you to put your guests' comfort and happiness above all—not just because that's good hosting, but because their high spirits are the crackling electricity that powers your celebration. If the guests are miserable for any reason—they're hot, cold, wet, bored, deafened by the music, or packed in with too many at a table—the good feelings will escape your event like air out of a balloon. They won't care that their suffering is taking place in a particularly lovely historical mansion with original wainscoting. Nor will they necessarily notice how striking your centerpieces are. Quite the opposite: If your guests can stop sweating or shivering long enough to notice your hard work on the decorating, they may even feel somewhat hostile at the obvious attention you gave to some minor details while ignoring the big issues that matter most to them.

But wait. "Wet?" How do guests get wet at a party? At an event other than a frat party or a wet T-shirt contest? I'm glad you asked, because this brings me to a particular rant: cheap tents. There are tents so wonderful you would think you were in the ballroom of a gorgeous mansion! Then there are the ones I always seem to be partying under. They hold in heat when the weather is hot; they cannot be heated adequately when it's cold out. They keep the rain off your head but, depending on the terrain, not necessarily off your feet. And if, heaven forbid, you have to move between tent and building and the weather is bad, you may end up walking through a sort of tropical waterfall on your way in and out.

All this can be avoided with the help of a good tent rental adviser. The more difficult issue with tents that can't be as easily addressed is this: If you purposely book a room that's too small to accommodate all your guests and use a tent for the "overflow," you will violate one of most sacred principles of *MitzvahChic*, the one about treasuring your friends and family and making them all feel equally valued. Because you will then be forced to decide who sits inside the building and who sits in the tent, creating a sort of caste system, an A-team/B-team feeling among your friends. You may have all sorts of practical reasons for whatever you decide—Grandma's got bursitis so she's got to sit inside and then so does the rest of the family—but the people in tent Siberia aren't going to see it that way. As far as they're concerned, there is a main room . . . and they're not in it.

Interestingly, as I write this, a mitzvah event of my acquaintance was just held where this exact scenario took place. The hostess had spent an entire year full-time planning this party. She chose a pretty room that was too small and apparently never considered the impact it would have on some people to be consigned to the tent, during fairly chilly weather to boot. In the end, she received high marks for taste and elegance on the details of the party, but I'm fairly sure she has no clue how many of the tent people are still grumbling.

Even if you could know for sure that the weather would be divine, the tent perfect, and your incredibly understanding friends not the least disturbed about being sent to the tent, it's still a bad idea. Because the entertainment is going to happen in only one place: the main room or the tent. It's not only alienating for some guests to be seated away from where they can see and hear what's going on, it drains off party energy and disturbs the flow to have people off in another room, needing to be called in every time something's about to happen.

This is something you need to plan around also in places like historical houses where there typically are several small dining rooms rather than one big ballroom where everyone can sit together around or near the dance floor. I love old mansions; they've got a lot of soul. I even got married in one and it had a wonderfully intimate feel plus there were lots of great backdrops for photographs. My husband and I enjoyed ourselves, obviously. But by pure party standards, our wedding was not great. I was not yet a party genius and I made a lot of mistakes. The dance floor was tiny and it was in a room other than where people were sitting and eating. The band was good, but you could barely hear it and the party just never developed any momentum. Once dinner was over, it didn't feel like there was any reason to stay, and people just floated away.

Parties, we know now, work somewhat like nuclear fission. You amass all the atomic material and then use a catalyst to start a chain reaction. With parties, you load up the room with all your favorite people, get their spirits high and their enthusiasm going, and then there's a reaction and the whole thing just takes off. The chemistry of parties is not as predictable as the chemistry of nuclear devices, but if you follow the rules, you can be reasonably confident of the *kapow* you're looking for.

So now we know that your guests need to be comfortable and they need to be together in order to form critical party mass. What else should you be thinking about when picking the place? In general, you get better food at a cheaper price if you go to a place where serving food is their everyday business—in other words, a restaurant, a hotel, or a country club. Not many restaurants have a big party room with a dance floor that can accommodate a lot of guests. But if your community has one, that will almost certainly be your best value.

Otherwise, any place that a caterer is willing to go can be set up for a party, but all the bother and inconvenience may get expensive. Typically, many museums, art galleries, and such rent themselves out for parties. But the cooking facilities will vary greatly—your caterer may have to import virtually an entire kitchen—and you will also have to pay for rental of tables, chairs, and everything else that a restaurant would just naturally include in the per-person price. Probably a lower per-person price, to boot. You also have to consider, if you decide to send your caterer into unknown terrain, if he can do his best work under the conditions he'd have to deal with. You may also find, if you choose a venue other than a restaurant, that for insurance purposes you are required to use their in-house caterer or choose from an approved list they maintain. Assuming you like their cooking, this is a great option, since you will then be guaranteed to have someone who knows the facility, how to make the most of it, and how to deal with any obstacles.

Depending on where you live, you could have literally hundreds of options in banquet halls. In most cities these include museums, zoos, sports stadiums, and even the train station.

To find out about venues in your community, network with parents whose kids are a few years older than yours and with other parents actively planning their children's b'nai mitzvah. Ask the DJs and caterers you're considering which places seem to work best for parties of the size you're planning. On MitzvahChic.com there's a vendor directory with photos of the interiors of several inns, restaurants, and clubs plus info on services available, how many guests the room will hold, and sometimes even a per-person price range for food and liquor. The directory will give you a good overall feel for what's generally available and what things cost in your area. If you thought an all-inclusive dinner would be $50 per person and it turns out that prices really start at $75, that is an early warning to revise your budget (if possible), trim the guest list, or consider some cost-effective alternative to a sit-down dinner. Like lunch.

You are unlikely to see—even in a directory as *fab* as mine—all the more unusual locations that are available. It takes a more creative thinker to see the possibilities in some venues, and many people don't want the bother and risk of working out all the logistics required to turn an unusual location into an up-and-running party space. So you'll see the kind of places most people are familiar and comfortable with, but certainly not all the options. Go through the directory and talk to lots of people to come up with your list of possible sites. Then follow the same procedure to evaluate each one. First, use common sense to disqualify anything that's obviously unsuitable—too small, too distant, space too chopped up, not available on your date. Once you have a short list of heavy contenders, visit each one to discover the nuances that can't be conveyed by photos or statistics.

Having spent considerable time at the zoo, for example, I can attest that the rare mammal house—mentioned in the party literature as one possibility—is, to me, too smelly for any party where food will be served. Unless you're purposely trying to keep expenses down by limiting how much people eat. The only real alternative to nonsmelly buildings used to be the reptile house—imagine the fun of eating dinner with all those slithery things watching you!—and the bird house where the birds fly around loose. To many hosts, neither seemed like an ideal option. But now our local zoo has wonderful new alternatives with real party style, so it always pays to go look.

You may find, once you make those tough no-reptile decisions, that you're left with just the old standbys: hotels and country clubs. Many people, and I used to be one of them, don't like hotels and country clubs because they find them ordinary and uninspired. I have changed my mind, though, because with my new maturity as party genius and creator of *MitzvahChic*, I have come to realize that there are more important things than making people eat in places they've never eaten before. If you accept that the ideal setting is one where guests are comfortable and can all be together in one room with a dance floor, hotels and country clubs—and most synagogue auditoriums, for that matter—are perfect.

But they're dull, you say. They all look alike. True, but they're also blank canvases ready to receive your artistry. Parties get their personalities from the people who create them. Once you fill up the room with "you"— your friends, your design touches, and expressions of your heartfelt emotion—it will seem like no other place on earth. Remember, a bar mitzvah celebration is not dinner or lunch with a band and a bar; it's a group contemplation of a very special moment in your family's life. The more you focus everything on that, the more moving and exceptional it will be.

The challenge, then, should not be defined as finding a place no one's been before or a food they've never tasted before or an entertainment they've never seen before. Though such novelties *are* fun. The real challenge is to do what everyone has done before but make it different by making it your own. So if the best choice—the most comfortable and best-laid-out room in town—also happens to be the one everyone uses, go ahead and book it anyway and don't worry that the experience won't be unique. The magic is not in the room; it's in you.

Choosing the Music

The conventional wisdom is that there are two choices when it comes to music: live music and DJs. Families usually split along generational lines: The parents prefer a band while the kids want a DJ. Whichever you choose, you will have a lot of decisions to make.

Some bands/orchestras are established—they always have at least the same number of musicians and often the same people playing together. By keeping a constant roster, the orchestra develops a signature sound. It becomes known for being great at playing certain styles of music and, once that becomes the basis of its popularity, it stays with that winning formula. Other bands are more fluid and dynamic. The leader draws from a pool of musicians who regularly play together and he can customize the sound for you by assembling instruments according to your interests. Hence, if your taste runs more to rock and roll than big band, the leader can tweak the mix accordingly.

DJs also present you with a huge menu of options. Minimally, you should expect three people to work your party: the MC, or master of cere-monies, who will essentially run the party; the DJ, who works the equip-ment; and a dancer. The dancer's job is to teach/lead dances, help run the games, and generally encourage as much audience participation as possi-ble. Entertainers recognize that although many guests are reluctant to par-ticipate, they'll have more fun if they do, so the dancers and MC can be pretty aggressive.

Sometimes it will be suggested that the MC and DJ jobs can be done by the same person. If you accept this option, just know going in that there will be less interaction and "leadership" coming from that person, since it's just common sense that it's not possible for one person to run the music and run the party with the same energy and dynamism as two. A company that proposes this option should charge less than one that sends a bigger crew. So when looking at proposals, be sure you're comparing apples with apples.

When people upgrade from this basic three-person package, it's usually by adding more dancers. That may be a good idea when you have a lot of guests because it gets more people out there inciting the crowd.

With some DJs, the sky's the limit in terms of what they offer and how many people they can bring along to make it all happen. Some can stage activities as elaborate as sumo wrestling in those inflatable suits and Velcro jumping as popularized by David Letterman. One DJ sent me a brochure that featured a list of no fewer than seventeen different entertainment packages. The list ended with the notation "and much, much more!" After you read the list, you may say to yourself, "More? What else is there? Surely he can't mean alligator wrestling?" Hmm, sounds like a party you should have in the reptile house of the zoo! Here's his package:

- Karaoke
- Magicians
- Caricaturists
- Psychics
- Face painters
- Fire eaters
- Belly dancers
- Casinos
- Sports games
- Impersonators
- Singing telegrams
- Mascots/cartoon character
- Pinball
- Make your own music videos
- Video games

This DJ clearly defines his role broadly—he sees himself not as a music man but as an entertainment director. He is so right! Whether you have a band or a DJ, the musical host runs the party. You should love his or her personality because it's going to set the tone for your whole event. All people who go into this line of work have one thing in common: They're natural hams or, at least, they're not the shy, retiring types. Beyond that, the DJ world is made up of people of all backgrounds, experience, tastes, attitudes, and personal styles. You don't want to wait until your event to discover that the DJ you've hired sounds like the lounge lizard that Bill

Murray used to spoof on *Saturday Night Live,* or a fugitive from a Catskills resort of the *Dirty Dancing* era. You don't want someone who makes the kind of comments you would never make in a million years, or someone who is burnt out, who is on his fifteen hundredth bar mitzvah . . . and it shows. You can't have someone who could do it in his sleep or who might—*wait a minute, look at his eyes!*—actually *be* doing it in his sleep. *Cyber-DJ . . . flip the switch and he comes to life!*

DJs appear at parties to be playing some music, schmoozing a bit, and leading people through games and dance contests. They're actually performing some larger functions. First and most important to everyone's enjoyment, the DJ ideally keeps the kids under control. That means they more or less stay in the room and don't throw food or drinks or misbehave in any other major way. You have to expect a certain amount of youthful misbehavior, considering that youngsters of bar and bat mitzvah age are hormonally challenged adolescents having (or craving) their first taste of teenage independence. They're noticing the opposite sex and feeling self-conscious and apprehensive yet simultaneously emboldened and wild. They have no clue what they're doing, and they act, to the adult eye, like lunatics.

Young teens of today don't behave as their parents did at their age. They are far less intimidated by adults and by the formality of a dress-up occasion. They don't worry about etiquette; they worry about having a good time. In a mixed group of kids and adults, most will behave acceptably. If you put them in a room by themselves with a DJ, be prepared for the worst. Ideally, you should choose a DJ who maintains control by captivating the kids and keeping them busy. If the party is sizable and the DJ is a solo artist working with just a dancer or two, you should line up one or more extra adults to help keep order.

Beyond the issue of keeping control over the kids hangs one final question: How "inspired" and "fun" is the DJ? Good DJs have an instinctive grasp of how parties should flow from the timid first moments to all-out good time. They can sense the mood and make corrections to keep the party on track.

I hope it's clear by now that when you book the music, you are looking for someone who can do more than just competently play CDs. You're looking for the right mix of a personality you like, good control, and a talent for shaping mood. You don't need to use a checklist to determine if someone's got all the right qualities—you'll know it when you see it. But you do have to go out and look. You absolutely must go and see all potential candidates working actual parties that are as similar to yours as possible. There is no other way to know who they are and how they behave.

Many DJs have videotapes of themselves working a party. Most bands, though, are serious musicians who will give you an audiotape or CD that showcases the music, but not necessarily one that includes the patter between numbers or shows how the leader interacts with the guests or handles the all-important special moments of the celebration. This you must divine for yourself through the personal visit.

Keep in mind that another matter you are deciding in your choice of a music leader is how "onstage" you wish to be. If you, the bar mitzvah parents, are rather shy and want to have minimal time in the spotlight, choose someone who can ably carry the ball for you. If you're more outgoing and interested in playing a larger role, you have the option of going with a more laid-back musical host, since you can assume some of the leader's duties.

Later in this book, I encourage all parents to plan on getting up at some point during the celebration (or service) and saying something to and about your child. I know this is hard for many people—fear of public speaking is in the top five fears expressed by most people. And, though I am a party genius, I am certainly no exception. I find it very hard to be the center of attention.

So I know it's difficult to be onstage, particularly if you're shy, but I encourage it anyway because getting up and saying what's in your heart is the essence of *MitzvahChic*. You may be uncomfortable briefly thinking about making a speech or actually making one, but after you've done it, the moment will mean so much to your child, to your friends and family, and even to you that you will consider it well worth the effort. See "Writing a Great Speech and Finding the Courage to Give It" for tips on doing just that. And one final word about the music: Don't ever let it get so loud that guests can't talk without screaming at the top of their lungs.

Should There Be Special Entertainment?

Remember for a moment the list that DJ sent me. Which wasn't even complete because there's much, much more! There are some fun ideas on that list, but do they make sense here? More to the point, are they *MitzvahChic?* The test of an idea's suitability is this: Is it relevant to your child and to the occasion? Even if it doesn't pass this test, a special activity or entertainment could be lovely if

- It brings people together in a group activity
- It creates warmth
- It expresses something special about the family

A good friend is a native of Ireland and a Jew by choice. At her daughter's bat mitzvah, a troupe of young girls from a school of Irish dancing performed and then paired up with young guests to show them how to do the dances. Was it relevant in strictly Jewish terms? No. Was it wonderful? Yes, because my friend shared with us something that was very special to her and her entire family. And that was just the beginning. Another family member got up and sang an Irish ballad. The bat mitzvah's father, a distinguished violinist, accompanied him. Several musician colleagues played at other times in the celebration. It was a wonderful party because the hosts shared themselves, and that inspired other people to do the same. You also got a very clear, poignant sense of how these dual traditions—Irish and Jewish—had come together to form this unique family.

We don't all have talented family or friends who can step up to the plate at a time like this. But, as my friend engaged the little girls who danced, you can often hire someone to get the idea across. Every family has a special history, special qualities and interests. This is an opportunity to share them and even better understand for yourself who you are and the influences that have shaped you. Whatever you present at the bar mitzvah—entertainment, speeches, even decor—should be designed either to deepen people's understanding of you or to engender a feeling of connectedness between you and all the people who are important to you. It should transmit affection. Perhaps also a sense of Jewish ideas and heritage.

There are lots of options out there—find them in the MitzvahChic .com vendor directory. Also look in this book at "Party Ideas for Each Torah Portion" and "Eight Complete Parties That Will Leave You *Farklempt!*" You may easily find an idea that can be the additional entertainment. Also, if your motivation is to entertain the kids at the party, be sure to look at "The Kids Have the Last Word" to see what kids actually find entertaining.

If you look within and discover there is nothing particular you want to share with your guests or no way to turn the things you'd like to share into a meaningful entertainment or activity, you can turn to an entertainment that always works because it's so perfect for the bar mitzvah occasion—Jewish music and dance. Klezmer bands are great—the music sounds vaguely like Dixieland jazz and, as is the case with Motown, has an instant let's-get-jiggy effect on people.

Jewish/Israeli folk dance is also a great way to bring people together. The music is haunting and the dances are beautiful. Unlike the dances of some cultures where the basic steps are very complex and daunting to learn, Jewish folk dance consists of just a small number of simple movements put together in different combinations that repeat over and over. Hence, a good leader can easily teach a roomful of people several simple dances in the course of a bar mitzvah party. It's a very cool feeling to be part of a large group of people—your village—all dancing together while wonderful, evocative music plays in the background. Of course, most people don't want to do this the whole time, but a couple of folk dance sets interspersed with popular dancing help to keep both fresh and interesting.

The final thing to be said about Jewish music and dance is that they open a window on the ancient world. They become a "way through" to a time that is part of our history but not our experience. Ethnomusicologists say that music tells a lot about the culture that makes it. The Jewish musical tradition is full of passion and fire and poignancy and beauty. It's Jewish history told in a different language and it's great to experience, even if it's just this once. For non-Jews, it's another way to explore the culture and the meaning of the day. So you will doubtless see many of your non-Jewish guests joining in with enthusiasm . . . and having the time of their lives.

five The Little Party Details That Really Matter

"God is in the details."

So now you're well under way. You've booked a comfortable room, hired a DJ you love who's adored by kids and adults alike, and nailed the other big decisions. What's left to do on the party-planning end of the bar mitzvah?

The Theme

To be honest, I've never liked the usual themes for bar and bat mitzvahs because the event already has a theme: A child is coming of age and accepting the duties of Jewish adulthood. The themes that get layered on top by party planners and fun-loving parents obscure and distract everyone from this real theme. Plus, in trying to say something about the bar mitzvah, they usually reduce him to one cliché: *He loves basketball! She's into horses!*

Great, we want to know that. But that is only one tiny fact about your child, and probably the most obvious one. I advocate saying as much about your child in as many ways as you can think of: in speeches, in decorations, in games, in toasts from the guests. If she's an artist, litter the room with color photocopies of her work. Make party favors by laminating them as place mats or having miniature copies made into refrigerator magnets. Let people perceive her through these expressions of self. If there are no such visual aids at hand, you can still incorporate into the decor photographs that will help tell her story. This party is, after all, about her, the step she's taking today, and about the Torah, the sacred writings that define what it means to be a Jew.

In "Party Ideas for Each Torah Portion" and "Eight Complete Parties That Will Leave You *Farklempt!*" you will see many ideas for linking your party to the Torah portion, the Jewish holidays, and the big ideas of life. And making it really fun and beautiful at the same time. Don't settle for one of the usual themes until you look these over.

The Invitation

The party starts way before the first hors d'oeuvre is passed. For the family, the approach to the bar mitzvah is a long runway that begins at the bris or baby naming—the first expression of your decision to raise your child as a Jew. For your guests, the bar mitzvah starts when they receive the invitation. It previews the experience and sets the tone. If the invitation is a gold Mylar statuette with a call to "Join us at the Oscars—Rachel's Up for Best Girl Ever!" you know what you're in for. If, on the other hand, it says, "Celebrate with our family as our son reads from the Torah about Joseph's world of dreams," you immediately feel drawn into an event that is clearly going to be about more than a decorating scheme.

If you follow the time line at the end of this book and the suggestion that you get very familiar with the Torah portion early on in the planning process, you will definitely be prepared to write an invitation that's more compelling than most you've received. Whatever speaks to you in the portion, give voice to it in the invitation. Don't worry about breaking etiquette rules on wording. This celebration should express something your family feels about the journey. The more emotional content you give your family and friends, the more moving the experience will be for all of you.

For those who just want basic wording, here are some suggestions:

We invite you to join us in ceremony
and celebration when our son

Griffin Aubrey

is called to the Torah as a Bar Mitzvah
Saturday, December 9

MitzvahChic

11:00 a.m.
Reform Congregation Kol Ami
[Address]
Zachary and Lauren Stevens

Please share our pride and happiness
on Saturday, November 24,
as our daughter

Julia Alexis
Raphaella Arielle

becomes a Bat Mitzvah
at Temple Beth Am
[Address]
at 10:30 a.m.
Gabriel and Jena Jordan

Other Popular Invitation Openers

"It is with great pleasure that we invite you to join us when our son _____ is called to the Torah as a Bar Mitzvah . . ."

"Only yesterday we celebrated her birth. Today we celebrate in prayer as our daughter and sister _____ is called to the Torah as a Bat Mitzvah . . ."

"With hearts full of love and joy we invite you to celebrate with us when our son _____ is called to the Torah . . ."

"We invite you to share a very special moment in our lives when our beloved daughter _____ is called to the Torah . . ."

"On this special day of love and tradition we invite you to share our happiness when our son _____ becomes a Bar Mitzvah, a son of the Commandment . . ."

Personalizing Invitation Wording to the Portion

To draw guests into your experience of the Torah portion, identify the theme that has most captivated your child and family. It could be a relatively minor point within the many themes of the text, but if it's an idea that your child connects with, it's the one to use! For example, one friend's child had the portion Ki Teze, a parashah in which Moses recounts many laws by which Israel must live. One of these—the prohibition against taking a mother bird "along with its young"—caught her heart, for it may well be the first recorded suggestion in Western literature that animals can feel emotional pain. The bat mitzvah, who adores animals and plans a veterinary career, was astonished to discover that her religion had pioneered this concept. She has chosen to make animal welfare her mitzvah project as well as a theme of her celebration. Although her party hasn't happened yet, I'm guessing there's a good chance the meal will be vegetarian. Her invitation, not yet written, might say . . .

> *"We invite you to share our pride and happiness when our daughter*
> *_____ reads from the Torah about the preciousness of*
> *life, both animal and human . . ."*

What Else to Include

Naturally, the invitation will also include a card inviting guests to a reception, a reply card plus envelope, and perhaps a map. One piece of information always wanted but rarely given is the party's end time. This is something parents really need to know when their children are attending your party by themselves. Put it in and you will be the hero of your community!

Another excellent idea that helps everyone get into the mood is to enclose with the invitation a card that says something like this: "In becoming a bar mitzvah, Jake assumes the responsibilities of Jewish adulthood. Please use this blank card to tell him what you feel he should know to be a good Jew and a good man." Not everyone will return this card—and you shouldn't hound anyone who doesn't feel a strong impulse to reply—but the responses you do get will be thoughtful and lovely. You can then put the ones that are not too personal into a scrapbook to share at the party, or you can just pull out quotes you particularly like for your speech or type them in a calligraphy script onto "table tents" to place on the tables.

Candlelighting

Every successful party brings people together. Imagine for a moment how your children would feel if you gathered them together one day and announced, "I like Jacob better than Molly." Jacob would be thrilled, of course; Molly would be devastated. And would you expect them to play happily together after that? No. Even after the initial shock wore off, the memory and hurt feelings would linger.

This is an extreme metaphor for how guests experience the typical candlelighting. Perhaps it's more akin to waiting to be chosen for a team. Some people have happy memories of that experience; others shudder still as adults thinking about it. It would be marginally okay if hosts limited the candlelighting honors to family only, but when they honor some friends and not others, they hurt people unnecessarily and deal a major blow to the goodwill in the room. Who wants to come to a bar mitzvah and be told very clearly, "You're not our favorite friends"?

It's not even appropriate to leave anyone out. Every person you think to invite to an occasion like this has contributed in some way to you and your family. If they haven't, why are they here? Your friends are the village that has helped you to raise your child, even if they did nothing more than sympathize when you were frustrated over the math homework. It seems completely wrong to decide now whose contributions you do and don't value.

Candlelightings are not a Jewish "ritual," though we've embraced them as such. The ceremony was actually invented in the 1950s by a caterer who thought the bar mitzvah party needed a "big moment." Unlike other bad ideas from the '50s—poodle skirts, doing housework in high heels, and plastic furniture—this one is still with us today, as young and vibrant as ever! It persists not because people love it. In fact, when we announced at my son's party that we weren't going to have a candlelighting, people actually broke into applause. That's because, on top of being an emotional minefield, candlelightings are long and boring for the guests to sit through and they bring the party's momentum to a grinding halt.

Candlelightings appear to persist because no one has come up with a good alternative. *Any* alternative that recognizes all your friends is a better choice, but here are two specific ideas. Whatever you end up doing, consider also reserving one candle and lighting it in memory of the departed loved ones in your family, victims of the Holocaust, or all those whose lives have been a blessing to humanity.

- **A Group Candlelighting**—Buy an individual votive or tea light candle for each person and put them on the dining tables. *Important:* Place each candle in some sort of protective glass holder since that's a lot of little candles on a table and you don't want anyone's sleeve to catch fire when he or she is reaching for the salt. *Very important:* Have at least one lit candle already on the table and give everyone a long fireplace match to use to transfer the fire to his or her candle. Make a speech saying how much you treasure them all and ask them to rise and light the candles together. *Voilà!* The room will fill with the most beautiful light and all your friends, without exception, will glow as well.

- **A Round of Toasts**—This is so much more interesting for everyone than watching people light candles and pose for pictures. Let guests know in advance that in lieu of a traditional candlelighting, they will have the opportunity to make a toast or say something directly to the bat mitzvah. Ask some close friends to definitely prepare something so they can get the ball rolling. Have your child ask one or two of his closest friends. When the adults see kids getting up to speak, they'll feel emboldened and realize their message doesn't have to be as eloquent as the Gettysburg Address. Open it up to everyone. Have a lit candle on a table by the cake; as each person finishes his or her remarks, a parent or the bat mitzvah can give the person a candle out of a holder to light and put into the cake. Then you don't have to worry about the number of candles in the cake.

If your initial reaction is to reject these ideas because your child has waited a lifetime to write a poem to favorite people and to honor them with it, just keep in mind that it doesn't have to be an either/or situation. Your child can make a speech recognizing special people and you can still include everyone when it comes time for the candlelighting itself.

The chapters "Party Ideas for Each Torah Portion" and "Eight Complete Parties That Will Leave You *Farklempt!*" contain suggested activities that can easily take the place of a candlelighting. In "Writing a Great Speech and Finding the Courage to Give It," you will see quotes on friendship that you can use as a springboard in finding the words to tell your friends how you feel about them and having them with you on this day. You've seen to their physical comfort; this is the vehicle for addressing their emotional desire to feel connected to you at a powerful moment in your life. It is also a *middah*—one of the twenty-four Jewish virtues—called *Ohev Zeh et Zeh/Mechabayd Zeh et Zeh:* to "love and honor others."

Tribute Videos

These are usually charming video collages of toddlers in splash pools, moving through the years to first soccer games, first lost teeth, first dance recital, and right up to the present. It's a perfectly wonderful idea . . . just keep it short. There's a huge difference between having photos and mementos around where guests can encounter them at their own pace and forcing everyone to sit down and watch a home movie, even one that's sweet and professionally produced.

If you're interested in having a video, consider doing one that really fits the occasion and would become a family heirloom. Bat mitzvah is about passing the Torah from hand to hand, each generation linking to the ones before and after. Many video companies out there will help you create an "oral history" video containing historical documents, interviews with elderly relatives talking about your family's life in the old country and how it came to America, and finally introducing the current generation. This puts your child's bat mitzvah into a fascinating context and may actually help her appreciate why it means so much to your family—and to all Jews—when a child chooses to embrace Judaism.

It would also be an incredible gift for other family members to receive their own copies. They can be expensive—in some families, a whole group of people gets together to pay for it so they can have copies to pass down in their families as well.

Occupying Small Children

This is not an actual mitzvah, but it is a blessing indeed. There will inevitably be elementary-age or younger children at your event. Rather than depending on their parents to keep them happy, why not take some simple steps yourself to see that it happens? This is one of those details that make guests feel extremely appreciated and cared for—and I don't mean just the parents who would otherwise be chasing the kids! Everyone feels more comfortable and relaxed if the kids in the room are happily and peacefully occupied.

- Ask any older teenagers who are there as guests—and who may not be that interested in partying with the thirteen-year-olds or the adults—to "babysit" for pay. This way the family obligation of attending the party is not a wasted night for them.
- Set aside one table in the banquet hall to be the kid activity table. You can put on the same fancy tablecloth as on the other tables, but then throw on a big clear vinyl table topper to prevent damage to the good cloth. Put out baskets of markers, coloring or activity book pages, beads and plastic lanyard "thread," and any other tidy craft materials they'd enjoy. This not only keeps the kids busy, it creates a meeting place for all the little kids. With a little luck, most of them will end up staying there and eating with their new friends.

Icebreaking for Strangers

Every host finishes the seating plan with a number of guests who don't fit with any other group, and these people—total strangers to each other—always get seated together. To ease their discomfort and grease the social wheels, make a joke out of it by putting cards like these on the table. Does this simple icebreaking idea work? Well, all I can say is that I did it, and some strangers got to be such good friends that now they get together and don't invite me!

Coffee Talk
Table 7

We always thought it would make a great party game for the people thrown together at a table to try to divine what twisted logic caused the hosts to put them together.

Well, apart from the usual recipe for conversational chemistry—chatty people with quiet ones, oil execs with environmentalists—there are some specific bonding theories being tested here. Here are some clues as to why we thought *you* might hit it off. Now, *talk amongst yourselves!*

1. Several of you are captains of industry.
2. Several of you have a strong connection to the city that doesn't sleep.
3. Two of you are in the same profession.
4. Not a similarity but a difference between you: Two of you attended Raquel Welch's *most recent* wedding and did *not* see the rest of you there.

Coffee Talk
Table 10

We always thought it would make a great party game for the people thrown together at a table to try to divine what twisted logic caused the hosts to put them together.

Well, apart from the usual recipe for conversational chemistry—chatty people with quiet ones, oil execs with environmentalists—there are some specific bonding theories being tested here. Here are some clues as to why we thought *you* might hit it off. Now, *talk amongst yourselves!*

1. Several of you live on the same street.
2. One couple lived abroad.
3. At least two of you are in the same profession.
4. Interesting factoid: One of you is building a robot.

six The Torah for the *Farchadat* (confused)

Now of course, dear readers, you are not *farchadat* (loopy and confused) at all! *Farchadat* people would probably not buy a book about how to pack more meaning into a bar mitzvah and make it more beautiful and fun at the same time. They would say, "Meaning? Don't bother me; I'm picking table-cloths!" They wouldn't see the bar mitzvah as a unique opportunity to find and nurture their Jewish roots. And I doubt that they would appreciate how attractive and exciting it feels to do a great job of infusing heart, soul, and style into one fabulous event. No, the *farchadat* would be content with the clichés and would never reach for something extraordinary. I've picked this chapter name not to tease *them* but to assure *you* that if you want to do something more—learn about Torah—you most certainly can.

It's pretty simple, actually. Everything in Judaism begins and ends with the Torah. It is the sine qua non of the Jewish tradition: Truly without the Torah there is no Judaism. The Torah is referred to in the Torah as God's gift to the Jewish people. We are known as the "chosen people" because God chose to give us the Torah. Although it is just one part of the Bible—specifically, the first five books or Chumash (Hebrew) or Pentateuch (Greek), as it is also called—it is the heart and soul of the faith, the source of all its laws and mystery. Yet despite its importance, the Torah is not very long. Much longer is the Talmud, a multivolume set of books where scholars interpret and debate the meaning of the Torah.

The reason b'nai mitzvah are joyous events is that the young man or woman gets the privilege of reading the Torah—symbolically receiving the Torah just as the nation of Israel received it thousands of years ago. Still, for as long as we've had the Torah, what does the average person know about it? Most of us have never read the Torah, or certainly not read it start to finish. Most of us learn the contents of the Torah in random disorganized bits and pieces—the quotations we've heard, the Bible stories we learned as children, the rituals whose basis we don't really understand. And although many of today's bar mitzvah dads had their own bar mitzvahs and studied at least one Torah portion in the process, a great many bar mitzvah moms did not have bat mitzvahs themselves. That means that half the parents raising the current generation of b'nai mitzvah may never have seen a Torah scroll up close, much less studied its message.

One glory of the bat mitzvah is that it creates an opportunity for the whole family—whatever their history—to receive the Torah anew, to plunge in, discuss, and perhaps gain a desire to know more. To smooth your way, I read the Torah, and I've summarized it for you by portion in the following pages. This means that wherever your child's portion falls, you can easily read up on what came before and see what follows so you will know how her part fits into the whole.

Using the Torah Summary to Choose a Date

If you have flexibility on when your child's bar mitzvah will take place, you may also want to consult this summary as a way of choosing among dates. After the name of each portion, I've listed the dates on which that portion will be read, going out several years. This means that even people with very young children can find out which portion their child will likely have. I like knowing such things way ahead—it influences my thinking in subtle ways. In the process of doing this work, I discovered what portion my then-eight-year-old would have . . . and I was very excited because its themes speak to me and our family. So do your friends a favor: When you read this, call them up and tell them which Torah portion their kids will have. They will be thrilled and amazed . . . and it may get them excited too. Be advised that at the Shabbat afternoon service, the Torah portion changes to the one for the following Shabbat. So if you're planning a havdalah service, your child's portion will actually be the one indicated for the week after his or her date.

Books and Videos That Bring the Torah to Life

Below each portion summary, I've suggested other resources—novels, nonfiction books, poetry, videos, websites—that will help expand and stimulate your thinking about your child's portion. Not because I'm trying to lead you to any particular conclusions, but because I hope to inspire you on this one occasion to do what Jews have reveled in for millennia: Read some Torah, think about what it means, argue about it, rejoice that it's yours. The best source material on the Torah is, well . . . the Torah itself, an edition with detailed footnotes. You will find these in abundance. In most editions, the footnotes take up more space than the Hebrew text and English translation combined.

The absolute best overall study guide I've found for a family interested in looking at Torah together—so good, in fact, I consider it almost required reading—is actually a teacher's manual titled *Teaching Torah* by Sorel Goldberg Loeb and Barbara Binder Kadden. It is one of a series of study guides published by A.R.E. Publishing; other titles include *Teaching Jewish Virtues*, *Teaching Jewish Holidays*, and *Teaching Mitzvot*. All are written by different authors but have in common clarity, inventiveness, and simple language for kids and regular people who are not scholars. *Teaching Torah* gives, for each portion, a synopsis, relevant selections from Midrash, activities to help the mitzvah child and family "experience" the text, and even suggestions on suitable mitzvah projects.

Another series of study guides written on the "young adult" level and, I'm told, highly readable are the *A Torah Commentary for Our Times* books written by Rabbi Harvey J. Fields. These are published under the imprint of the Union of American Hebrew Congregations and are available through your local bookseller or amazon.com, also reachable through www.MitzvahChic.com. Also worth a look, particularly for a bat mitzvah and her family, is *The Women's Torah Commentary: New Insights from Women Rabbis on the 54 Weekly Torah Portions*, edited by Rabbi Elyse Goldstein and published by Jewish Lights Publishing.

You can also find dozens of commentaries on each Torah portion by going online. See "Writing a Great Speech and Finding the Courage to Give It" for the addresses of these websites.

When you get to the Torah summary and my section of "Things to Read/View," you'll see that some are classics and some are provocative, written by people just looking for an argument or to get your blood going. That's what I looked for, a different slant: a familiar story told by an obscure character, writings by foreigners, poetry, self-help books that address the dilemmas faced by biblical characters, people advancing such provocative notions as the old sins aren't really sins anymore. Anything that made me think and will likely do the same for you. Because Judaism is a religion that's about having passion for ideas.

Once you've exposed yourself in this chapter to the real "theme" material of the bar mitzvah, I believe you will feel even more connected to and excited about your upcoming event. Not only that, but any residual sense of loss you have about abandoning that great Spider-Man theme for the party will be, I believe, *so over*.

"Firsts" in the Torah

Having sat down and read the Torah start to finish, I can say it was fascinating both from a historical and an ethical perspective. I understood for the first time how all the different Bible stories flow together as a continuous story. I also reached the inescapable conclusion that Judaism is far more interesting and compelling than any theme you could dream up for a bar or bat mitzvah.

It's here that some of the first codes of moral and civil law are recorded; where we get the concept of atonement, the Ten Commandments, the Golden Rule, and a seemingly intuitive grasp of science in the dietary laws, the prescriptions for leprosy, and in the idea that a field should "rest" uncultivated for one year every seventh year. The Torah establishes a daughter's right to inherit from her father, hence a woman's right to own property—a modern idea that is still not universally held throughout the world.

These may not seem like radical ideas to the contemporary mind, but consider the times in which the Torah was written. A primitive people concerned only with their own survival suddenly began embracing a philosophy with concepts of right and wrong, fairness, and decency. Even if you're unsure what you believe about the existence of God, you have to feel a sense of wonder about how a tribal people could have such an immense impact on the development of humanity. And, in the process, change the course of the entire human race. As Leo Tolstoy put it, "The

Jew is that sacred being who has brought down from heaven the everlasting fire and has illumined with it the entire world. He is the religious source, spring, and fountain out of which all the rest of the people have drawn their beliefs and their religions."

To the newcomer, the Torah reads as an epic narrative of first the creation of the universe, then the world's destruction by flood, and finally the evolution of a family from one couple—Abraham and Sarah—to a nation called Israel journeying to the Promised Land. Along the way, God educates them on His laws and expectations. As a document, it appears to be also a record of marriages and births of the people of the time. The narrative frequently stops for long flights recounting who begat whom, citing dozens and dozens of names.

How the Torah Is Made and Organized

The word *Torah* literally means "instruction" or "direction." The scroll consists of the first five books of the Bible: Genesis, Exodus, Leviticus, Numbers, and Deuteronomy. The Hebrew Bible also has additional sections: Nevi'im (Prophets) and Ketuvim (Writings). The Hebrew Bible consists of the Christian Bible's Old Testament.

All Torahs are hand lettered using vegetable ink and a quill pen from a turkey or goose. The *sofer* (scribe) who does the work prepares himself spiritually first and pronounces each word aloud before copying it from an existing Torah. The writing is in Hebrew without vowels or punctuation.

The Torah is divided into weekly portions, each called a parashah or sidra and read in order starting the first Shabbat after Simchat Torah and concluding the following Simchat Torah. Except for those rare congregations that read the complete Torah over three years instead of one and except for all the congregations in Israel—which, because of a difference in the Israeli and American Jewish religious calendar, are periodically one week out of sync with our schedule—every synagogue worldwide reads the same Torah portion during a given week. Each parashah has an accompanying haftarah (conclusion) reading that comes from Prophets. On the following pages, the haftarah reading is noted following the description of the Torah portion. Since the Ashkenazic (Eastern and Central European) and the Sephardic (Spanish and Portuguese) Jews in some cases use different haftarah readings, the Sephardic is indicated in parentheses.

In looking at the list of reading selections, keep in mind that due to the specialized market for these books and tapes, they're not all generally available to flip through in a bookstore. Some are written by Christian scholars and Bible teachers and will certainly contain Christian references and interpretations. In situations where these are the only books available (the biographies of Hagar, Esau, and Leah come to mind), they may still merit a look since they should also contain worthwhile factual material.

I suggest that before selecting anything from this list to buy, read, or view, you look up the book or video on a website such as amazon.com for a more complete picture.

One more overall suggestion for families interested in experiencing the Torah through biblical archaeology, check out www.archpark.org.il.

For families interested in taking a *real* journey of spiritual engagement, growth, and transformation—as individuals, as a family, and as Jews—learn about the family enrichment adventure retreats and other resources offered by my friend Rabbi Goldie Milgram at www.reclaimingjudaism.org.

And now my regular person's summary of the Torah, the place where everything begins and ends. Be sure to check "Things to Read/View" for several portions, as most books and films apply to more than one portion.

TORAH SUMMARY

BERESHIT

READ ON

10/21/06
10/6/07
10/25/08
10/17/09
10/2/10
10/22/11
10/13/12
09/28/13
10/18/14
10/10/15
10/29/16
10/14/17
10/6/18

Note: If you are having a havdalah service, you will have the portion noted for the week *after* your date. Check with your rabbi or cantor.

PORTION HIGHLIGHTS

Bereshit is the Hebrew word for "in the beginning." This portion contains the Creation story: the origin of the universe, beginning of the human race, and creation of the Sabbath. The Adam and Eve story. Eve bears Cain and Abel; Cain slays Abel and, when asked where he is, replies, "Am I my brother's keeper?" Adam and Eve have Seth. God grieves at the wickedness of man and wishes to blot all flesh from the earth. But Noah finds grace in the eyes of the Lord.

Haftarah: Isaiah 42:5–43:11 (42:5–21)

THINGS TO READ/VIEW

The Diaries of Adam and Eve by Mark Twain. A charming love story said to be Twain's eulogy to his beloved wife

VHS: *Adam and Eve* (Arts & Entertainment's *Biography* series)

Messengers of God by Elie Wiesel. Known for his Holocaust books, Wiesel here renders fascinating modern insights using classic Midrash

VHS: *Cain and Abel* (A&E's *Mysteries of the Bible* series)

How Good Do We Have to Be? A New Understanding of Guilt and Forgiveness by Rabbi Harold S. Kushner

VHS: *The Real Eve.* Modern DNA research proves that much of the human race is descended from perhaps just one woman

NOAH

READ ON

10/28/06
10/13/07
11/1/08
10/24/09
10/9/10
10/29/11
10/20/12
10/5/13
10/25/14
10/17/15
11/5/16
10/21/17
10/13/18

PORTION HIGHLIGHTS

Noah and the Flood. Noah builds the ark, gathers two of each creature. It rains for forty days and nights. Once the rain ends, they wait several months as the ark comes to rest on top of Mt. Ararat and, months later, all waters recede. God tells Noah and family to "be fruitful and multiply" and makes a covenant never to destroy the world by flood again. Noah's descendants begin to build a city with a tower "with its top in heaven." God confounds their language so they can't understand each other.

Haftarah: Isaiah 54:1–55:5 (54:1–10)

THINGS TO READ/VIEW

Website: www.arksearch.com

VHS: *Noah* (1987; A&E's *Biography* series)

VHS: *The Search for Noah's Ark* (A&E's *History's Mysteries* series)

VHS: *Quest for Noah's Flood* (National Geographic)

Noah's Ark by Rien Poortvliet. Lavish artwork with discussion

In Search of the Lost Mountains of Noah: The Discovery of the Real Mt. Ararat by Robert Cornuke and David Halbrook. The case for Noah landing in Iran, not Turkey

Quest for Discovery: The Remarkable Search for Noah's Ark by Richard and Dick Bright. 1984 expedition

The Torah for the *Farchadat* (confused)

LECH LECHA

PORTION HIGHLIGHTS

History of the Patriachs. Because of famine, Abram takes his wife, Sarai, and nephew Lot to Egypt. On returning to Canaan, the family becomes so prosperous that the land cannot support them, and Lot goes to Sodom. Abram helps the kings of Sodom and Gomorrah in war but refuses to take payment. God makes a covenant with Abram, changing his name to Abraham and Sarai's to Sarah and telling him he will be father of a multitude of nations. The covenant requires male circumcision. God reveals that after many barren years, Sarah will bear a son, Isaac.

Haftarah: Isaiah 40:27–41:16

THINGS TO READ/VIEW

Sarah by Orson Scott Card. Sarah's story from age ten

Abraham: A Journey to the Heart of Three Faiths by Bruce Feiler. The story of the "father" of Judaism, Christianity, and Islam by the author of the bestselling *Walking the Bible* and *Where God Was Born*

VHS: *Abraham* (1994; Turner Original Films) starring Richard Harris. Accurate, detailed, and quite good

VHS: *Walking the Bible* (2006; PBS)

VAYERA

PORTION HIGHLIGHTS

The Destruction of Sodom and Gomorrah. God agrees to spare Sodom if ten righteous men can be found within. Two angels come to Sodom's gate and Lot takes them into his home. They instruct him to leave with his family and not to look back. Lot's wife looks back at the cities being destroyed and turns to a pillar of salt. Isaac is born; Sarah demands that Abraham send his illegitimate son, Ishmael, away with his maidservant mother, Hagar. In the wilderness, God reveals to Hagar that Ishmael will be head of a great nation. God asks Abraham to sacrifice Isaac, but an angel stops him at the last moment. God rewards Abraham's devotion by blessing him and multiplying his seed "as the stars of heaven."

Haftarah: II Kings 4:1–37 (4:1–23)

THINGS TO READ/VIEW

Sarah by Orson Scott Card. Sarah's story from age ten

Hagar by James R. Shott. A romance by a Christian author detailing Hagar's journey from slave to matriarch

VHS: *Abraham* (A&E's *Mysteries of the Bible* series)

Messengers of God by Elie Wiesel. Known for his Holocaust books, Wiesel here renders fascinating modern insights using classic Midrash

GENESIS IN GENERAL

Genesis. Bill Moyers's video series of his talks with guests of different faiths. A companion book: *Talking About Genesis: A Resource Guide*

CHAYE SARAH

READ ON

11/18/06
11/3/07
11/22/08
11/14/09
10/30/10
11/19/11
11/10/12
10/26/13
11/15/14
11/7/15
11/26/16
11/11/17
11/3/18

PORTION HIGHLIGHTS

Death and Burial of Sarah. Sarah dies at age 127 in Kiriath-arba in the land of Canaan. Abraham buys a field with a cave at one end and buries Sarah in the cave. Abraham sends a servant with ten camels to the city of Nahor to find a wife for Isaac. The servant waits by a well and asks God to show him which girl to choose, deciding he will select the one who is kind enough to offer water to him and the camels. Rebekah does just that, and the servant follows her home to meet her mother and her brother Laban and ask for her hand. Isaac's joy with Rebekah eases his grief for his mother. Abraham dies at 175. Isaac and his half brother, Ishmael, bury him in the cave with Sarah.

Haftarah: I Kings 1:1–31

THINGS TO READ/VIEW

Rebekah by Orson Scott Card. A fanciful, semifactual book about her life

GENESIS IN GENERAL

The Beginning of Desire: Reflections on Genesis by Avivah Gottlieb Zornberg. Scholarly and somewhat hard to read, but an effective weaving of biblical, rabbinic, and literary sources to bring stories to life in a book organized by Torah portion

TOLEDOT

READ ON

11/25/06
11/10/07
11/29/08
11/21/09
11/6/10
11/26/11
11/17/12
11/2/13
11/22/14
11/14/15
12/3/16
11/18/17
11/10/18

PORTION HIGHLIGHTS

Jacob. Rebekah is barren, but Isaac entreats God to let her conceive. She soon does, and God tells her that two nations are in her womb: One people shall be stronger and the elder shall serve the younger. The hairy Esau is born first and Jacob follows with his hand on Esau's heel. Esau is a cunning hunter; Jacob is quiet. One day Esau, faint with hunger, begs Jacob for food. Jacob gives it in exchange for Esau's birthright. The family prospers. When Isaac is old and dying, he asks Esau to bring him venison and receive a father's blessing. Rebekah overhears and sends her favorite, Jacob, in Esau's clothing to deliver a meal of roasted goat. Isaac, his eyes failing, gives the one blessing he has to bestow to Jacob instead of Esau. Esau hates Jacob and vows to kill him. To save him, Rebekah sends Jacob to her brother Laban in Haran. Esau goes to the land of his uncle Ishmael to find a wife.

Haftarah: Malachi 1:1–2:7

THINGS TO READ/VIEW

Self, Struggle & Change: Family Conflict Stories in Genesis and Their Healing Insights for Our Lives by Norman J. Cohen

Esau by James R. Shott. Another in Shott's popular Christian *People of Promise* series

GENESIS IN GENERAL

The Genesis of Justice: 10 Stories of Biblical Injustice That Led to the 10 Commandments and Modern Morality and Law by Alan Dershowitz. Genesis viewed as a quest for justice

The Torah for the *Farchadat* (confused)

VAYETZE

PORTION HIGHLIGHTS

Jacob's Dream. On Jacob's first night abroad, he dreams of angels on a ladder reaching to heaven and receives the prophecy that his descendants will inherit the land promised to Abraham and Isaac. In Haran, Jacob asks his uncle Laban for his daughter Rachel's hand in marriage in return for seven years of service, but Laban deceives him, giving him Leah instead. In exchange for Jacob's promise to serve an additional seven years, Laban gives him both women. With his two wives and their two maidservants, Jacob has twelve children—his youngest and the only child of Rachel is Joseph. After many years and some complications with Laban over how to divide the herds and wealth that Jacob has helped to vastly increase, Jacob takes his family and returns to his homeland. On leaving, Rachel steals her father's idols. Laban pursues, but the idols are not found. God tells Laban in a dream not to take revenge; Jacob promises the thief will die, thereby inadvertently cursing his beloved. (At this point, Jacob has eleven sons and one daughter. The birth order is Reuben, Simeon, Levi, Judah, Dan, Naphtali, Gad, Asher, Issachar, Zebulun, Dinah, Joseph.)

Haftarah: Hosea 12:13–14:10 (11:7–12:12)

THINGS TO READ/VIEW

The Red Tent by Anita Diamant. A bestseller; story of Jacob told by his only daughter, Dinah

Leah by James R. Shott. A Christian author's story of Jacob's wife

VHS: *Jacob* (1994; Turner Original Films). Starring Matthew Modine

VAYISHLACH

PORTION HIGHLIGHTS

Jacob alerts Esau that he is on his way home and hears that Esau plans to meet him with 400 men. Afraid, Jacob sends large herds as gifts for Esau. On the journey, Jacob spends one night alone by a river and wrestles with a "man" who won't stop until Jacob blesses him. The man (actually an angel) changes Jacob's name to Israel because "thou hast striven with God and with men, and hast prevailed." When Jacob meets Esau, Esau embraces him and they weep. Jacob's only daughter, Dinah, meets a prince, Shechem, who wishes to marry her. Thinking Dinah was defiled, Jacob and sons plot revenge. They agree to the marriage on condition that Shechem and all men of his city are circumcised. While the men are in pain, Jacob's sons slaughter them. Rachel dies giving birth to a second son, Benjamin. Isaac dies at 180.

Haftarah: Hosea 11:7–12:12 (Obadiah 1:1–21)

THINGS TO READ/VIEW

The Red Tent by Anita Diamant. A bestseller; story of Jacob told by his only daughter, Dinah

Messengers of God by Elie Wiesel. Known for his Holocaust books, Wiesel here renders fascinating modern insights using classic Midrash

Self, Struggle & Change: Family Conflict Stories in Genesis and Their Healing Insights for Our Lives by Norman J. Cohen

GENESIS IN GENERAL

The Women of Genesis: From Sarah to Potiphar's Wife by Sharon Pace Jeansonne. You go, girls!

VAYESHEV

PORTION HIGHLIGHTS

Joseph and His Brethren. Joseph, the child of Jacob's old age, is the best loved and he receives a coat of many colors. Joseph's siblings are jealous. Joseph has a dream that the sun, moon, and eleven stars bow down to him. When he joins his brothers tending the flocks, they plot to kill him, but Reuben makes them relent. Instead, they take his coat, throw him into a pit, and later sell him to the Ishmaelites. The brothers return Joseph's coat, stained with goat's blood, to Jacob and he is inconsolable. Joseph is sold to an Egyptian, Potiphar, and finds favor, becoming overseer of the house. Falsely accused of attempted seduction of Potiphar's wife, he is imprisoned. There he meets Pharaoh's butler and baker, also prisoners, and astounds all by correctly interpreting their dreams to mean the butler would regain his position and the baker would be hanged.

Haftarah: Amos 2:6–3:8

THINGS TO READ/VIEW

Joseph by Charles R. Swindoll. Christian author. Joseph brought to life as the victim of a dysfunctional family. A volume in the Great Lives series

The Story of Joseph and the Family of Jacob by Ronald S. Wallace. A fresh look at Joseph's story and its relevance today; includes New Testament references

Messengers of God by Elie Wiesel. Known for his Holocaust books, Wiesel here renders fascinating modern insights using classic Midrash

DVD: *Joseph and the Amazing Technicolor Dreamcoat.* Andrew Lloyd Webber musical starring Donny Osmond

MIKETZ

PORTION HIGHLIGHTS

Two years later, Pharaoh dreams of seven lean cows eating seven fat cows and seven thin ears of corn swallowing up seven plump ears. Troubled, Pharaoh calls for an interpreter. At the butler's suggestion, Joseph is brought from the dungeon. He tells Pharaoh the dreams mean there will be seven years of plenty followed by a seven-year famine so severe that the time of plenty will be forgotten. Warned, Pharaoh stores up food for the coming famine. He makes Joseph his second in command. When the famine comes, Joseph's starving brothers come to Egypt to buy corn, but they don't recognize him. He accuses them of being spies. They tell Joseph of their lost brother and the other son, Benjamin, later born to the same now-deceased mother.

Haftarah: I Kings 3:15–4:1

THINGS TO READ/VIEW

Joseph by James R. Shott. Another in Shott's popular Christian *People of Promise* series

VHS: *Joseph* (1994; Turner Original Films). Starring Paul Mercurio of *Strictly Ballroom* fame. Well done

VHS: *Power of Dreams* (Discovery Channel). Looks at the science and cultural importance of dreaming

GENESIS IN GENERAL

The Genesis Trilogy by Madeleine L'Engle. The popular author of *A Wrinkle in Time*, splits Genesis into three tales, including Joseph's story and the Creation story; has Christian references

VAYIGASH

PORTION HIGHLIGHTS

Joseph feasts with his brothers but hides a silver cup in Benjamin's bag. When the brothers leave, Joseph's men pursue and accuse them of stealing. When the cup is found, Benjamin is ordered enslaved in Egypt, but Judah offers himself in Benjamin's place, saying that their father could not bear the loss of Benjamin after losing Rachel's beloved other child, Joseph. Joseph is moved and reveals himself to his brothers. They fear his wrath, but Joseph kisses them and says it was God who sent him to Egypt so he could later deliver them and others from famine. He sends them to bring Jacob and their families back to live nearby, where he can help them through the famine. Jacob's heart faints at the news that Joseph lives and they have a tearful reunion. During years of famine, the family trades all they have to buy food and seed. Pharaoh "buys" everyone's land in exchange for food but allows them to continue farming it, asking only that one-fifth of the crops are paid to him. Jacob's family is fruitful and multiplies.

Haftarah: Ezekiel 37:15–28

THINGS TO READ/VIEW

Forgiveness, the Greatest Healer of All by Gerald G. Jampolsky, M.D. The author is a self-help guru who also wrote the bestselling *Love Is Letting Go of Fear*

Self, Struggle & Change: Family Conflict Stories in Genesis and Their Healing Insights for Our Lives by Norman J. Cohen

DVD: *Joseph and the Amazing Technicolor Dreamcoat.* Andrew Lloyd Webber musical starring Donny Osmond

VHS: *Joseph, Master of Dreams* (A&E's *Mysteries of the Bible* series)

VAYECHI

PORTION HIGHLIGHTS

After seventeen years in Egypt, Jacob is dying at age 147. He asks Joseph to bury him in the cave that now holds his grandparents, Abraham and Sarah; his parents, Isaac and Rebekah; and his wife Leah. Jacob blesses Joseph's two sons, then speaks of his own twelve sons, each the father of a tribe of Israel. He blesses them, then dies. Joseph's brothers fear that with Jacob gone, Joseph will finally seek vengeance against them. Joseph says, "Fear not; for am I in the place of God?" Joseph dies at 110 but tells the family that God will surely bring them to the land promised to Abraham, Isaac, and Jacob. This ends the Book of Genesis.

Haftarah: I Kings 2:1–12

THINGS TO READ/VIEW

Jacob's Dozen: A Prophetic Look at the Tribes of Israel by William Varner. A look at Jacob's deathbed prophecies for each tribe and whether they came true

Sacred Voices: Women of Genesis Speak by Sherri Waas Shunfenthal. Speak in poetry, that is. You may be moved *and* you may find a lovely passage for that speech

SHEMOT

PORTION HIGHLIGHTS

Israel in Egypt: The Oppression and the Redemption. This parashah begins Exodus. The pharaoh who loved Joseph and his family is gone. The new king thinks the children of Israel (Jacob) are too numerous and he enslaves them. They continue to multiply greatly until Pharaoh orders all male children born to slaves be killed at birth. One mother puts her infant son in a basket in the river and it floats to where Pharaoh's daughter is bathing. The baby's sister, Miriam, follows and offers to find a nurse for the infant. Thus, Moses's birth mother gets to help raise him. As a young man, Moses sees an Egyptian beating a slave and kills him. Moses is then forced to flee to Midian. There he marries and later hears God call out to him from a burning bush, telling Moses to bring His people out of Egypt. Moses asks Pharaoh to let the people go, but he responds by treating them more harshly than ever.

Haftarah: Isaiah 27:6–28:13; 29:22, 23 (Jeremiah 1:1–2:3)

THINGS TO READ/VIEW

The Midwife's Song by Brenda Ray. An engaging novel of Moses from the time of birth

Stone Tables: A Novel by Orson Scott Card. An entertaining writer as at home writing biblical fiction as science fiction

The Five Books of Moses: A Translation with Commentary by Robert Alter. *Publishers Weekly* said, "This may well be the best one-volume introduction to the Torah ever published in English"

VHS: *Moses* (1996; Turner Original Films). Starring Ben Kingsley. One in a series of TNT Bible portraits, all acclaimed for quality, accuracy, and appeal

VA'ERA

PORTION HIGHLIGHTS

Renewed Promise of Redemption. God reminds Moses that He made a covenant with Abraham to give his descendants the land of Canaan. Moses tells this to the children of Israel, but they "harkened not unto Moses for impatience of spirit, and for cruel bondage." Moses and his brother Aaron go to see Pharaoh. To demonstrate God's power, Aaron throws down his rod and it becomes a serpent; Pharaoh's magicians do the same, but Aaron's serpent swallows all the others. Next, God visits the first seven of ten plagues on Egypt: turning the river to blood, frogs, gnats/beetles, flies, death of the cattle, boils, and hail. During each, Pharaoh relents briefly, but once the plague ends, the Lord hardens his heart again.

Haftarah: Ezekiel 28:25–29:21

THINGS TO READ/VIEW

VHS: *Moses* (1987; A&E's *Biography* series)

Messengers of God by Elie Wiesel. Known for his Holocaust books, Wiesel here renders fascinating modern insights using classic Midrash

The Life of Moses by Edmond Fleg. Fleg is a French poet and this work has been called a classic. Brief but loaded with content from Scripture, Talmud, and Midrash

VHS: *The Exodus Revealed* (A&E). Documentary showing archaeological evidence of a mass Hebrew migration

BO

PORTION HIGHLIGHTS

The eighth plague is locusts and the ninth is darkness. Before the final plague, death of the Egyptian firstborn people and beasts, God warns Moses that his people must be ready to leave as soon as this plague is executed, for Pharaoh will "thrust you out." God instructs the congregation of Israel to paint the side posts and lintels around their doors with lamb's blood, then hastily roast and eat the lamb with unleavened bread and bitter herbs. The blood will be a sign for the destroyer to "pass over" those houses. When Israel leaves, there are about "600,000 men on foot, besides children." They had dwelt in Egypt for 430 years. The Lord commands that they keep the service of Passover, eating the unleavened bread and explaining the meaning of the rituals.

Haftarah: Jeremiah 46:13–28

THINGS TO READ/VIEW

Moses—The Prince, the Prophet: His Life, Legend & Message for Our Lives by Levi Meier. Kirk Douglas called this book "illuminating," and *he's* Spartacus

Moses, Man of the Mountain by Zora Neale Hurston. Unique and vivid. The author was an African-American woman who offers great insight: preserving the story while paralleling it to slavery in America

BESHALACH

PORTION HIGHLIGHTS

The Redemption From Egypt. God leads the people by way of wilderness to the Red Sea. They carry Joseph's bones with them. God goes before them in a pillar of cloud by day and a pillar of fire by night. Pharaoh decides it was a mistake to let the slaves go and chases them with 600 chariots plus horsemen and the army. The Lord divides the sea so the Israelites can cross and then lets the waters back, destroying all the Egyptians. The people begin to starve, and God provides water and food, instructing them to gather double manna on the sixth day so that they rest on the seventh. The people face their first enemy in Amalek, but Joshua chooses men to fight, and as long as Moses holds up his hands, Israel prevails. So they prop up his arms until sunset.

Haftarah: Judges 4:4–5:31 (5:1–31)

THINGS TO READ/VIEW

The Particulars of Rapture: Reflections on Exodus by Avivah Gottleib Zornberg. Scholarly. One advantage: organized by Torah portion so you don't have to read anything extra

VHS: *Who Was Moses?* (2000). A documentary in which archaeologists and scientists seek and find proof of Moses

YITRO

READ ON

2/10/07
1/26/08
2/14/09
2/6/10
1/22/11
2/11/12
2/2/13
1/18/14
2/7/15
1/30/16
2/18/17
2/3/18
1/26/19

PORTION HIGHLIGHTS

Jethro. In the wilderness three months after leaving Egypt, Moses is camped at the base of Mt. Sinai. He is reunited with his wife, Zipporah, and their sons, Gershom and Eliezer, when Zipporah's father, Jethro, brings them. Jethro advises Moses to stop spending whole days settling arguments among the people by setting rules and appointing leaders to help him. God tells Moses to tell the people if they will listen to Him and keep His covenant they shall be "Mine own treasure from among all peoples" and to prepare for God to speak to Moses on the mount. There Moses receives the ten commandments: (1) the sovereignty of God; (2) the unity and spirituality of God; (3) against perjury and profane swearing; (4) the Sabbath; (5) honor of parents; (6) sanctity of human life; (7) sanctity of marriage; (8) sanctity of property; (9) against bearing false witness; (10) against covetous desires.

Haftarah: Isaiah 6:1–7:6; 9:5, 6 (6:1–13)

THINGS TO READ/VIEW

Losing Moses on the Freeway: The Ten Commandments in America by Chris Hedges. Essays on the power and relevance of the ancient laws in modern life

VHS: *The Ten Commandments* (1956). The classic starring Charlton Heston. Majestic but not as content rich or accurate as TNT's *Moses* (see description earlier) or as musical as *Prince of Egypt* (below)

Smoke on the Mountain: An Interpretation of the Ten Commandments by Joy Davidman and C. S. Lewis. The romance of doomed Davidman with Lewis was the subject of the film *Shadowlands.* An atheist when she met Lewis, her book is very sharp and well written

MISHPATIM

READ ON

2/17/07
2/2/08
2/21/09
2/13/10
1/29/11
2/18/12
2/9/13
1/25/14
2/14/15
2/6/16
2/25/17
2/10/18
2/2/19

PORTION HIGHLIGHTS

Civil legislation. This portion spells out laws having to do with the rights of persons, the Hebrew servant, murder, personal injuries (this is where "eye for an eye" appears, but it was meant only in case of murder), offenses against property (through neglect of an animal, theft, injury caused by a beast, damage by cattle or fire, laws of safekeeping), moral offenses (seduction, sodomy, polytheism, oppression of the weak, witchcraft, loans, and pledges), truth in justice, respect toward God and rulers, offerings of first fruits, unlawful meat, impartiality in justice, love of enemy, the Sabbath year and day, the three annual pilgrim festivals, an exhortation (to faithfully adhere to these laws and receive the reward of a happy existence in the Holy Land). Moses reads the book of the Covenant to the people and they agree to obey. Moses goes to the top of the mount to ratify the Covenant and stays forty days and nights.

Haftarah: Jeremiah 34:8–22; 33:25, 26

THINGS TO READ/VIEW

Broken Tablets: Restoring the Ten Commandments and Ourselves edited by Rachel S. Mikva. An essay on each commandment, most by rabbis

VHS: *The Prince of Egypt* (1998; Dreamworks). Animated musical version of Moses' story; beautifully scored and quite affecting, slightly marred by Disneyesque goofiness

The Ten Commandments: From the Shadow of Eden to the Promise of Canaan by Dennis S. Ross. Thought provoking and fairly breezy

Losing Moses on the Freeway: The Ten Commandments in America by Chris Hedges. Essays on the power and relevance of the ancient laws in modern life

TERUMAH

PORTION HIGHLIGHTS

This portion contains detailed instructions on the building of the tabernacle and its furnishings. The first object described is the ark, which is to hold the two tablets inscribed with the Ten Commandments. Then the mercy seat and cherubim, the table of showbread, the curtains of the tabernacle, the curtains and coverings of the tent, the boards of the tabernacle, the veil, the altar of burnt offerings, and the court of the tabernacle.

Haftarah: I Kings 5:26–6:13

THINGS TO READ/VIEW

VHS: *Ark of the Covenant* (A&E's *Ancient Mysteries* series). Biblical scholars discuss their lifelong search for the ark and the evidence that drives them on

The Sign and the Seal: The Quest for the Lost Ark of the Covenant by Graham Hancock. English journalist recounts how he accidentally stumbled onto evidence that the ark really exists

God Dwells With His People: A Study of Israel's Ancient Tabernacle by Paul M. Zehr. Quotes both Jews and Christians; lots of fine photos and drawings

TEZAVEH

PORTION HIGHLIGHTS

The oil for the lamp; the vestments of the priests; the ephod (a short, close-fitting coat); the breastplate; the robe; the plate, miter, and other priestly garments. It also explains the consecration of the priesthood, the daily sacrifices, and the altar of incense.

Haftarah: Ezekiel 43:10–27

THINGS TO READ/VIEW

The Tabernacle of Israel: Its Structure and Symbolism by James Strong. Scholarly and incredibly detailed. For those inquiring minds who *really* want to know

VHS: *Ark of the Covenant* (A&E's *Ancient Mysteries* series). Biblical scholars discuss their lifelong search for the ark and the evidence that drives them on

KI TISA

PORTION HIGHLIGHTS

This portion specifies the law of the shekel (every time a census of the warriors was taken, every adult Israelite was to pay a half shekel), the laver (to hold water for washing), the anointing oil, the holy incense, the chief artificers and their task, and the Sabbath (keeping it holy). When Moses did not return from his forty days on the mount on the exact day he was expected, the people thought he was dead and, feeling helpless, made a golden calf to worship. When Moses returns to camp he angrily destroys the tablets with the Ten Commandments. He burns the golden calf, grinds it into powder, casts it on water, and makes the people drink it. He stands at the gate and says, "Whoso is on the Lord's side, let him come unto me." Moses asks God to forgive the people. God remakes the tablets and reinstates his covenant with Israel.

Haftarah: I Kings 18:1–39 (18:20–39)

THINGS TO READ/VIEW

The Midwife's Song by Brenda Ray. An engaging novel of Moses from the time of birth

Stone Tables: A Novel by Orson Scott Card. An entertaining writer as at home writing biblical fiction as science fiction

VHS: *Moses* (1996; Turner Original Films). Starring Ben Kingsley. One in a series of TNT Bible portraits, all acclaimed for quality, accuracy, and appeal

Broken Tablets: Restoring the Ten Commandments and Ourselves, edited by Rachel S. Mikva. An essay on each commandment, most by rabbis

VAYAKHEL

PORTION HIGHLIGHTS

This section plus Pekudei are the final sections of Exodus. These portions describe in detail the actual construction of the sanctuary and how every divine instruction was loyally and lovingly executed. All these portions prominently mention Moses' brother, Aaron, and Aaron's sons. They are Levites, descendants of Jacob's son Levi, and they are the priests and caretakers of the tabernacle.

Haftarah: I Kings 7:40–50 (7:13–26)

THINGS TO READ/VIEW

The Tabernacle of Israel: Its Structure and Symbolism by James Strong. Scholarly and incredibly detailed. For those inquiring minds who *really* want to know

God Dwells With His People: A Study of Israel's Ancient Tabernacle by Paul M. Zehr. Quotes both Jews and Christians; lots of fine photos and drawings

PEKUDEI

PORTION HIGHLIGHTS

See preceding portion, Vayakhel. When all elements of the sanctuary are in place, and God has instructed Israel on the rituals to be performed within it, the portion states that "the cloud covered the tent of meeting and the glory of the Lord filled the tabernacle." Whenever the cloud was "taken up" from over the tabernacle, the Israelites journeyed on. But they stayed put if the cloud remained. By custom, whenever one of the five books of the Torah is completed, the congregation exclaims, "Be strong, be strong, and let us strengthen one another"—words that recall the ancient warriors.

Haftarah: I Kings 7:51–8:21 (7:40–50)

THINGS TO READ/VIEW

The Sign and the Seal: The Quest for the Lost Ark of the Covenant by Graham Hancock. English journalist recounts how he accidentally stumbled onto evidence that the ark really exists

God Dwells With His People: A Study of Israel's Ancient Tabernacle by Paul M. Zehr. Quotes both Jews and Christians; lots of fine photos and drawings

VAYIKRA

PORTION HIGHLIGHTS

Leviticus begins. The Lord instructs on making proper burnt offering of an animal or bird, and what a "meal-offering" should consist of. The Lord also states the rules "if his offering be a sacrifice of peace-offerings"—sacrifices made in fulfillment of a vow or in thanks for something received or hoped for. There is also a "sin-offering" made in repentance. The animal sacrificed depends on the wealth of the offender. If the *whole congregation* sins, there are specific instructions. The rest of the portion concerns sin and guilt offerings with instructions depending on the perpetrator and victim.

Haftarah: Isaiah 43:21–44:23

THINGS TO READ/VIEW

The Concept of Sin by Josef Pieper. A short book chronicling attitudes toward sin throughout the ages

In Defense of Sin, edited by John Portmann. Irreverent, provocative essays on sixteen kinds of sin. Portmann wrote *When Bad Things Happen to Other People,* a look at the shameful pleasure people take in the misfortunes of others

TZAV

PORTION HIGHLIGHTS

The first five chapters of Leviticus (the preceding parashah, Vayikra) instructed all the people on rites of sacrifice. This parashah is a manual on sacrifice addressed to Aaron and his sons, the priests. Most sacrifices call for the priests to be ritually washed, dressed, and sanctified with oil, and then to lay their hands on the animal to be sacrificed. Once the animal is slain, the blood is used to purify the altar, and parts of the animal are burned. In this portion, Aaron and his sons go through an inaugural consecration ceremony that requires them to stay in the sanctuary for seven days after the sacrifice.

Haftarah: Jeremiah 7:21–8:3; 9:22, 23

THINGS TO READ/VIEW

Losing Moses on the Freeway: The Ten Commandments in America by Chris Hedges. Essays on the power and relevance of the ancient laws in modern life

Five Cities of Refuge: Weekly Reflections on Genesis, Exodus, Leviticus, Numbers, and Deuteronomy by Lawrence Kushner and David Mamet. The rabbi and the prize-winning playwright share their observations as Torah study partners

SHEMINI

PORTION HIGHLIGHTS

On the eighth day, the newly installed priests begin the duties of their office when Aaron makes a sin offering on behalf of himself and his sons. He also makes a burnt offering, a meal offering, and a peace offering, which was for the people. Then Aaron blesses the people and the glory of God appears, consuming with fire all that's left of the burnt offering. In the midst of Aaron's joyous and exhalted first service as high priest, Aaron's eldest sons Nadab and Abihu place incense and "strange fire" on the altar in violation of God's law. They are consumed by the fire and killed. Moses orders the cousins of the dead to bury them and warns all not to perform rituals of mourning for fear of perhaps rousing God's anger further. The rest of the portion sets forth the dietary laws.

Haftarah: II Samuel 6:1–7:17 (6:1–19)

THINGS TO READ/VIEW

The Concept of Sin by Josef Pieper. A short book chronicling attitudes toward sin throughout the ages

In Defense of Sin, edited by John Portmann. Irreverent, provocative essays on sixteen kinds of sin. Portmann wrote *When Bad Things Happen to Other People,* a look at the shameful pleasure people take in the misfortunes of others

TAZRIA

READ ON

4/21/07
4/5/08
4/25/09
4/17/10
4/2/11
4/28/12
4/13/13
3/29/14
4/25/15
4/9/16
4/29/17
4/21/18
4/6/19

PORTION HIGHLIGHTS

Laws of Purification. This portion spells out purification after childbirth (how long the woman remains unclean and cannot enter the sanctuary, offerings to be made), the law of leprosy, diagnosis of leprosy, leprosy of garments, treatment of the leper (they were forced to live apart and follow customs of mourning as if already dead, mourning for themselves).

Haftarah: II Kings 4:42–5:19

THINGS TO READ/VIEW

Two Hearts One Fire: A Glimpse Behind the Mask of Leprosy by Howard Crouch and Mary Augustine. True story of how an army medic and a nun team up to help change the lives of leprosy victims in Jamaica

VHS: *Banished: Living with Leprosy* (Discovery Channel)

METZORAH

READ ON

4/21/07
4/12/08
4/25/09
4/17/10
4/9/11
4/28/12
4/13/13
4/5/14
4/25/15
4/16/16
4/29/17
4/21/18
4/13/19

PORTION HIGHLIGHTS

Here the discussion of leprosy continues with instructions on purifying a leper who appears "healed." Then, what to do about leprosy in a house (probably caused by fungus, dry rot, nesting parasitic insects, or incrustations). The rest of the parashah is about physical secretions that render a person "unclean" and therefore prohibited from coming into contact with anything related to the sanctuary.

Haftarah: II Kings 7:3–20

THINGS TO READ/VIEW

The Dark Light by Mette Newth. This novel about a thirteen-year-old girl in early 1800s Norway who contracts leprosy won a silver award from Parents Choice. Written for young adults, but it is quite graphic and dark

VHS: *Banished: Living with Leprosy* (Discovery Channel)

64   MitzvahChic

ACHARI MOT

PORTION HIGHLIGHTS

The deaths of Aaron's two eldest sons warned that any desecration of the sanctuary would be severely punished. Here the Lord spells out when and in what manner the high priest may enter the holy place. In this portion is the concept of sending an animal out into the wilderness to symbolically remove guilt and sin from the community. Next come the rules of ceremonial purification, instituting the Day of Atonement, further discussion of food laws, and rules prohibiting unlawful marriages, unchastity, and molech worship. This was key, as it was common in many ancient cultures for even close family members to marry each other.

Haftarah: Ezekiel 22:1–18 (22:1–16)

THINGS TO READ/VIEW

The Concept of Sin by Josef Pieper. A short book chronicling attitudes toward sin throughout the ages

In Defense of Sin, edited by John Portmann. Irreverant, thought-provoking essays on sixteen kinds of sin. Portmann wrote *When Bad Things Happen to Other People,* a look at the shameful pleasure people take in the misfortunes of others

KEDOSHIM

PORTION HIGHLIGHTS

Chapter XIX is the center of Leviticus, which is the center of the Pentateuch, the five books of the Torah. This chapter is also considered the moral "center," expanding on the Ten Commandments and adding further moral instruction. It also contains the Golden Rule ("love thy neighbor as thyself"). Covered are holiness and imitation of God, fundamental moral laws, ritual laws, consideration for the poor, duties to our fellow man, prohibition of hatred and vengeance, prohibition of Canaanite customs, ethical injunctions, penalties for molech worship, unlawful marriages, necromancy, and laws on immorality.

Haftarah: Amos 9:7–15 (Ezekiel 20:2–20)

THINGS TO READ/VIEW

Simple Courtesies: How to Be a Kind Person in a Rude World by Janet Gallant. The book that proves, finally, that it's nice to be nice. Practical application of the Golden Rule in modern everyday life

Join the Golden Rule Revolution—Practice One Habit Each Month of the Year by Elaine Parke and Melvin H. Steals. An especially good book for teens

EMOR

PORTION HIGHLIGHTS

Regulations Concerning Priests and Sanctuary. Rules for an ordinary priest, increased restrictions for the high priest, physical blemishes in a priest (any physical defect prevents officiating in the sanctuary), rules for priests sharing in a sacrificial feast, quality of offerings, *Chillul Hashem* (profaning the divine name), and *Kiddush Hashem* (hallowing the name of God), the sacred seasons of the Jewish year: Passover, the Omer, Shavuot, days of memorial (Rosh Hashanah) and atonement (Yom Kippur), Feast of Tabernacles. Finally, the need to keep the lamps and showbread maintained during holidays and the penalty for blasphemy.

Haftarah: Ezekiel 44:15–31

THINGS TO READ/VIEW

Biblical Literacy: The Most Important People, Events, and Ideas of the Hebrew Bible by Rabbi Joseph Telushkin. Covers the entire Torah. Simple and straightforward, a great flip-through reference *and* a good read

Five Cities of Refuge: Weekly Reflections on Genesis, Exodus, Leviticus, Numbers, and Deuteronomy by Lawrence Kushner and David Mamet. The rabbi and the prize-winning playwright share their observations as Torah study partners

BEHAR

PORTION HIGHLIGHTS

The system of Sabbaths was Sabbath at the end of the week; Pentecost at the end of seven weeks; the seventh month held sacred with festivals; the sabbatical year (every seven years); and the Jubilee every seven sabbatical years (forty-nine years). Every seventh year, the fields were to go uncultivated for the entire year in order to "rest," a practice honored by Alexander the Great and Julius Caesar. During the Jubilee every fiftieth year, Hebrew slaves and their families were freed and nearly all property reverted to its original owner. This prevented poverty by keeping property from staying in the hands of just a few.

Haftarah: Jeremiah 32:6–27

THINGS TO READ/VIEW

The Sabbath by Abraham Joshua Heschel. Folks with a poetic nature will love this book. More than you thought could be said, beautifully expressed. Will definitely provide good speech material

Moses, Man of the Mountain by Zora Neale Hurston. Unique and vivid. The author was an African-American woman who offers great insight: preserving the story while paralleling it to slavery in America

BECHUKOTAI

READ ON

5/12/07
5/24/08
5/16/09
5/8/10
5/21/11
5/19/12
5/4/13
5/17/14
5/16/15
6/4/16
5/20/17
5/12/18
6/1/19

PORTION HIGHLIGHTS

Concluding Admonition. This parashah concludes Leviticus, which—except for occasional narrative about Moses and Aaron—is largely a manual of rules and procedures plus discussions of ethics and morals. These chapters are a warning to keep God's laws as given. They contrast the blessings that await those faithful to God with the terrible fate that will befall those who turn away from or are disloyal to God.

Haftarah: Jeremiah 16:19–17:14

THINGS TO READ/VIEW

Five Cities of Refuge: Weekly Reflections on Genesis, Exodus, Leviticus, Numbers, and Deuteronomy by Lawrence Kushner and David Mamet. The rabbi and the prize-winning playwright share their observations as Torah study partners

BAMIDBAR

READ ON

5/19/07
5/31/08
5/23/09
5/15/10
5/28/11
5/26/12
5/11/13
5/24/14
5/23/15
6/11/16
5/27/17
5/19/18
6/8/19

PORTION HIGHLIGHTS

Numbers begins. A month after erecting the tabernacle, Moses is ordered to gather all men of military age (twenty plus)—603,550. Only the Levites (priests) are excluded. God orders all to encamp in a square with the tent of meeting in the center and the twelve tribes arrayed three on each side. The Levites, who include Aaron and Moses, form an inner square to keep non-Levites from approaching the holy vessels. The Levites became the priests as a reward for not worshipping the golden calf. Before that, the priestly honor and duty would have fallen to the firstborn of all the tribes. The rest of the portion numbers the Levites and rules of service.

Haftarah: Hosea 2:1–22

THINGS TO READ/VIEW

Biblical Literacy: The Most Important People, Events, and Ideas of the Hebrew Bible by Rabbi Joseph Telushkin. Covers the entire Torah. Simple and straightforward, a great flip-through reference *and* a good read

NASO

PORTION HIGHLIGHTS

This parashah continues numbering the Levites and details their duties transporting the tabernacle. Next it covers removal of lepers from camp and the "trial by ordeal" (drinking the "water of bitterness") for women suspected of marital infidelity. Then the portion looks at the Nazirite "vow" for devotees choosing a higher level of self-dedication than is required of the community. Then we see the priestly blessing: "The Lord bless thee, and keep thee; the Lord make His face to shine upon thee and be gracious unto thee; the Lord lift up His countenance upon thee, and give thee peace." Finally, the portion details the gifts given by the princes of the twelve tribes at the dedication of the altar.

Haftarah: Judges 13:2–25

THINGS TO READ/VIEW

Five Cities of Refuge: Weekly Reflections on Genesis, Exodus, Leviticus, Numbers, and Deuteronomy by Lawrence Kushner and David Mamet. The rabbi and the prize-winning playwright share their observations as Torah study partners

BEHAALOTECHA

PORTION HIGHLIGHTS

This portion starts with discussion of the menorah and then the Levites, their special position and duties. Then Passover and a second Passover held a month later for those who were unclean or absent. There's retelling of God as a fiery cloud and details of silver trumpets used to summon the congregation or to signal a journey or war. The people journey from Sinai toward Moab and the Holy Land. Moses asks his father-in-law, Jethro—here called Hobab—to be a guide. The people are initially excited to be going and march three days without stopping, but later there are rebellions. Moses is discouraged about handling all the grumblers and the Lord tells him to pick seventy elders to help. Moses' siblings Miriam and Aaron speak out against him, and they're rebuked by the Lord; Miriam is turned into a leper, but Moses asks God to heal her.

Haftarah: Zechariah 2:14–47

THINGS TO READ/VIEW

Biblical Literacy: The Most Important People, Events, and Ideas of the Hebrew Bible by Rabbi Joseph Telushkin. Covers the entire Torah. Simple and straightforward, a great flip-through *and* a good read

Five Cities of Refuge: Weekly Reflections on Genesis, Exodus, Leviticus, Numbers, and Deuteronomy by Lawrence Kushner and David Mamet. The rabbi and the prize-winning playwright share their observations as Torah study partners

SHELACH-LECHA

READ ON
6/9/07
6/21/08
6/20/09
6/5/10
6/18/11
6/16/12
6/1/13
6/14/14
6/13/15
7/2/16
6/17/17
6/9/18
6/29/19

PORTION HIGHLIGHTS
The Spies and Their Report. Moses sends one man from each tribe to "spy out" Canaan. On return, they report that the land indeed flows with milk and honey as the Lord promised, but only two men—Caleb and Joshua—think Israel can conquer it; the other ten are afraid. The people panic; many consider a return to Egypt rather than face battle. Joshua and Caleb urge them to believe that God will help them prevail. Just as the mob is ready to stone them, an enraged God appears and condemns the people. When Moses asks for mercy, God relents, but He strikes down the ten spies who spoke against advancing into the Holy Land. When the Israelites do attack, they have some initial success but then they are crushed and won't attack again for thirty-eight years. God continues to hint that a later generation will occupy the land and He instructs on rituals to perform—involving offerings, challah, and tzitzit (fringes)—when they actually enter Canaan to stay.

Haftarah: Joshua 2:1–22

THINGS TO READ/VIEW
The Five Books of Moses: A Translation with Commentary by Robert Alter. *Publishers Weekly* said, "This may well be the best one-volume introduction to the Torah ever published in English"

Be Equipped by Warren W. Wiersbe. Wiersbe is a Christian teacher, but if you can get past the Jesus references, this is one of the few books available that talk in detail about the three latter books of the Torah

Losing Moses on the Freeway: The Ten Commandments in America by Chris Hedges. Essays on the power and relevance of the ancient laws in modern life

KORACH

READ ON
6/16/07
6/28/08
6/27/09
6/12/10
6/25/11
6/23/12
6/8/13
6/21/14
6/20/15
7/9/16
6/24/17
6/16/18
7/6/19

PORTION HIGHLIGHTS
The Great Mutiny. Korach, a Levite who was cousin to Moses and Aaron, and Dathan and Abiram of the tribe of Reuben rise up against Moses with 250 men. Korach was jealous of Moses' special relationship with God. Reuben's tribe was angry because they felt, as descendants of Jacob's eldest son, it was their birthright to rule Israel. Because the entire community was discontent, the mutineers were supported by many more than just the 250 warriors. Moses tells all that God will determine the end of the conflict, and the following day, the earth opens and swallows up all who stood with the traitors; the 250 are consumed in fire. The next day, more people rise up in anger about the deaths and God prepares to kill all of them, but Aaron rushes out among them with incense as atonement and stays the plague so that some are spared. To end the cycle of revolt and death, Moses places a rod with each tribe's name in the tent, saying the one that buds will be the tribe chosen by God to lead. The next day, Aaron's rod representing the Levites is budding and fruitful with almonds. This is Moses' tribe as well. The people finally repent.

Haftarah: I Samuel 11:14–12:22

THINGS TO READ/VIEW
Aaron's Rod by D. H. Lawrence. A novel that compares the wonder and miraculous power of Aaron's flowering rod with the captivating power wielded by main character Aaron Sisson when he plays his flute. Lawrence wrote such controversial novels as *Lady Chatterley's Lover, Sons and Lovers,* and *Women in Love,* if that helps

CHUKAT

READ ON

6/23/07
7/5/08
7/4/09
6/19/10
7/2/11
6/30/12
6/15/13
6/28/14
6/27/15
7/16/16
7/1/17
6/23/18
7/13/19

PORTION HIGHLIGHTS

This parashah instructs on sacrificing a red heifer to remove defilement caused by contact with a dead body. Next, we resume the story begun in Shelach-Lecha about Israel failing to conquer Canaan in an attack from the south. Thirty-eight years have now passed. The people who participated in that battle were rebellious and initially doubted God when the spies said Canaan couldn't be taken. Hence, they were condemned to die in the wilderness without reaching the Promised Land. Later generations now prepare to complete the journey. Miriam, sister to Moses and Aaron, dies. The people rebel again because they're thirsty. God tells Moses to speak to a rock to bring forth water, but instead he hits it twice with his rod. Because of his disobedience and doubting God, Moses and Aaron will also not be granted the favor of settling in the Holy Land. The king of Edom won't let the Israelites cross his land to enter Canaan, so they make a terrible journey around. Aaron dies. The Israelites defeat the Amorites and Og, king of Bashan. They stop in Moab facing Jericho.

Haftarah: Judges 11:1–33

THINGS TO READ/VIEW

Biblical Literacy: The Most Important People, Events, and Ideas of the Hebrew Bible by Rabbi Joseph Telushkin. Covers the entire Torah. Simple and straightforward, a great flip-through reference *and* a good read

Losing Moses on the Freeway: The Ten Commandments in America by Chris Hedges. Essays on the power and relevance of the ancient laws in modern life

The Midwife's Song by Brenda Ray. An engaging novel of Moses from the time of birth

Stone Tables: A Novel by Orson Scott Card. An entertaining writer as at home writing biblical fiction as science fiction

BALAK

READ ON

6/30/07
7/12/08
7/4/09
6/26/10
7/9/11
7/7/12
6/22/13
7/5/14
7/4/15
7/23/16
7/8/17
6/30/18
7/20/19

PORTION HIGHLIGHTS

Balak, king of Moab, is afraid of the Israelites and calls for Balaam to put a curse on them, but God speaks to Balaam and tells him not to. Balaam is—like Job and Jethro—unconnected to Israel but worships the same God. He's portrayed in the Torah at times as a heathen sorcerer and at other times a true prophet. When Balak's men return to again implore Balaam to come, God tells him to go with them but to do only God's bidding. An angel with a sword blocks their way, but only Balaam's donkey sees it and reacts by veering away. Balaam beats the donkey until God's voice speaks through her mouth, saying Balaam will tell Balak only the words God tells him. The first two prophecies Balaam receives lavishly praise and bless Israel; the third contains the famous quote, "How goodly are thy tents, O Jacob, Thy dwellings, O Israel!" Balak is enraged to hear blessings in place of curses and dismisses Balaam. In parting, Balaam gives the prophecy that the foes of Israel fall helpless. Moab and Midian conceive a plan to make Israel bring curses upon itself: They invite the Israelites to a sacrifical festival to take part in sinful rites. God sends a plague that kills twenty-four thousand who participated, but a priestly act saves many more.

Haftarah: Micah 5:6–6:8

THINGS TO READ/VIEW

Balaam's Revenge—and Other Uncommon Tales from the Old Testament by Rob Alloway. Not sure of the author's religious orientation, but his decision to write about the odder lesser-known tales from the Torah makes this book look promising

PINCHAS

PORTION HIGHLIGHTS

Aaron's grandson Phinehas is the priest who saved Israel from further punishment by stabbing one guilty Israeli man and his Midian lover. Phinehas receives the reward of hereditary high priesthood. The Midianites, though, are punished because they plotted the downfall of Israel out of hatred, not fear of invasion, as the Moabites did. A census is taken of Israel's men age twenty or older. The Levites are counted separately since, as priests, they do not fight. The land will be apportioned according to the size of each tribe. Joseph's descendant Zelaphchad died in the wilderness leaving only daughters—they ask to inherit just as a son would and the law is made to allow it. God tells Moses it's time to choose his successor—Joshua. The rest of the parashah details offerings for feast days and other purposes.

Haftarah: I Kings 18:46–19:21

THINGS TO READ/VIEW

The Daughters Victorious: Fictional Recreation of the Biblical Story of the Daughters of Zelaphchad by Rabbi Shlomo Wexler

Joshua in the Promised Land by Miriam Chaikin. For nine- to twelve-year-olds, so it might also be just enough for an adult who's pressed for time

Joshua: Mighty Warrior and Man of Fearless Faith by W. Phillip Keller. Keller is the son of Christian missionaries and this is an interesting biography where it does not veer into Christian interpretation

MATOT

PORTION HIGHLIGHTS

The first chapter of this portion deals with how solemn and binding religious vows are, and when a woman's vows can be voided by husband or father. Moses sends one thousand men from each of the twelve tribes to attack Midian; Phinehas goes along, holding the holy vessels and trumpets for alarm. They prevail, and the portion then details how the warriors are to be purified and the spoils divided. The tribes of Reuben and Gad, and the half tribe of Manasseh (son of Joseph) ask Moses if they can settle east of the Jordan River and avoid fighting to gain the other side. Moses replies that if they will fight with the rest of Israel to win the territory west of the Jordan, they can then have the eastern lands they want. Moses points out you must be "clear before the Lord, and clear before Israel"—be accountable to God and your fellow man.

Haftarah: Jeremiah 1:1–2:3

THINGS TO READ/VIEW

Leviticus, Numbers, Deuteronomy (Berit Olam series), edited by Stephen K. Sherwood. Look in these three books for the narrative art of the Torah

VHS: *Who Was Moses?* (2000). A documentary in which archaeologists and scientists seek and find proof of Moses

MASEE

PORTION HIGHLIGHTS

The first chapter recounts the entire journey from Egypt to Moab. In every stage of the journey and at every stop, the Israelites were taught, admonished, or encouraged in some way. God commands Israel to drive out all inhabitants of Canaan, the Holy Land, so it will be occupied by only those whom He has chosen and who keep his laws. Otherwise, He says, Israel will ultimately be driven out as well. Next, the portion sets the boundaries of the Holy Land and sets aside forty-eight cities for the Levites. This will spread the priests among the people. Also given are three "cities of refuge" on each side of the river to provide asylum for those who commit accidental homicides. The portion then talks about legal procedures for murder and manslaughter and the law for daughters who inherit land to keep it from passing, through marriage, to another tribe. This ends Numbers.

Haftarah: Jeremiah 2:4–28; 3:4 (2:4–28; 4:1, 2)

THINGS TO READ/VIEW

The Midwife's Song by Brenda Ray. An engaging novel of Moses from the time of birth

Stone Tables: A Novel by Orson Scott Card. An entertaining writer as at home writing biblical fiction as science fiction

Moses: A Narrative by Anthony Burgess. Burgess is the author of *A Clockwork Orange,* so one thing is certain: This book is not boring

VHS: *Moses* (1996; Turner Original Films). Starring Ben Kingsley. One in a series of TNT Bible portraits, all acclaimed for quality, accuracy, and appeal

DEVARIM

PORTION HIGHLIGHTS

This begins Deuteronomy. This book is Moses' "farewell discourses" and hymn to Israel. This parashah begins by telling where and when Moses spoke the discourses. In his first one, Moses reviews the journey from Egypt and how spies scouting the Promised Land so panicked the people that they wished to return to Egypt. Because they forgot God, that generation was doomed to die in the wilderness. Thirty-eight years later, the new generation began the invasion that would win them their homeland. The portion then recalls certain events: the command to start from Horeb, the election of seventy judges and their charge, Moses disobeying God at Meribah and his punishment of never living in the Holy Land. Moses speaks of Israel's victories and allotment of the lands won.

Haftarah: Isaiah 1:1–27

THINGS TO READ/VIEW

VHS: *Moses* (1987; A&E's *Biography* series)

Moses, Man of the Mountain by Zora Neale Hurston. Unique and vivid; the author was an African-American woman who offers great insight: preserving the story while paralleling it to slavery in America

VHS: *The Exodus Revealed* (A&E). Documentary showing archaeological evidence of a mass Hebrew migration

Tenth of Av by Kenneth Roseman. A book for nine- to twelve-year-olds about the destruction of the Temple that puts *them* in the action

VAETCHANAN

PORTION HIGHLIGHTS

Continuation of the First Discourse. When God smiles on Israel by granting victories, Moses hopes he too will be forgiven and allowed to enter the Holy Land. But it's not to be, and he must prepare to let his successor, Joshua, assume his place. God is making an example of Moses to dramatize that all transgressions are punished but also that great men are held to a higher standard. Now the discourse becomes an appeal to keep God's commandments without alteration and to remember various experiences when Israel disobeyed and got disastrous consequences. He specifically warns against idolatry, though there's a sense that it should be tolerated in heathens outside Israel as long as they too are a just and moral people. The Second Discourse teaches the *spirit* of the covenant and the obligations Israel has as the people chosen to receive it. Moses reviews the commandments and then sums up the first two by saying, "Hear, O Israel: the Lord our God, the Lord is One," the phrase we know as the Shema. Next comes the exhortation to love God with "all thy heart, and with all thy soul, and with all thy might." To put these words on your heart, teach them to your children, talk of them at home and on your way, when you lie down and when you rise up . . . The portion ends with reminders of the perils of forgetting and the charge to hold the Passover seder.

Haftarah: Isaiah 40:1–26

THINGS TO READ/VIEW

Joshua in the Promised Land by Miriam Chaikin. For nine- to twelve-year-olds, so it might also be just enough for an adult who's pressed for time

Smoke on the Mountain: An Interpretation of the Ten Commandments by Joy Davidman and C. S. Lewis. The romance of doomed Davidman with Lewis was the subject of the film *Shadowlands*. An atheist when she met Lewis, her book is very sharp and well written

Losing Moses on the Freeway: The Ten Commandments in America by Chris Hedges. Essays on the power and relevance of the ancient laws in modern life

Tenth of Av by Kenneth Roseman. A book for nine- to twelve-year-olds about the destruction of the Temple that puts *them* in the action

EKEV

PORTION HIGHLIGHTS

This portion begins with the rewards of obedience to God. Then a charge to love God and fulfill his commandments. In the wilderness, the Israelites were totally dependent on God and completely cared for by Him. Now that they're about to start life in a fertile land and experience self-reliance, they are reminded to remember and obey. Contains the quote "Man doth not live by bread only but by every thing that proceedeth out of the mouth of the Lord . . ." The discourse continues with more recounting of the Israelites' experiences and reminders of what God wanted in every case and what He wants them to do now.

Haftarah: Isaiah 49:14–51:3

THINGS TO READ/VIEW

The Midwife's Song by Brenda Ray. An engaging novel of Moses from the time of birth

Stone Tables: A Novel by Orson Scott Card. An entertaining writer as at home writing biblical fiction as science fiction

VHS: *Moses* (1996; Turner Original Films). Starring Ben Kingsley. One in a series of TNT Bible portraits, all acclaimed for quality, accuracy, and appeal

RE'EH

PORTION HIGHLIGHTS

Summarizing the Second Discourse so far, this portion starts, "Behold, I set before you this day a blessing and a curse . . ." The blessing will happen if the Israelites follow the commandments; the curse, if they do not. Next comes the codification of all laws stated up until now, dealing with worship and religious institutions, governing the people, criminal law, domestic law, and finally miscellany like first fruits and prayers to go with them.

Haftarah: Isaiah 54:11–55:5

THINGS TO READ/VIEW

Biblical Literacy: The Most Important People, Events, and Ideas of the Hebrew Bible by Rabbi Joseph Telushkin. Covers the entire Torah. Simple and straightforward, a great flip-through reference *and* a good read

Broken Tablets: Restoring the Ten Commandments and Ourselves, edited by Rachel S. Mikva. An essay on each commandment, most by rabbis

SHOFTIM

PORTION HIGHLIGHTS

This parashah continues the code of law, focusing on government of the people. There are, among other things, provisions for the selection of a king, discussion of the priests and Levites, and warnings against soothsayers and wizards. There are sections on criminal law and warfare in which there is an interesting concept not to devastate the land being conquered, in particular not to harm trees. If the trees are not vital to man by providing food, they may be cut down to make bulwarks for battle. The portion ends with details of rituals to perform when a slain man is found and the murderer is unknown.

Haftarah: Isaiah 51:12–52:12

THINGS TO READ/VIEW

The Ten Commandments: From the Shadow of Eden to the Promise of Canaan by Dennis S. Ross. Thought provoking and fairly breezy

Losing Moses on the Freeway: The Ten Commandments in America by Chris Hedges. Essays on the power and relevance of the ancient laws in modern life

KI TEZE

READ ON

9/2/06
8/25/07
8/13/08
8/29/09
8/21/10
9/10/11
9/1/12
8/17/13
9/6/14
8/29/15
9/17/16
9/2/17
8/25/18

PORTION HIGHLIGHTS

This portion begins with family laws: marrying captives of war, rights of firstborns, and disobedient children. Then come laws having to do with humanity: burial of an executed criminal, restoring lost property, and helping others lift fallen beasts. Miscellaneous laws: modesty in dress, sparing the mother bird, adding parapets (protective walls) to roofs, against mixing seeds for planting (or an ox and ass in the same yoke or wool and linen in the same garment), and the wearing of tzitzit. Next come laws on marriage, followed by a second group of miscellaneous laws, then laws of equity and humanity. The portion concludes with a charge to remember Amalek, a coward who had sneaked up behind to attack the weakest and slowest people as Israel marched from Egypt, and how he was without pity and humanity.

Haftarah: Isaiah 54:1–10

THINGS TO READ/VIEW

VHS: *Moses* (1987; A&E's *Biography* series)

The Life of Moses by Edmond Fleg. Fleg is a French poet and this work has been called a classic. Brief but loaded with content from Scripture, Talmud, and Midrash

VHS: *The Exodus Revealed* (A&E). Documentary showing archaeological evidence of a mass Hebrew migration

VHS: *Hester Street.* Film that shows a Jewish divorce

KI TAVO

READ ON

9/9/06
9/1/07
9/20/08
9/5/09
8/28/10
9/17/11
9/8/12
8/24/13
9/13/14
9/5/15
9/24/16
9/9/17
9/1/18

PORTION HIGHLIGHTS

Rituals for presenting first fruits and tithes in the sanctuary. Every third year, one of the three yearly tithes was given to the poor, and landowners had to pay all old debts. Moses' Third Discourse is on the enforcement of the law. When the Israelites enter the Promised Land, they are to perform four rituals: writing the law on twelve stones on Mt. Ebal, erecting an altar, ratifying the Covenant, and pronouncing curses on any who perform one of twelve misdeeds. The Levites are to stand around the ark in the valley between Mt. Ebal and Mt. Gerizim and have everyone face Ebal when pronouncing the "Doom" and Gerizim when saying the blessings. Moses also gives warnings of the terrible fate that will befall the Israelites if they don't keep God's law. The concluding warning is to follow all the words of law in this book or "thou mayest fear this glorious and awful Name, the Lord thy God . . ."

Haftarah: Isaiah 60:1–22

THINGS TO READ/VIEW

Biblical Literacy: The Most Important People, Events, and Ideas of the Hebrew Bible by Rabbi Joseph Telushkin. Covers the entire Torah. Simple and straightforward, a great flip-through reference *and* a good read

Broken Tablets: Restoring the Ten Commandments and Ourselves, edited by Rachel S. Mikva. An essay on each commandment, most by rabbis

Five Cities of Refuge: Weekly Reflections on Genesis, Exodus, Leviticus, Numbers, and Deuteronomy by Lawrence Kushner and David Mamet. The rabbi and the prize-winning playwright share their observations as Torah study partners

The Torah for the *Farchadat* (confused)

NITZAVIM

READ ON

9/16/06
9/8/07
9/27/08
9/12/09
9/4/10
9/24/11
9/15/12
8/31/13
9/20/14
9/12/15
10/1/16
9/16/17
9/8/18

PORTION HIGHLIGHTS

The Third Discourse continues with Moses warning that individuals with evil in their hearts cannot hope to be protected from God's rebukes by hiding among the righteous. He says that "the things that are revealed belong unto us and to our children for ever . . ." On the power of repentance, Moses says if Israel seeks God, Israel will find mercy. In conclusion, Moses notes that a choice lies before them: "I have set before thee life and death, the blessing and the curse; therefore choose life, that thou mayest live, thou and thy seed."

Haftarah: Isaiah 61:10–63:9

THINGS TO READ/VIEW

The Ten Commandments: From the Shadow of Eden to the Promise of Canaan by Dennis S. Ross. Thought provoking and fairly breezy

VAYELECH

READ ON

9/16/06
9/8/07
10/4/08
9/12/09
9/4/10
9/24/11
9/22/12
8/31/13
9/20/14
9/19/15
10/8/16
9/16/17
9/15/18

PORTION HIGHLIGHTS

The Final Days of Moses. Moses tells the people that the Lord and Joshua will lead them into the Holy Land. He has committed the Torah to writing and now gives it to the priests and commands them to gather the people periodically and read it to them. God tells Moses that after he dies, the people will go astray, and God commands Moses to compose a song and teach it to Israel so that it "shall testify before them as a witness" and keep them from forgetting God. Moses tells the people that because they're already being rebellious during his final days, he knows they will be even more so when he's gone. He speaks the words of the song to them.

Haftarah: Isaiah 55:6–56:8

THINGS TO READ/VIEW

Joshua in the Promised Land by Miriam Chaikin. For nine- to twelve-year-olds, so it might also be just enough for an adult who's pressed for time

Joshua: Mighty Warrior and Man of Fearless Faith by W. Phillip Keller. Keller is the son of Christian missionaries and this is an interesting biography where it does not veer into Christian interpretation

VHS: *Moses* (1987; A&E's *Biography* series)

READ ON	PORTION HIGHLIGHTS
9/30/06	
9/15/07	
10/11/08	
9/26/09	
9/11/10	
10/1/11	
9/29/12	
9/7/13	
9/27/14	
9/26/15	
10/15/16	
9/23/17	
9/22/18	

PORTION HIGHLIGHTS

The Song of Moses. When Moses led the Israelites out of Egypt, he began his ministry with a song of praise at the Red Sea. Here it ends with another song. This one begins with a cry to the heavens to give ear, then contrasts God, a "rock" of faithfulness, with the foolish, fickle people. The song recalls Israel's birth as a nation and God caring for the people in the wilderness only to be provoked by their faithlessness and dishonorable behavior. God punished them by hiding His face from them and causing a vile nation to rise up against them. But God stays His vengeance to keep Israel's enemies from giving themselves and their gods credit for their victories. "See now," the song says, "there is no god with Me . . . And there is none that can deliver out of My hand." The song tells how God will judge and avenge Himself on Israel's enemies and concludes with a call to the nations to join Israel in its song of deliverance. Moses tells the people to set all these words on their hearts. God tells Moses to go up Mt. Nebo to behold Canaan and die.

Haftarah: II Samuel 22:1–51

THINGS TO READ/VIEW

The Midwife's Song by Brenda Ray. An engaging novel of Moses from the time of birth

Stone Tables: A Novel by Orson Scott Card. An entertaining writer as at home writing biblical fiction as science fiction

VHS: *Moses* (1996; Turner Original Films). Starring Ben Kingsley. One in a series of TNT Bible portraits, all acclaimed for quality, accuracy, and appeal

VHS: *Moses* (1987; A&E's *Biography* series).

VHS: *The Exodus Revealed* (A&E). Documentary showing archaeological evidence of a mass Hebrew migration

READ ON

No dates as this portion is read on Simchas Torah and not on Shabbat.

PORTION HIGHLIGHTS

The people line the route Moses takes to the mountain, and he blesses them as he passes. When he is past all, he turns, sees them for the last time, and blesses them, mentioning each tribe by name and saying, "The eternal God is a dwelling-place, and underneath are the everlasting arms." Moses goes to Nebo, to the top of Pisgah, and looks upon the Promised Land and dies according to God's decree. He is 120 years old, but "his eye was not dim, nor his natural force abated." Moses is buried in the plain of Moab in an unmarked grave. The portion concludes that "there hath not risen a prophet since in Israel like unto Moses."

Haftarah: Joshua 1:1–18 (1:1–9)

THINGS TO READ/VIEW

Worth a look for all the Haftarah portions is

VHS: *Prophets: Soul Catchers* (A&E's *Mysteries of the Bible* series)

seven Basics of the Service

What Is a Bar or Bat Mitzvah?

A bar mitzvah is a ceremony and a person. Becoming a bar or bat mitzvah literally means to become "a son or daughter of the commandment." Under Jewish law, children are encouraged but not obligated until they reach the age of thirteen (age twelve for girls) to observe the commandments. The bar mitzvah ceremony marks the beginning of a lifelong obligation to study Judaism's beliefs and practices, and obey its laws. It also confers the right to lead religious services, to count in a minyan (the minimum ten people needed for a religious service), to form binding contracts, and to marry. Jewish law, however, does not consider thirteen-year-olds to be full adults—the Talmud recommends higher ages for marriage and living independently from the family. Bar/bat mitzvah is a bridge from childhood to accountability.

Although we prepare for months for the bar mitzvah ceremony and celebration, a Jewish boy becomes a bar mitzvah automatically on his thirteenth birthday and no ceremony is actually required. Learning Hebrew and reading Torah on this occasion is not the culmination of a Jewish education—it's the prologue and preparation for a lifetime of study and worship.

The Torah doesn't mention bar mitzvah or any special procedures for a boy turning thirteen; it's in the Talmud that the concept first appears. The Talmud holds that Abraham was thirteen when he smashed his father's idols and became the first Jew. Abraham's twin grandsons Jacob and Esau were also thirteen when they went forth on their separate paths, one to found the nation of Israel and the other to follow idolatry. In Talmudic terms, then, thirteen is the age you start the lifelong process of becoming who you're going to be. By the time the Talmud was codified in the sixth century, the rabbis basically all agreed that thirteen was the right age to start following the commandments. While there was debate about how to mark the milestone, one sage was adamant that the formal ritual of an individual child receiving the commandments was as important and sacred in its way as Moses receiving the commandments on Mt. Sinai.

It's also clear that the bar mitzvah had legal as well as religious importance. It was customary on the occasion for the child's father to recite the *shepetarani* prayer—"Blessed is He who has released me from responsibility for this child's conduct"—putting the community on notice that the father no longer considered himself liable for damages or agreements stemming from the child.

The bar mitzvah ceremony as it is today probably started in Germany and Poland around 1300–1500. While Jews in those countries could worship openly, the Jews of Spain and Portugal were persecuted and had to worship in secret. There, a boy would be taught nothing about Judaism until he was of bar mitzvah age. Only then was he considered "adult enough" to keep the secret.

Although the bar mitzvah is hundreds of years old, the origin of the bat mitzvah is much murkier. The most widely accepted version is that it dates back to just 1922, a scant two years after American women received the right to vote. On May 6 of that year, a progressive New York City rabbi named Mordecai Kaplan, who had previously bucked tradition by counting women in a minyan, held a bat mitzvah ceremony for his daughter, Judith. There is a competing belief, though, that some rendition of the bat mitzvah existed in eighteenth-century Italy. Whichever version is true, today all branches of Judaism, except the Orthodox, perform comparable rites for bar and bat mitzvah.

The Shabbat Service

The service is in five basic parts. In Orthodox and many Conservative synagogues, it begins with introductory prayers, songs of praise, meditations, and readings, but most Reform synagogues reduce these. This introductory section concludes with a Reader's Kaddish; a Kaddish is a prayer that praises God.

The next section starts with the *Barchu*—a call to worship—followed by two blessings that acknowledge God as Creator and the gift of Torah as proof that God loves us. All lead up to the recitation of the Shema, the prayer that is so central to Jewish life that it's typically the first one taught to children and the last one a Jew will speak before dying. The Shema comes from a portion near the end of the Torah when Moses, in the first of three discourses to Israel, sums up the first two commandments and exhorts the nation to "Hear, O Israel: the Lord our God, the Lord is One."

Shema means "hear" in Hebrew. The three discourses of Moses recount the history of the nation of Israel and admonish the people to keep God's law. This part of the service is likewise full of reminders of what God has wrought and what He wants the Jewish people to do. It condenses the core of Jewish belief and includes prayers to the God who creates, to the God who shows love to the Jewish people through the gift of Torah, and to the God who redeemed the Jewish people from Egyptian bondage. This section of the service concludes with *Mi Chamocha* recalling God as Israel's redeemer. *Mi Chamocha* comes from a special passage (found in the Torah portion called *Beshalach*) that's referred to as the "Song at the Sea" or the "Song of the Reeds." This is one of many songs found in the Torah and recounts how God parted the Red Sea for the Israelites and then let it close over the pursuing Egyptians.

Next in the service are the prayers of the traditional daily liturgy. In a non-Shabbat service, this is called the Amidah (the "standing" prayer) and, on Shabbat, *Tefillah*. The Amidah starts by invoking the God of our ancestors and stating that God is the source of life. Then comes the sanctification of God's name (the passage that requires a minyan), followed by pleas for healing, sustenance, forgiveness, and the restoration of Jerusalem. The prayers also affirm God's strength and holiness, and the holiness of Shabbat. They express our thanks to God and recognize that He is the source of peace.

Next come the prayers and rituals surrounding the reading of the Torah. A family member or the clergy open the holy ark, a cabinetlike structure usually front and center in the sanctuary and called, in Hebrew, *Aron ha Kodesh,* and bring forth the Torah scroll. At this point, your synagogue may perform a ritual called *L'dor va-dor,* passing the Torah from generation to generation. The scroll is physically passed from grandparents to parents to the child. In some synagogues, it's the custom to include siblings, Hebrew school teachers, and others as well. In some Reform and Reconstructionist congregations, this ritual may also include non-Jewish grandparents and parents who have supported the child throughout his Jewish education. Some synagogues then have a Torah procession—the Torah is carried through the sanctuary.

Once the Torah is back on the bimah, the cover, breastplate, and other ornaments are removed and it is opened to the proper place for reading. Various people will be called for their aliyah; they chant a brief prayer both before and after a section of the Torah is read. In many synagogues, the bat mitzvah will be just one of several people reading from the Torah. Following the Torah reading, your child will most likely read from the haftarah portion. During this part of the service, the bat mitzvah typically also presents the *dvar Torah,* a "word of Torah," a speech discussing the meaning of the portion. Parents may also give a short speech, and the child may make a separate speech thanking all the people who helped her prepare for this day.

Finally, it's on to the concluding prayers. These include *Aleinu,* a special prayer that reminds Jews of their unique destiny and looks ahead to the coming of the Messiah and a time of perfect peace. The service concludes with the Mourner's Kaddish, a prayer for mourners to say but one that gives thanks for life and extols the goodness of life. There is usually a closing hymn.

In Orthodox congregations, there will then be a musaf (additional) service. Conservative synagogues typically hold a shorter version of this service, and Reform synagogues eliminate it entirely.

Personalizing the Service

If your rabbi and cantor are receptive, here are some ways to personalize the service.

Add Readings

When you have a strong need or desire to include a person or an idea in the service, this is often the best way to do it. In particular, if you have non-Jewish family members who cannot recite the standard blessings and cannot have an aliyah, you can ask your rabbi about giving them something else to read. The Psalms are very appropriate for this purpose, particularly since they're embraced by Jews and Christians alike and contain no conflicting theologies. There are also good liturgical books, such as *Likrat Shabbat* (Prayer Book Press of Media Judaica), that contain more contemporary poems and readings that complement the service. *Likrat Shabbat* is out of print, but many rabbis and synagogue libraries have a copy.

In addition, you can investigate popular Jewish authors like Anne Frank and Elie Wiesel for literary passages that serve as meditations on themes of the service and the bar mitzvah event. Contemporary Passover Haggadahs are a good place to check, as they've often already identified interesting readings and authors for you. Here are some suggested books to look at for additional material.

To Life! A Celebration of Jewish Being and Thinking by Harold S. Kushner

The Book of Blessings: New Jewish Prayers for Daily Life, the Sabbath, and the New Moon Festival by Marcia Falk

The Book of Jewish Sacred Practices: Clal's Guide to Everyday & Holiday Rituals & Blessings, edited by Rabbi Kula Irwin and Vanessa L. Ochs, PhD

Traditions: The Complete Book of Prayers, Rituals, and Blessings for Every Jewish Home by Sara Shendelman and Avram Davis

Woman-Oriented Books

The Jewish Woman's Book of Wisdom: Thoughts from Prominent Jewish Women on Spirituality, Identity, Sisterhood, Family and Faith, edited by Ellen Jaffe-Gill

Bringing Home the Light: A Jewish Woman's Handbook of Rituals by E. M. Broner

The Global Anthology of Jewish Women Writers, edited by Robert Kalechofsky

Add Music

There is so much beautiful Jewish music that finding something wonderful is often as easy as letting the cantor know you're interested. In traditional synagogues, musical instruments cannot be played on Shabbat, but singing is always appropriate. Ask your cantor if you may add music to the service and get suggestions of what would be most suitable. Make it easy for the congregation to sing along by printing the lyrics in a prayer booklet (see next entry).

Create a Special Prayer Booklet

This is not only a lovely keepsake afterward, but it gives you a place to explain the service to your guests, add thoughts you may not be able to include in the service, print lyrics to the songs that will be sung in the service, thank the people who are performing the aliyot and acknowledge the contributions of others. If your child is artistic, she can illustrate the booklet, thus making it even more special. Some booklets are simple one-page guides to the service, the synagogue, and the meaning of the child's portion. Others are very elaborate and include translations of every prayer plus commentary, a copy of the *dvar Torah* plus the bat mitzvah's favorite poems and personal writings, and comments from close relatives. If you're interested in creating a prayer booklet, ask your rabbi for samples of those that other families have produced.

Present a Tallit

In some synagogues, it's a given that the parents or grandparents will present the bar mitzvah with a tallit (prayer shawl) during the service. Many families, in keeping with the day's theme of passing down what is holy from generation to generation, bestow a tallit that has been in the family for generations. Others make it a special project to find a tallit that has personal significance because it was purchased from a charity or from Israel or is handmade or has other special qualities. The bar or bat mitzvah can even make a tallit, if desired. See "Crafts for Style and Therapy" for one simple, child-friendly approach. If you're interested in presenting a tallit and the ritual is not standard in your synagogue, ask your rabbi if and how it could be done.

Honor Departed Loved Ones

Your synagogue may already have recommendations on how best to do this. Some simple ideas you can include in the service are to kindle a light in remembrance of loved ones, put their names in your prayer booklet, read a prayer or sing a favorite song in their honor, speak of them in your speech or read their names during the prayers, or place an empty chair on the bimah to represent them. One family had a quiet but eloquent idea: They placed a table in the entryway with framed photographs and a small card that read simply, "With us in spirit."

What to Tell Your Friends About the Service

Jews and non-Jews alike need some help when it comes to the service. Synagogues all have different policies; the only guests who will be absolutely sure what to do and how to do it are members of your synagogue. And since your friends want so earnestly not to embarrass you or cause a problem, many will be anxious about attending the service unless you give them clear instruction.

It's not necessary to send a policy manual along with the invitation, but do use common sense and tell people what they need to know. If your synagogue has a strict dress code that could easily be violated—women are required to cover their arms and legs—you need to send a note with the invitation. Often, there will be a special dress code for people who will be on the bimah—head coverings required for both genders; no pants for women; skirts not to be above the the knee, etc. In this case, you need inform only the people who will be up there, usually your closest family members.

In addition, there may be general rules in the sanctuary that everyone needs to know. Photos cannot be taken, cell phones are to be turned off, *kippot* are required for all men, etc. You can handle this in a couple of ways. If the regular synagogue program that congregants receive from the ushers on the way in doesn't make these rules clear, you can publish them in your own prayer booklet. It's friendlier and more effective, though, just to ask a couple of your friends from the synagogue to stand at the door with the ushers and hand out *kippot* to all the men as they enter. Then your reps are also available to answer any other questions people have or to issue a well-timed warning about the cameras, pagers, and cell phones.

One issue that *always* comes up in Conservative synagogues—because they often have bins of complimentary *kippot* and tallitot (and no instructions) at the door—is that non-Jewish guests don't know whether or not to put on these items. That's just one example of the technical things non-Jews need to know. Many guests would also appreciate knowing what the service itself is about: the symbols and meanings and how this rite of passage compares to Christian rites. For them, Rabbi Jeffrey K. Salkin has graciously created a poetic and copyright-free explanation in his book *Putting God on the Guest List*. You are free to photocopy this—it's Appendix 1 in the book—and hand it out.

Now, returning from the sublime to the occasionally silly, here is a list of other things non-Jews want to know.

The Top Ten Things Non-Jews Want to Know About the Bar or Bat Mitzvah

1. *Anyone can wear a* kippah*; only Jews wear the tallit.*

The *kippah* is worn as a gesture of respect to God in the sanctuary. In Reform synagogues, it's usually optional; in Conservative synagogues, it's usually required for men and optional for women. Wearing the tallit is a mitzvah—a commandment meant for Jews only. A Jewish guest, even if he is not from your synagogue, may don the tallit at his option, but it's not usually required. Non-Jews should not wear the tallit at any time.

2. *If it's a long service, people will come late.*

Most Christians are accustomed to religious services that last around an hour at most. A service at many Reform temples will be sixty to ninety minutes. Every other branch of Judaism, however, has services that can average three hours or more. Imagine your non-Jewish guests' surprise when the pace has barely slowed after two hours! Best to let them know ahead of time.

3. *People will go in and out of the sanctuary during the service.*

This would never happen in a church, but in many synagogues where the services are long, the kids run in and out and up and down the aisles. If no one is stopping them, it's because there's general resignation that many people of all ages cannot sit still through a service of three hours or more.

4. *Non-Jews don't have to do everything the congregants do.*

Non-Catholics, when attending Mass at a friend's church, are not expected to kneel or to pray in a way that's inconsistent with their beliefs. It also is not be appropriate for them to take part in a rite, like Holy Communion, that is for Catholics only. Similarly, non-Jews should not say prayers that assume the speaker is Jewish, prayers that refer, for example, to God's Covenant with the Jewish people. Catholics do everything together in their services; they may assume they are to join in here as well. The rules are pretty simple: Non-Jews, out of respect, should stand when the congregation stands. Other than that, they need only listen and, if they wish, participate during responsive readings that have general themes like peace.

5. *You don't have to know Hebrew to get something out of the service.*

In fact, a lot of Jews don't know very much Hebrew, but like Catholics attending Mass in Latin, they know certain parts of the service just from hearing them over and over. There's much that non-Jews would find interesting in a Shabbat service. If your synagogue conducts its service mostly in Hebrew and the prayer book doesn't include English translation, think about creating your own prayer booklet with translations of the main prayers or one that at least explains the service overall. You're welcome to use the section in this chapter that talks about the service. In the alternative, you could ask the rabbi to briefly explain from the pulpit the meaning of the prayers and rituals as they're being performed. If you're already looking at a three-hour service, though, you might not want to add to it.

6. *A bar mitzvah sometimes means a weekend.*

If you're a close friend of the family and the service is Saturday morning, you could easily spend nearly a whole weekend on bar mitzvah activities.

In a typical scenario for a Reform or Reconstructionist family, there may be dinner before the Friday night service, followed by the service itself and an *oneg Shabbat* afterward. Saturday morning is the service with the child's Torah reading. It's followed by a community *oneg Shabbat,* which may—if the main party is that night—be followed by a Kiddush lunch. After everyone's been up late Saturday night, the weekend may wrap with a Sunday brunch. At Conservative and Orthodox synagogues, there will most likely not be a Saturday afternoon or evening party—guests will attend the service on Saturday and the party will be on Sunday. Guests who are not close friends, family, or out-of-towners are typically not invited on Friday night or—assuming the main party happened on Saturday—on Sunday for brunch. And not everyone has this many gatherings. The point is, if you want everyone's whole weekend, send an itinerary that says so.

7. *A bar mitzvah is most like a Christian confirmation.*

Many religions have a ritual that recognizes when a child is mature and accountable for obeying the rules. In Catholicism, children prepare and at seven receive their first Holy Communion. This is a bit like bar mitzvah because being able to receive Communion presumes that the child can know when he's sinned and can confess and repent in preparation for Communion. Bar mitzvah likewise makes children responsible for understanding and obeying God's laws, but at a much later age. The Christian milestone that is most like bar mitzvah in the sense that the child is symbolically ushered into the adult community is confirmation.

8. *On the other hand, a bar mitzvah is nothing like a Christian confirmation.*

If a confirmation party is a paper airplane, a bar mitzvah is a Learjet. It's bigger, sleeker, noisier, and "more" in every way. Christian children never experience fuss on this scale at any point in their religious education. A bar mitzvah party is more like a wedding than a kids' party. If you want to know which guests are Christians attending their first bar mitzvah, just look for the dropped jaws.

9. *Dress code varies by region.*

Where I live, "church" has become casual in recent years; "temple" has not, particularly when you're an invited guest attending a bar or bat mitzvah. When there is no dress code cited, it's always appropriate and respectful for women to wear dresses, suits, or dressy pantsuits, and for men to wear suits. In my town, even the kids dress up. People dress as they would for a formal wedding. Unless it's an evening service followed by a party— then they dress up even more. (If you're considering a "black tie optional" party following an evening service, check with your synagogue since many do not allow formal wear in the sanctuary.)

10. *Your gift should not be based on your hosts' income.*

With cash gifts, the two considerations in figuring the amount are how close you are to the family/child and what's appropriate for you based on your financial circumstances. The other standards people tend to use— how affluent the hosts are and how much they're spending on you are totally irrelevant.

The tradition is to give in multiples of $18, the numeric equivalent of *chai*, the Hebrew word for "life." Follow, generally, your customary giving patterns. If you're of modest means and would normally give a niece or nephew $25 for a birthday, give $36–$54 to the mitzvah child in recognition that this is bigger than the standard birthday; if you'd more typically give a niece $50, give the bar mitzvah $72–$108. Or you can give less and supplement with a small gift or even a heartfelt letter, which is especially flattering if you take the time to find out and speak to the child's interests. If you're very close to the child/family, live in an affluent community, and are in outstanding financial shape, the standard is around $150–$200. Well-heeled family members in such affluent areas give $200+. Of course, in modest areas or small towns, these numbers may seem high; in very wealthy places, they will seem low. But for many people they're valid.

eight For the Non-Jewish Parent

If you're a non-Jewish parent planning a bar mitzvah, you may already feel like the proverbial "fish with a bicycle." You may feel that at best, people see you as irrelevant and at worst, a potential speed bump on the otherwise smooth bar mitzvah highway. Whatever you feel, you should not feel lonely. In a 2000 study, fully 33 percent of Jews responding said that they were married to someone of another faith.

The bar mitzvah can be the catalyst for reawakening old hurts, anxieties, and questions from the past. If you're very lucky, your Jewish in-laws liked you almost from your first introduction and bit their tongues when your wedding plans were being made, even though they were dying to know whether you planned to convert and, if not, how "Jewishly" things would be handled. Since then, they've been very respectful of your marriage and your right to participate in religious activities to whatever extent you feel sincerely moved. When your first child was born, they held their breath to see if there would be a bris or a baby-naming or some outward sign that you intended to raise the child as a Jew. And now that your child is Jewish and it's time for the bat mitzvah, they have total faith in your commitment to the team and total confidence that you will do everything to their satisfaction.

Okay, that was a lovely little trip to la-la land; now let's talk about *your* situation. There are parents who let their married children make all their own decisions about religious observance, but it's unlikely that they belong to your spouse. Before you get too resentful, though, you should know that family problems that grow out of interfaith marriages are hardly unique to families where Jews marry gentiles. There can be just as many issues when Catholics marry Protestants or even when a Protestant marries a different kind of Protestant!

Why Intermarriage Upsets People

What is unique to the Jewish community is the sense that the religion's continued existence is threatened by intermarriage. There are about 14 million Jews worldwide. It sounds substantial, but it's a pittance compared to the 2 billion Christians and 1.3 billion Muslims. Intermarriage is a threat because children of these unions can be raised in the non-Jew's religion or with some combination of traditions that doesn't result in the child having a clear Jewish identity in adulthood.

To complicate matters further, there's disagreement on who *is* Jewish. Judaism is matrilineal, meaning that only the children of Jewish mothers are agreed across all branches to be automatically Jewish. In 1983, the Reform movement affirmed a controversial decision to regard the children of Jewish fathers and non-Jewish mothers to be Jewish if they are being raised as Jews; the Reconstructionist movement follows the same policy.

There are many valid issues for the intermarried and an equal number of people and organizations interested in helping families find their way. The attitude of the Jewish Outreach Institute is to welcome non-Jewish spouses into the Jewish community so that the children of these marriages will have a chance to belong and to form a Jewish identity. I like to think non-Jewish spouses are welcomed also because it's the right thing to do. Certainly, as a practical matter, a non-Jew who receives kindness and acceptance is far more likely to see Judaism as a beautiful and ethical faith and to want to raise the kids as Jews. Be aware, though, that there are some people who will just never be okay with people marrying out of their religion, and you might be amazed at how technical the distinctions can be. There is no religious hair so skinny that it can't be split by a well-meaning crank. Don't let such people define you or suck the happiness out of your experience.

For all the non-Jewish parents of b'nai mitzvah out there—and those who love them—these are the challenges I see to a joyful, unconflicted mitzvah experience.

Feeling Accepted by Your Jewish Family

As noted, you may have gone for years without any outward sign that your Jewish in-laws or spouse had any misgivings about you being a non-Jew. They might actually have forgotten that you're not Jewish. Now that this very important ceremony approaches, everyone remembers and suddenly the anxieties resurface: How Jewish is she? Will he understand how much this means to "us"? Will she plan the event appropriately? Who will handle the "Jewish father" duties?

You may be asking yourself the same questions. However the decision to raise the kids as Jews was originally made, you may be revisiting the emotions now. Maybe you really admired the religion and felt strongly that you wanted your children to be Jewish. In that case, you're probably very excited about celebrating this milestone. Maybe you had bad memories of your own religious upbringing and welcomed the chance for your kids to experience something else. If that's the case, perhaps you approach the bar mitzvah with eagerness tinged with sorrow. Or maybe religion just didn't matter to you, so why not Judaism? If that was how it came about, you may be struggling with your ambivalence even now.

Interestingly, rabbis say that when intermarried parents come in for the bat mitzvah kick-off meeting, they never know which parent will be more gung-ho. In a surprising number of cases, it's the non-Jewish spouses who are more enthusiastic because they don't have any emotional baggage from their own Jewish upbringing. People who, as adults, embrace a faith because of its beauty and lyricism are far less likely to dwell on the negatives than someone who sat through years of services . . . and disliked almost every minute of it.

So I guess the good news is that if you're conflicted or unsure how you feel about the coming *simcha*, you may not be alone—even within your own family. The harder issue is that at the same time you're struggling with your own feelings—about your child's adolescence, about being Jewish or not being Jewish at this particular moment, about how the Jewish establishment is going to treat you during this process and how you're going to feel about it—you're also somewhat under fire from the outside. Your family is under greater pressure to define itself, the Jewish grandparents are anxious about where you stand and how you'll handle the project, and their friends and associates may be unwittingly fanning the flames by asking a lot of good-natured questions about how it's all coming along.

Not to play favorites, but I think a non-Jewish mother has a more difficult time than a non-Jewish father when planning a bar mitzvah. First, because her children are in that gray zone where—to some Jewish people—they're not even Jews. And there's a sense that the mother put them there by not converting when she had the chance. Second, the moms tend to project-manage the bar mitzvah even if the final decisions are made as a couple. So the moms are naturally the brunt of whatever unhappiness the grandparents or others express about the arrangements.

Finally, I think it's especially hard for the non-Jewish mom because the clichés about Jewish mothers, like most clichés, have an element of truth. Jewish women are known for having the courage of their convictions and the willingness to speak up—all qualities to love and admire . . . unless they belong to your mother-in-law. The normally intense, occasionally troubled relationship between the woman who raised a son and the woman who later married him can become really difficult at times like this. Especially if the mother-in-law lacks confidence in her daughter-in-law and doesn't respect boundaries. If the relationship has been strained all along, it's hardly going to improve now.

Many parents feel very challenged and judged when planning a bar mitzvah. Heavy is the weight of society, family, and their own expectations on their backs. At a moment like this, the whole family should work extra hard to be supportive of each other and restrained in their comments and behavior. To a family in a fragile, vulnerable state of mind, even modest criticism—and even when it's expressed as helpful advice—can seem harsh and divisive.

I haven't even talked about what the non-Jewish extended family can add to the pot—everything from anger at being on the team that "lost" when the children's religion was chosen to simple confusion about how they can be a meaningful part of the celebration now. Suffice it to say, family dynamics can become fierce. The best way to dampen ardent feelings is to appeal to everyone's higher nature. Make it clear at the beginning—and repeat as necessary—that this is a project with a goal. And the goal is to make sure that when your child mounts the bimah on the big day, she'll know that her entire family is united behind her. She should not be troubled or distracted by any sense of conflict, divided loyalties, hostility, or sadness. This is the time for adults to act like adults and put aside their agendas to focus on what's most important: "their" child's well-being.

If you're from the non-Jewish side of the family, it's time to recognize that however you feel about it, this child is Jewish. Respect that; honor that. If you're from either side of the family and have a major problem with a detail of the plans, politely explain your position. Distinguish between real issues and matters of taste. If you're strictly kosher, for example, and no appropriate food has been ordered for you and other kosher guests, that's a real issue. If you're being asked to participate in a ritual and don't feel comfortable, that's also a real issue. Not liking the particular country club chosen is not a real issue. Neither is it appropriate to nurse a grudge because you were allowed to invite only a certain number of guests when your "payback" list is much longer. If you are the parents of the bar mitzvah, get used to listening. Then, weigh the input and respond with as much patience and compassion as you can muster. Remember that your son is also their grandson . . . nephew . . . brother.

Feeling Accepted by the Jewish Community

As you know from the earlier discussion, Conservative synagogues are bound by official policy to view your children as non-Jews if their father is the only Jewish parent and the children haven't formally converted, even if their hearts tell them otherwise. If the children's mother is Jewish, there's no problem for the kids. But, male or female, the non-Jewish parent will have a more limited role in the bat mitzvah than he or she would have at a Reform or Reconstructionist shul. Forward-thinking parents investigate all these issues—the status of the children and the eventual role of the non-Jewish parent—up front when they join a synagogue. But many of us instead join the synagogue where our friends belong without thinking much about the implications down the road.

Intermarried families will find varying degrees of welcome at different synagogues, but the non-Jewish family members will not be treated as equals at any of them, even the most liberal. You should all know right away, though, that if you're not allowed to perform a certain ritual or say a prayer, it's not because the clergy wish to shun you or make you feel slighted. It's simply that Jewish practice requires that non-Jews be excluded from certain rites. Non-Jews are not supposed to speak such phrases as *"Asher bachar banu"* meaning "Who has chosen us" or others that refer to God's Covenant with the Jewish people. Many prayers that parents normally say in their child's bar mitzvah service presume that the speaker is Jewish. It's not appropriate for a non-Jew to say them, as this amounts to saying a prayer "in vain" or offering a prayer that is not true in some way.

Other popular rituals—lining up the family on the bimah and passing the Torah from grandparents to parents to the bat mitzvah—may at the discretion of the clergy include the non-Jewish family, however. That's because many synagogues recognize that although the Torah was not strictly the non-Jewish family's to give, the family has played a key role in delivering it by supporting the child in her Jewish education. The most compassionate and supportive synagogues will wherever possible have alternative prayers that the non-Jewish family members can recite so that the whole family can participate equally, if not identically.

Some synagogues, for example, replace the traditional aliyah *Barchu* that the parents chant before the Torah reading with a non-Jewish aliyah like the one that appears in Rabbi Jeffrey K. Salkin's book *Putting God on the Guest List* (in the chapter "The Changing Jewish Family"). This prayer begins, "O God of all humanity: We lift our voices in gratitude that the Torah has come into the world through the Jewish people . . ." The message of this prayer is very clear, states Rabbi Salkin: "I am proud that my child is a Jew. I am proud that the Torah is part of the spiritual inheritance of the entire world. I am grateful to have been part of that process."

Other synagogues allow the non-Jewish family to participate before the *Barchu* or after the *Aleinu*, the two "bookends" marking the part of the service that is obligatory for Jews and only Jews. In this case, the non-Jewish parent or family could read from the Psalms or recite the *Shehekheyanu*, the prayer that thanks God for "keeping us, sustaining us, and allowing us to reach this day."

Ask as early as possible what the non-Jewish family members will be doing in the service. Network with other intermarried families at your synagogue who've been through the process to see if there's any flexibility about adding non-Jewish prayers or other "moments" where the non-Jewish family can participate. If there's no opportunity to add to the service and you're unsatisfied with the level of participation you'll be allowed, the only alternatives—none of them ideal—are to make your peace with the situation, switch synagogues, or seek private tutoring and have your bar mitzvah outside of a synagogue. You could also talk to the group that helps draft these rules—the synagogue's Ritual Committee—to see if they'd consider any changes to existing policies.

Although there are limitations placed on non-Jewish family members in every synagogue, you should not assume it reflects ill will. On the contrary, many Jews rightly feel a debt of gratitude to a non-Jew who has set aside his own tradition and unselfishly given a child to the Jewish faith. That gift deserves to recognized and honored.

Non-Jews, whether guests or family, also need information about the bat mitzvah service and synagogue customs so they can feel comfortable attending the service. In "Basics of the Service," you will find information you should give to your non-Jewish guests as well as a description of "service booklets" families have prepared to explain what happens in the service. You don't need to write a novel, but distributing a little information will calm the fears of nervous guests and contribute to everyone's relaxation and enjoyment.

The "Basics of the Service" chapter suggests tools and knowledge that can help you shape your family's mitzvah experience to most closely resemble your ideal. When this day of ceremony is complete, your family should feel moved, inspired, and joyous about your decision to raise your children as Jews. If the behavior of any individuals threatens to ruin this for you, just remember Linus's famous remark from *Peanuts:* "I love humanity; it's people I can't stand." You can love the religion and what it aspires to be without having to embrace all its members. Here are two organizations that will help with whatever intermarried dilemmas you may experience.

Resources for Intermarried Families

The Jewish Outreach Institute provides support and resources for the intermarried and their families. Its website, www.joi.org includes directories of programs, a bulletin board, questions and answers, a library of resources, and many other services. Contact them at 1270 Broadway, Suite 609, New York, NY 10001; (212) 760-1440.

InterfaithFamily.com can help you make interfaith family connections in your geographic area and online. The site features interesting articles, discussion groups, links, and other helpful resources. You can reach them offline at PO Box 9129, Newton, MA 02464; (617) 965-7700.

There are also quite a few books on the subject of interfaith families. Let these organizations or the other interfaith families you know guide you to the best of these.

nine Writing a Great Speech and Finding the Courage to Give It

Bar/bat mitzvah speechwriting is not just for grown-ups, and your first speechwriting effort will probably be in support of your child when writing the *dvar Torah* (a "word of Torah"). If you follow the suggestion on the time line at the end of this book that your family discuss one idea from your child's Torah portion each week, your child should feel very prepared to write the *dvar Torah*. If not, here to help is a list of organizations with websites that keep archives of commentaries on the Torah portions you can use in devising your own word of Torah.

Helping Your Child with the *Dvar Torah*

Union of American Hebrew Congregations (Reform), 633 Third Avenue, New York, NY 10017-6778; (212) 650-4000; www.uahc.org.

Jewish Reconstructionist Federation, Beit Devora, 7804 Montgomery Avenue, Suite 9, Elkins Park, PA 19027-2649; (215) 782-8500; www.jrf.org.

United Synagogue of Conservative Judaism, 155 Fifth Avenue, New York, NY 10010-6802; (212) 533-7800; www.uscj.org (click on "Torah Sparks").

The Orthodox Union, 11 Broadway, New York, NY 10004; (212) 563-4000; www.ou.org. To find info on the Torah portion, click on "Learn Torah." This will take you to a drop-down list of many resources/commentators to choose from. I like Aish HaTorah (see next listing), but go ahead and explore.

Aish HaTorah, headquartered in Jerusalem, is based in the Orthodox movement, but its goal is not necessarily to compel people to embrace orthodoxy but to reconnect to their Jewish souls. Has a large network of offices in the United States and abroad. See their website, www.aish.com, for addresses and phone numbers. To find info on the Torah portion on their website, click on "Torah Portion" and you'll arrive at a lovely simple page that gives a choice of several commentaries. I like "The Family Parsha" and "Lively Parsha."

Jewish Theological Seminary of America maintains a "distance-learning" website. Go to www.learn.jtsa.edu and click on "Parashat HaShavua" or "Parashat HaShavua Archives."

Your Speech to Your Child

If you were the greatest, most eloquent writer in the world, how would you tackle the job of summarizing your feelings for your child? Resuscitated people who say they've glimpsed heaven report that there are luminous colors there we've never seen on earth. Perhaps there are also words there wondrous enough to express what we hold in our hearts for our children, but I don't know what they are. We're stuck with the thousands of words we know, none of which seem up to the task.

So it's probably best right now to make your peace with the idea that whatever you say in a speech to your child, however long you go on, it's never going to feel completely right or sufficient. If you're making a speech from the bimah, the clergy and congregants would most definitely prefer that you keep your remarks short and to the point. You will have many more chances at the party to speak at length.

Parent speeches seem to fall into a few categories: the ones that are purely about the love, joy, and pride we feel as parents; the ones that instruct the child on embracing Judaism; and those that do both. There is at least one other type of speech: the spoken résumé. This chronicles the child's every achievement from birth. It sounds like a "love and pride" speech because the information is presented that way—"and then after you led your team to victory in the semifinals, we were so proud that you were chosen MVP . . ."—but we're not fooled now, are we? These parents feel that certainly on this day, they've got bragging rights and they aim to use them.

I don't want to be judgmental because my children move me to tears and, when faced with "doing right" by them in a speech, I'm just as perplexed and stammering as the next mom. I honestly don't know what to say or, more important, what our kids need to hear at a moment like this. So I did an informal survey of the child experts I know.

What Kids Want Their Parents to Say

No one wanted to generalize too much, feeling that one-size-fits-all advice never really applies to anyone. But I heard some surprisingly simple and commonsensical things. First, kids don't want to be embarrassed, so forget about telling those adorable stories from their baby and childhood years. And second, kids want you to recognize the hard work of bar/bat mitzvah preparation, but don't detail their struggles. Your child does not want to be viewed as anything other than the cool, commanding individual he or she appears to be today.

It may sound strange, but I think many parents do feel that something changes about their child on bar or bat mitzvah day. Or perhaps something changes about themselves. The tussles over Torah study are finished. You can't hold his hand anymore; he goes on alone from here. There's a great sense of dignity and majesty around him. You may already have heard him chant his portion in the kitchen, but it's quite another matter to see him up on the bimah, beautifully dressed, standing before the huge Torah scroll. And to see all eyes turn to him—they don't see the baby you held in your arms or the goofy boy he was just yesterday. Today, he *is* a man.

I spent my son's bar mitzvah day in awe of who he had become. Griffin had been growing up all along, but somehow I didn't really see it until I looked through those other people's eyes. He was poised . . . masterful. He had such presence. I was so proud, yet I could also feel my heart breaking. He didn't belong just to me anymore; he was going out into a bigger world . . . handsome, confident, not looking back.

What does your child want you to say before she goes? That you know how hard she worked, how much it took to get here. That you could never take for granted how complicated it is to be young and on the verge of adulthood—wanting to go, longing to stay. That you love the person she is and admire the person she's becoming. That no matter how far away she goes, you will always be her home.

I didn't know going in what I should say in my speech and I was unprepared for how emotional I felt, but I was able to read the words I had written the night before. This is what they said:

Since Dad and I are both writers, I expect some people may look to us and think, here, finally, are the people who can find the words that express what is in every parent's heart at a moment like this. But, of course, we aren't those people . . . because there are no words. Just feelings of love and pride that are almost overwhelming. Pride about the kind of person you are, about all you've achieved, but also a pride that comes from a personal sense of having contributed something really special to the world.

Lots of parents use this moment to plot a course for their child's life. I don't have any particular ambition for you. You have so many gifts; you could do anything, really. But I would say, it's not so important to set the world on fire; rather to kindle love in people's hearts and to be a force for what is good in the world. I wish you an extraordinary life, that is, one filled with the everyday miracles of love, friendship, children, useful work, and a sense of how precious it all is. You have been a wonderful son and you will be a great man —a great husband, father, and friend. I am so happy to have a front-row seat. And I am so grateful to be your mother.

Listen to Other Parent Speeches

In choosing your own words, it's a very good idea to attend as many bar and bat mitzvah services at your own synagogue as possible leading up to your own big day. If the synagogue allows parent speeches from the bimah, you will certainly hear enough to know what sounds right to you. You can even grab little phrases here and there that you might want to use. Not to diminish what is special in each one, but parent speeches over the course of a year become a de facto essay contest since everyone is trying to do his or her best with the same topic. You be the judge of who succeeds. Go and learn from them. In addition to the creative inspiration, it will make you very excited about how you're going to feel when it's your family's turn.

Quotes to Get You Going

Often the hardest part of writing is getting started. If you're hung up, don't keep trying to think of that all-important first line yourself when there's so much great material out there. Use a quote! Since you will probably give at least two speeches—one to your child and one welcoming your guests—this selection contains quotations on life, children, and friendship. If you'd rather not write the first line, second line, or any line, you can read a poem, literary passage, or blessing instead of a speech. Check "Basics of the Service" under "Personalizing the Service" for sources.

Quotes on Life and How Best to Live It

The best and most beautiful things in the world cannot be seen or even touched. They must be felt with the heart.

—HELEN KELLER

Today a new sun rises for me; everything lives, everything is animated, everything seems to speak to me of my passion, everything invites me to cherish it.

—ANNE DE LENCLOS

Our obligation is to give meaning to life and in doing so to overcome the passive, indifferent life.

—ELIE WIESEL

We make a living by what we get; we make a life by what we give.

—WINSTON CHURCHILL

There are only two ways to live your life. One is as though nothing is a miracle. The other is as though everything is a miracle.

—ALBERT EINSTEIN

Love the moment and the energy of that moment will spread beyond all boundaries.

—CORITA KENT

Whatever you can do, or dream you can, begin it. Live each day as if your life had just begun.

—JOHANN WOLFGANG VON GOETHE

What lies behind us and what lies before us are tiny matters compared to what lies within us.

—RALPH WALDO EMERSON

Everything you can imagine is real.

—PABLO PICASSO

Don't be afraid to take a big step if one is indicated. You can't cross a chasm in two small jumps.

—DAVID LLOYD GEORGE

Life isn't about finding yourself. Life is about creating yourself.

—GEORGE BERNARD SHAW

It is not how much we do, but how much love we put in the doing. It is not how much we give, but how much love we put in the giving.

—MOTHER TERESA

We can do no great things, only small things with great love.

—MOTHER TERESA

To be Jewish is to be an idealist.

—ANONYMOUS

Courage is not the absence of fear, but rather the judgment that some-thing else is more important than fear. The brave may not live forever, but the cautious do not live at all. From now on you'll be travelling the road between who you think you are and who you can be. The key is to allow yourself to make the journey.

—A FATHER WRITING TO HIS DAUGHTER IN THE FILM *THE PRINCESS DIARIES*, SCRIPT BY GINA WENDKOS, FROM THE NOVEL BY MEG CABOT

Do it trembling if you must, but do it.

—ANONYMOUS

The true measure of a man is how he treats someone who can do him absolutely no good.

—SAMUEL JOHNSON

Do just once what others say you can't do, and you will never pay attention to their limitations again.

—JAMES R. COOK

I haven't failed; I've found 10,000 ways that don't work.

—BEN FRANKLIN

Never doubt that a small group of committed citizens can change the world. Indeed, it's the only thing that has.

—MARGARET MEAD

Twenty years from now you will be more disappointed by the things you didn't do than by the ones you did. So throw off the bowlines, sail away from the safe harbor. Catch the trade winds in your sails. Explore. Dream.

—MARK TWAIN

Nothing will ever be attempted if all possible objections must be first overcome.

—SAMUEL JOHNSON

Keep your eyes on the stars, keep your feet on the ground.

—THEODORE ROOSEVELT

You will find as you look back upon your life that the moments that stand out, the moments when you have really lived, are the moments when you have done things in a spirit of love.

—HENRY DRUMMOND

It is never too late to become what you might have been.

—GEORGE ELIOT

Throw your dreams into space like a kite and you do not know what it will bring back, a new life, a new friend, a new love, a new country.

—ANAÏS NIN, THE DIARIES OF ANAÏS NIN

To find the best in others, to leave the world a bit better whether by a healthy child, a garden patch, or a redeemed social condition; to know even one life has breathed easier because you lived. This is to have succeeded.

—RALPH WALDO EMERSON

Don't give in! Make your own trail.

—KATHARINE HEPBURN

Even if you're on the right track, you'll get run over if you just sit there.

—WILL ROGERS

If I have the belief that I can do it, I shall surely acquire the capacity to do it even if I may not have it at the beginning.

—MAHATMA GANDHI

Hold fast to dreams, for if dreams die, life is a broken-winged bird that cannot fly.

—LANGSTON HUGHES

If you're going to tell people the truth, be funny or they'll kill you.

—BILLY WILDER

It is not easy to find happiness in ourselves, and it is impossible to find it elsewhere.

—AGNES REPPLIER

Far better it is to dare mighty things, to win glorious triumphs, even though checkered by failure, than to take rank with those poor spirits who neither enjoy much nor suffer much, because they live in the gray twilight that knows not victory nor defeat.

—THEODORE ROOSEVELT

Reality is wrong. Dreams are for real.

—TUPAC SHAKUR

The grace of God means something like: Here is your life. You might never have been, but you are because the party wouldn't have been complete without you. Here is the world. Beautiful and terrible things will happen. Don't be afraid. I am with you. Nothing can ever separate us. It's for you I created the universe. I love you.

—FREDERICK BUECHNER

Be at peace with your God, whatever you conceive him to be, and whatever your labor and aspirations in the noisy confusion of life. Keep peace with your soul. With all its sham, drudgery and broken dreams, it is still a beautiful world.

—MAX EHRMAN

To love and be loved is the greatest happiness of existence.

—SYDNEY SMITH

We don't remember days, we remember moments.

—CESARE PAVESE

One word frees us of all the weight and pain of life. That word is "love."

—SOPHOCLES

Nothing is impossible to a willing heart.

—ANONYMOUS

Do what you can, with what you have, where you are.

—THEODORE ROOSEVELT

Nothing shines as brilliantly as work created with pride and passion.

—ANONYMOUS

It is impossible to win the great prizes of life without running risks.

—THEODORE ROOSEVELT

Everything I do, I do to make my heart sing.

—ANONYMOUS

Nothing is at last sacred but the integrity of your own mind.

—RALPH WALDO EMERSON

Never look down on anybody unless you're helping him up.

—JESSE JACKSON

If at first you don't succeed, you're running about average.

—M. H. ALDERSON

The greatest test of courage on earth is to bear defeat without losing heart.

—ROBERT GREEN INGERSOLL

There are no shortcuts to any place worth going.

—BEVERLY SILLS

Go the extra mile. It's never crowded.

—ANONYMOUS

Goals are dreams with deadlines.

—DIANA SCHARF HUNT

As long as I live, I'll hear waterfalls and birds and winds sing. I'll interpret the rocks, learn the language of flood, storm and the avalanche. I'll acquaint myself with the glaciers and wild gardens, and get as near the heart of the world as I can.

—JOHN MUIR

Each day comes bearing its gifts. Untie the ribbons.

—ANN RUTH SCHABACKER

Let your hopes, not your hurts shape your future.

—ROBERT H. SCHULLER

MitzvahChic

Life is either a daring adventure or nothing at all.

—HELEN KELLER

The most beautiful thing we can experience is the mysterious.

—ALBERT EINSTEIN

We find in life exactly what we put in.

—RALPH WALDO EMERSON

If there is no wind, row!

—ANONYMOUS

The happiest people don't have the best of everything, they just make the most of everything.

—ANONYMOUS

Life is a glorious banquet, a limitless and a delicious buffet.

—MAYA ANGELOU

Quotes on Children and Family

There is no friendship, no love, like that of the parent for the child.

—HENRY WARD BEECHER

It is not what a teenager knows that worries his parents. It's how he found out.

—ANONYMOUS

Children are the living messages we send to a time we will not see.

—JOHN W. WHITEHEAD

The value of marriage is not that adults produce children, but that children produce adults.

—PETER DE VRIES

Grandmas are moms with lots of frosting.

—ANONYMOUS

A man never stands as tall as when he kneels to help a child.

—KNIGHTS OF PYTHAGORAS

Adolescence is a period of rapid changes. Between the ages of twelve and seventeen, for example, a parent ages as much as twenty years.

—ANONYMOUS

If you want to recapture your youth, just cut off his allowance.

—AL BERNSTEIN

You don't have to suffer to be a poet; adolescence is enough suffering for anyone.

—JOHN CIARDI

If you bungle raising your children, I don't think whatever else you do well matters very much.

—JACQUELINE KENNEDY ONASSIS

If you can give your son or daughter only one gift, let it be enthusiasm.

—BRUCE BARTON

Of all nature's gifts to the human race, what is sweeter to a man than his children?

—CICERO

Some birds aren't meant to be caged, their feathers are just too bright. And when they fly away, the part of you that knows it was a sin to lock them up, does rejoice.

—*SHAWSHANK REDEMPTION*, SCRIPT BY FRANK DARABONT
FROM THE NOVELA BY STEPHEN KING

Quotes on Friendship

No road is long when you are traveling with good company.

—ANONYMOUS

Friendship is unnecessary, like philosophy, like art . . . It has no survival value; rather it is one of those things that give value to survival.

—C. S. LEWIS

Love is blind, but friendship closes its eyes.

—ANONYMOUS

Friendship is Love without his wings!

—LORD BYRON

Friendship is a sheltering tree.

—SAMUEL TAYLOR COLERIDGE

The greatest good you can do for another is not just to share your riches but to reveal to him his own.

—BENJAMIN DISRAELI

What is a friend? I will tell you . . . it is someone with whom you dare to be yourself.

—FRANK CRANE

I never came to you, my friend, and went away without some new enrichment of the heart; How can I find the shining word, the glowing phrase that tells all that your love has meant to me, all that your friendship spells?

—GRACE NOLL CROWELL

A friend is one to whom one can pour out all the contents of one's heart, chaff and grain together, knowing that the gentlest of hands will take and sift it, keeping what is worth keeping, and, with the breath of kindness, blow the rest away.

—ARABIAN PROVERB

A friend is someone who knows the song in your heart and sings it back to you when you have forgotten how it goes.

—ANONYMOUS

A friend is one who believes in you when you have ceased to believe in yourself.

—ANONYMOUS

The real test of friendship is: Can you literally do nothing with the other person? Can you enjoy together those moments of life that are utterly simple? They are the moments people look back on at the end of life and number as their most sacred experiences.

—EUGENE KENNEDY

Each friend represents a world in us, a world possibly not born until they arrive.

—ANAÏS NIN

The friend who can be silent with us in a moment of despair or confusion, who can stay with us in an hour of grief and bereavement, who can tolerate not knowing, not curing, not healing and face with us the reality of our powerlessness, that is a friend who cares.

—HENRI NOUWEN

A friend may well be reckoned the masterpiece of nature.

—RALPH WALDO EMERSON

If I die, I forgive you; if I live, we will see.

—SPANISH PROVERB

Overcoming Your Nervousness

It's normal to be nervous. It's heroic to give a brief speech anyway. On a day when we ask our child to get up in front of one hundred people and risk embarrassment, it seems only fair that we also venture it ourselves. This section contains suggestions for overcoming moderate nervousness. If you're extremely anxious and expect that your anxiety may cause you to lose sleep or make it impossible to enjoy your child's service, certainly you should not plan to give a speech. But read this section anyway, keep an open mind, and see how you feel as you get closer to the event.

Fear of public speaking is one of the all-time top phobias. For some reason, most of us would prefer torture to five minutes in the spotlight. If I had to name the fear, I would guess it's some combination of not wanting to look or sound like an idiot, not wanting to be vulnerable in public, and being unsure you have, or are worthy of, your friends' love and support.

The amazing thing about this fear is that we have it even though we've seen countless speakers lovingly and sympathetically supported by audiences not even as intimate and supportive as the one that surrounds us at our child's *simcha*. These people are your friends; you're safe with them. They already know and accept you. They're here for you. Moreover, everyone knows how hard it is to speak from the heart—one-to-one—much less on stage in front of a crowd.

No one's going to judge the weaknesses in your "performance." On the contrary, when someone gets up and says something we all feel—like what a miracle it is to love and be loved by a child—that's when the magic happens. There's instantly a special feeling in the room; the composition of the air seems to change the way ozone before a thunderstorm makes everything glow.

It's a sacred moment, a time to look within. So while you may think everyone is focusing on the shakiness in your voice, they're not paying attention to that. Nervousness is much less noticeable than it feels. And if people do notice, they're happy for you. Because having a voice that shakes with emotion means that you have loved deeply, one measure of a life well lived.

Preparation Is the Key

If you write a speech that you love, you should be excited about actually reading it on the big day. Notice I said "reading" it—a nervous person should not try to memorize, particularly since a lot of the worry will then center on whether, under pressure, you're going to be able to remember everything just the way you wrote it. Practice your speech aloud, though obviously not in front of anyone who should hear your words for the first time on the big day.

Write your speech on little index cards you can easily tuck into even a small pocket or purse. Reading from cards also gives you a place to look, so you can forget about how many people are actually sitting there listening. If you're speaking to your child, just look back and forth from that adorable face to the card. Pretend it's just you and him.

Keep it short—anyone can survive talking for three minutes. Force yourself to breathe slowly and deeply and to talk at a normal, not a hurried pace. Keep in mind that most people have stage fright only before they start speaking—once you're under way, you're going to feel fine and maybe even enjoy it.

And remember, according to Tom Antion, professional speaker and trainer, stage fright actually makes you better looking!

"Fear is your friend," he says. "It makes your reflexes sharper. It heightens your energy, adds a sparkle to your eye, and color to your cheeks. You are more conscious of your posture and breathing. With all these effects, you will actually look healthier and more physically attractive." For Tom's complete list of "Stage Fright Strategies," see his website at www.antion.com/articles/stagefright.htm.

And now, if you're still scared, think of it this way: You're the parent of a teenager—nothing's scarier than that! You can do this! If public speaking is a fear of yours (as it is of many of the world's top performers), make yourself give just a little speech. You will finish the bar mitzvah with not just great memories but also with feelings of real satisfaction and renewed confidence in your own abilities.

ten Making the Event More of a Mitzvah

I have touched in earlier chapters on how to make charitable giving part of your mitzvah event. Here, let's look at a whole range of opportunities to make this event a blessing and a true beginning for a child who's just consecrated himself to an ethical life and the enduring performance of mitzvot.

What Are the Mitzvot?

Although we talk about the Ten Commandments (mitzvot), there are actually 613. There are 248 positive mitzvot ("Do this") and 365 negative ("Don't do this"). Not all the mitzvot can be practiced by common people today—some deal exclusively with the practices of the priests; others stipulate how to deal with lawbreakers, a power that is no longer in the hands of the religious community. Many, though, are still practicable: believing in and worshipping God, reading the Shema, studying the Torah, putting up a mezuzah, saying grace after meals, keeping your word, giving to the poor, coming to the synagogue and rejoicing on the festivals, honoring and respecting parents, and many more. If you're interested in the complete list, ask your rabbi how to get a copy.

Mitzvah literally means "commandment," but it's also used colloquially to mean "a good deed"—the way it's used in the title of this chapter. This, according to Rabbi Jeffrey K. Salkin in *Putting God on the Guest List,* is because the Hebrew word found its way into Yiddish and became *mitzveh* with this diminished meaning. A mitzvah is part of the Jewish Covenant with God, a sacred obligation; it's not a deed to perform when you're in a mood to be lovely.

Where to Start

A rabbinical student gave a simple and perfect suggestion on how to help a child preparing for bar mitzvah to "live" the mission: When your child begins studying her Hebrew, have her choose one mitzvah to perform regularly. It should be something simple—saying the Shema at bedtime or getting a tzedakah box and putting something in it every day. Once the initial mitzvah becomes a habit, add another one to perform daily or weekly. You could decide, for example, to once a day offer a silent *bracha* after a meal.

We all like to join in when there's a big walkathon scheduled or a special day set aside to cook for the homeless, but the true path to a conscious, sanctified life is paved with small acts performed every day. Start down this road and see where it takes you. If, in support of your child, the family has begun talking Torah once a week (see the time line at the end of this book), you're already on your way. See if in the process you begin to feel more Jewish or at least more connected to ideas and a purpose larger than yourself.

Finding a Mitzvah Project

Most synagogues will require your child to do a mitzvah project, giving sustained volunteer effort over weeks or months to a charity. There are plenty of options, so your child should be able to choose a cause that connects with the Torah portion or with her own interests. Here are some great organizations that will help you find a good match or even help you start your own service club. If any of the web addresses don't work, start at the end of the address and keep lopping off sections that come after "/" until it finally works. Or go to the home page (the address ending with ".com" or ".org") and look for links to the page you want.

Note: This list is for information only! I don't endorse any charities.

Be sure to investigate and satisfy yourself as to the legitimacy of any charity before contributing or getting involved with it.

- **How Kids Can Raise Cash by Selling Their Stuff (or Yours).** Volunteering is excellent, but some kids want to generate cash for tzedakah so they can contribute in a tangible way. Of course it's hard because kids don't have much earning power at age twelve or thirteen, but now they can go beyond the lemonade stand or bake sale. eBay has a program—"Giving Works"—that allows you to sell items just as you would normally on eBay. But you can designate some or all of the sale's proceeds to go to a charity you choose. Check it out at www.ebay.com.

- **Get Matched With a Volunteer Job You'll Love**—VolunteerMatch lets you search in your community for volunteer opportunities that match your interests. Search in twenty-eight categories including animals, arts, computers, health, homeless, hunger, justice, and media. "Virtual" opportunities give you a chance to help even faraway groups. www.volunteermatch.org; (415) 241-6868

- **Start Your Own Social Action Group**—DoSomething helps teens organize their own social action groups at school. www.dosomething.org

- **116 Practical Mitzvah Suggestions**—Excerpted from Danny Siegel's *Gym Shoes and Irises (Personalized Tzedakah)* and published in conjunction with USY's Tikkun Olam ("heal the world") Program, these are ideas any bar/bat mitzvah child and family can do as a mitzvah project now and on an ongoing basis. www.ziv.org

- **Areyvut**—Recognizing the potential significance of the bar/bat mitzvah celebration in the lives of Jewish preteens, Areyvut is committed to providing young men and women with innovative opportunities to enhance their celebration by actively participating in challenging community-based projects. Their team of educators works with you to design projects that cater to each child's interests and personal development goals with the aim of igniting a lifelong commitment to social justice, charity, and kindness. areyvut.org; (212) 813-2950

- **SocialAction.com**—This is an online Jewish magazine dedicated to pursuing justice, building community, and healing the world. It has a huge index of links to help you find organizations engaged in important social action. www.socialaction.com

- **Kids for Kids**—Has programs, services, and activities for young victims of terrorism, their families, and friends: teen support groups and clubs, creative therapeutic activities, hospital visits, home care, and psychological clinics. They also give supplies and financial gifts to families in need. www.kidsforkids.net; New York phone (917) 254-4100 (rings in Jerusalem); Miami phone (305) 238-5600

- **Commission on Social Action and the Religious Action Center of Reform Judaism**—Helps families and b'nai mitzvah find social action projects and programs. www.rac.org/social/bank; 212-650-4160

- **Idealist.org**—Subtitled "Action Without Borders," this excellent website lists nearly thirty thousand organizations working around the world and lets you search them by interest. Also has a compelling list of charities/service clubs started by children and ones offering volunteer opportunities for kids, teens, and families. When the kids are older, there's a searchable directory of internships.

- **Familycares.org**—An organization supremely tailored to the needs of families with young children who want to find satisfying volunteer opportunities for the kids or the whole family.

- **Points of Light Foundation**—This organization helps you find a volunteer center in your community that maintains listings of local opportunities. www.pointsoflight.org/

Twinning

In the 1960s–'80s, it was common for a bar mitzvah to "twin" with a Jewish child in the Soviet Union who, because of religious oppression, was not able to become a bar mitzvah at his own service. Today, the distress of Jews in Russia is somewhat eased, but many children there still don't have the benefit of religious education. There are now also new opportunities to twin with children in Israel, including recent Ethiopian emigrants, or with a Righteous Gentile who helped to rescue Jews during the Holocaust. There are even a few programs of "Holocaust twinning" where the student shares his experience with the memory of a child who perished in the Holocaust before reaching bar mitzvah age.

The best example of what can happen when a family reaches for meaning (a true *MitzvahChic* story):

A bat mitzvah who decided to twin with the memory of a girl who died in the Holocaust asked Yad Vashem in Jerusalem to find for her, if they could, a girl from Poland (because the bat mitzvah's family was from there) named Malka (the bat mitzvah's Hebrew name). Yad Vashem sent the family the story of Malka Rosner who, it turned out, was survived by a brother who was then living in Florida. The family contacted Malka's brother and told him of their plan to honor his sister, hold her symbolic bat mitzvah, and tell her story through their daughter's event. The brother was overwhelmed and ultimately attended the bat mitzvah with his family, and they had an aliyah in the service. The entire experience, needless to say, was transformative to everyone who was involved or who merely attended.

- **Twinning With an Israeli AMIT Child**—For $250, your child can be twinned with a less fortunate Israeli child in an AMIT school. Your gift pays for an *oneg Shabbat* for the Israeli bar/bat mitzvah; your child will receive a bronze State of Israel Medal and a personalized certificate. Twins are encouraged to become pen pals. Visit their website at www.amitisrael.org, or send your check along with your child's name and date of bar/bat mitzvah to AMIT, 817 Broadway, New York, NY 10003.

- **Twinning With an Israeli, Russian, or Ethiopian Child**—Emunah of America provides a broad range of social services in Israel including the housing, care, and education of neglected and abused children and settlement of immigrant families. www.emunah.org; 7 Penn Plaza, New York, NY 10001; (212) 564-9045 or (800) 368-6440

- **Twinning With a Russian Child**—Two organizations offering this twinning are the Bay Area Council for Jewish Rescue and Renewal and Action for Post Soviet Jewry. In both, the twins get to share experiences and learn from each other. When it is time to become a bar/bat mitzvah, the American spiritually includes his or her twin in the ceremony. Bay Area Council: www.bacjrr.org; (415) 703-0800. Action for Post Soviet Jewry: www.actionpsj.org/twin.html; (781) 893-2331

- **Twinning With an Ethiopian Child**—The North American Conference on Ethiopian Jewry (NACOEJ) matches children worldwide with Ethiopian Jewish children living in Israel. In addition to the personal benefits of the friendships that often develop between twins, your financial gift helps to improve quality of life for all the Ethiopian Jewish children in the community. The council also offers handmade crafts and gifts that can be purchased for the bar mitzvah party. www.nacoej.org/bar_bat.htm; (212) 233-5200

- **Twinning With a Rescuer**—This program of the Jewish Foundation for the Righteous allows a child who is accepting the duties and responsibilities of an adult within the Jewish community to fulfill the mitzvah of tzedakah and to help the Jewish community repay a collective debt of gratitude. The child selects a particular rescuer to be twinned with and makes a donation to the JFR. The suggested minimum gift is $180. The bar/bat mitzvah receives a Twinning Certificate, and a presentation can be made from the bimah if your rabbi approves. www.jfr.org; (212) 727-9955

- **Holocaust Twinning**—There is no national program I'm aware of that is dedicated to matching b'nai mitzvah families with stories, but you can do this yourself. Visit the website of the Museum of Tolerance in Los Angeles for biographies of children lost in the Holocaust (www.museum oftolerance.com, then click on "Children of the Holocaust"); choose the child whose story most touches you. Tell his or her story at your child's service, make a donation in the child's memory to an appropriate charity, and pledge that you will hold that child's memory in your heart. Information on Holocaust children is also available from Yad Vashem (www.yadvashem.org).

  A particularly good charity to contribute to as part of a Holocaust Twinning effort is the Blue Card Fund, the only agency in the United States that provides cash to needy Holocaust survivors and, when necessary, to their psychologically affected children. It was founded more than sixty years ago by a group of compassionate people, themselves recent refugees from Nazi tyranny. This financial aid is rendered by check directly to the needy with a minimum of bureaucratic red tape. The Blue Card Fund is a nationwide organization that fills a need unmet by other agencies and public programs. Visit their website at www.bluecardfund.org.

Another Holocaust twinning resource is an organization running a local project in the Washington, DC, area. Contact Sam Spiegel, coordinator of the Remember-a-Child Project, at (301) 881-2454.

Buying Products with a Conscience

You're going to buy stuff anyway; why not get it from a charity that could really use the support? Here are some of the best opportunities. These are general ideas—"Party Ideas for Each Torah Portion" includes charitable ideas tied into the themes of specific Torah portions.

- **Voting Shares for the Bar/Bat Mitzvah in a Charitable Organization**—The World Repair Company is a youth-run organization that gives money to causes around the world. Anyone can buy shares of stock for $18 apiece as a gift to the bar/bat mitzvah. Or the child can use proceeds from the *simcha* to buy shares. Shares give the child voting rights in the organization and, hence, a voice in its work. www.worldrepair.net; (305) 778-7971

- **Invitations That Support Rescuers**—The Jewish Foundation for the Righteous sells an invitation that involves a bar/bat mitzvah family in the support of a Righteous Gentile who risked his or her own life to save Jews. If you don't wish to use the JFR's standard invitation, you can choose another by the Checkerboard Company, include the JFR's explanatory text with the name of the rescuer the family chooses, and make a donation of $5 per invitation. www.jfr.org; (212) 727-9955 or toll-free (888) 421-1221

- **Invitations That Support Autism**—Keshet sells full-color invitations (with matching response cards, celebration cards, and thank-you notes) that can be printed for any occasion. Text is added that says, "In honor of this occasion, a donation has been made to Keshet, an organization for children and young adults with special needs" www.keshet.org; (847) 205-1234

- **Place Cards and Centerpiece Ideas that Honor Strong Jewish Women** are available from the Jewish Women's Archive. Go to www.iwa.org and search under "bat mitzvah" or call (617) 232-2258.

- **Create Gorgeous Judaica for Your Event or at Your Event**—*Hiddur mitzvah,* the "beautification of a commandment," is the concept that says any ritual item should be as beautiful as possible in order to glorify God. The Hiddur Mitzvah Project lets you use glass mosaics to create items that become heirlooms or objects to donate. www.hiddurmitzvah.org

- **Handcrafted Ritual Items**—Lifeline for the Old (Yad L'Kashish) is a

Jerusalem-based organization that uses artistic elderly people to make special crafts. They have tallitot, tallit bags, *kippot,* challah covers, and all types of gifts, many embroidered or in beautifully painted silk. See "Tzedakah" in "Eight Complete Parties That Will Leave You *Farklempt!*" for photos of some of their items. www.lifeline.org.il/

- **Beautiful *Kippot* That Change Lives**—Brilliant colors and beautiful patterns are the hallmarks of the *kippot* crafted by the Maya women behind MayaWorks. Sales support the remote villages in Guatemala where these women live. Order early, as they are very busy. www.mayaworks.org; telephone is (773) 506-4905

- **Buy a Tallit Bag, Support a Family**—The North American Conference on Ethiopian Jewry offers richly embroidered bags that depict scenes from the Bible. These beautiful works of African art are made by Ethiopian Jews—each one takes a month to make and the purchase price will support a family for an entire month. They also sell matzo and pillow covers. www.NACOEJ.org (from home page, click on "Embroidery"); (212) 233-5200

- **Buy Trees as Party Favors**—The Jewish National Fund is the resource for buying trees to be planted in Israel. www.jnf.org; (800) 542-TREE

- **Products That Support Breast Cancer Research**—Available from Avon, www.avon.com, or The Susan G. Komen Breast Cancer Foundation, www.komen.org (click on "marketplace"). Also, buy the postage stamps that contribute to breast cancer charities to use when you're mailing your invitations.

Other Great Charitable Ideas to Use at Your Event

- **MAZON: A Jewish Response to Hunger**—*Mazon* means "food" in Hebrew, and this organization raises funds through Jews nationwide, donating 3 percent of the cost of weddings, bar and bat mitzvahs, and other joyous events. www.mazon.org; (310) 442-0020

- **Rachel's Table**—Picks up donations of surplus, unserved food from your party and delivers it to an emergency feeding program. You just need to call them ahead to arrange it. Some caterers who don't want to be bothered will tell you that this type of donation is illegal or inadvisable, but there are in some places "good samaritan" laws that protect donors from liability arising from food donation, so check the laws in your state and go for it! www.rachelstable.com; (413) 733-0084

- **Ziv Tzedakah Fund**—An inspirational kid-oriented website that recommends that when it comes to tzedakah, you take Nike's advice and "just do it." Recently added a great section on bar and bat mitzvah projects and simple things you can do to make your event more of a mitzvah. www.ziv.org; (973) 763-9396

Donating Money to Charities

The old standby is still a great idea, but how do you decide which organizations deserve your support? Get the information you need before you donate by visiting or calling Just Tzedakah.

- **Just Tzedakah**—The web resource for donors to Jewish charities. Features guidelines for giving, excerpts from Jewish sources that discuss the philosophy and law behind tzedakah, reports on charities, a "giving registry" that the bar/bat mitzvah or a well-wisher can set up. www.just-tzedakah.org; (240) 599-9196

Do-It-Yourself Opportunities

- Use as centerpieces baskets or arrangements of items to be donated after your party to a homeless shelter, school, hospital, library, etc. Good choices: baskets of food, toys, baby items, and stacks of books. (See "Tzedakah" in "Eight Complete Parties That Will Leave You *Farklempt*!") Note, if you donate books, place a bookplate in the front of each with the names of the guests at the table and note that the books are given in honor of those guests.
- Ask guests to bring a food item, small toy, or book to be donated and place a collection bin outside the sanctuary.
- Make a family donation to a charity in commemoration of the occasion.
- Investigate if any charities in your area offer for rent items needed for the service or party.

- Eliminate one planned expense from your party and instead donate the funds to charity.
- If you're creating any simple craft items for your party, hire an elderly or low-income worker to do the work.
- Give as party favors items purchased from a charity or a card noting that a donation was made in the guest's name to a charity.

eleven Party Ideas for Each Torah Portion

Using Torah and Holiday Themes at the Party

This is where we translate Torah and holiday themes into actual party ideas. Here you can also see how the holidays of the Jewish calendar match up with the Torah portions so, in planning decorations and activities for your party, you can draw on the portion, the holiday, or a broader theme from Torah. Of course, you don't strictly need a theme for your party in the sense that one motif pervades everything. If you like to tie everything together, check out "Eight Complete Parties That Will Leave You *Farklempt!*" a collection of intriguing and beautiful Torah-based theme parties worked out to the last detail. For a more individualistic approach, use an idea or two from this chapter or swap these ideas in and out of the "complete parties" to achieve just the right mix for you.

Why make party plans out of Jewish ideas? First, this celebration is about the Torah. If you engage yourself and others in even light discourse about the meaning of a Torah idea, you're fulfilling the mission of the day—for Jews, the mission of *every* day. Second, the concepts are fascinating and still relevant today to those who would pick them up and look at them. As Hayyim Nahman Bialik wrote in his poem "And if the Angel Should Ask," "Out of the dead letters welled forth songs of life."

Finally, you're going to make your party as beautiful and fun as you can, anyway—shouldn't it have heart and soul too? When guests come home and reflect that a celebration was truly magical, it's because it "worked" on all these levels, not just one or two.

If you've grown up Jewish with minimal exposure to other religions, you may not be aware of how special Judaism is. One unique aspect is that while most Christian denominations require that everyone accept without question the Bible interpretations set forth by the church and its clergy, Judaism is a dynamic religion in which everyone is encouraged to study and discuss. Hence our reputation for outspokenness and mental agility so eloquently captured in the expression "two Jews, three opinions."

It's our duty and privilege to think about the ancient words and what they mean, but if you're doing it in a party setting, there's no reason it shouldn't also be playful and fun. In the next section you will see Torah ideas linked to decorations, activities, games. This is not frivolous; this is a way of personalizing the great ideas of the faith and putting them to use in daily life.

As one quick example, consider the portion Vayetze. The Hebrew means "and he went out," referring to Jacob leaving his homeland. The words of the portion are ancient, but the feelings are familiar: We all eventually leave home. What does it mean to leave home? When you're a child, home is the house you live in and the people inside. Once you leave home, you can't make a new home of your own until you know what "home" means to you. What are the essential ingredients?

Now as a party host looking to use this idea, you have options. It would be interesting and discussion provoking to have everyone make a list of what they would take if they were leaving home or what they would need to make a home for themselves—a variation on the "What would you take to a desert isle?" idea. Then you could invite the extroverts to read theirs or simply pin them up on a corkboard. Or you could put on the table all the things the bar mitzvah misses the most when he's away at camp. Or, if you just wanted to play and have fun, you could put a stack of plain silver metal lunch boxes in the middle of the table, plus travel-themed stickers and paint pens, and let your guests decorate their own little suitcases. This is how Torah ideas become fun, compelling parties where people learn a bit about Torah, themselves, and each other.

Finding the Products and Charities Listed Here

The following pages contain many references to products you can buy or charities offering volunteer or giving opportunities. I include the website addresses for the charities, but not for most of the stores because products change so frequently. To find a product mentioned, visit my website, www.MitzvahChic.com. If you find that a product is no longer available and you need help finding an alternative, please email me—online treasure hunting is my favorite thing. If you find a great product on your own, I'd appreciate hearing about that as well and so would your village of fellow mitzvah planners! If you're not accustomed to shopping or finding information online, I would say anyone with a preteen in the house must have Internet access somehow, some way, and this is a perfect time to learn to use it. If that's really not a viable option for you, though, you can write to me for contact information for any charity or online store mentioned here and I'll do my best to supply it.

MitzvahChic
PO Box 30144
Elkins Park, PA 19027

Hunting Online by Yourself

For those who are new to Internet shopping, a few points to ponder. Many people are nervous about buying items online because they're concerned that their credit card information could be viewed and stolen. This is certainly a possibility, but the entire fate of the mushrooming ecommerce business rests on maintaining the public's trust, and most vendors are committed to keeping your information secure. Consider also that, up until several years ago, credit card paper receipts issued by stores and restaurants had your entire account number, expiration date, and signature on them, and the carbons from these often ended up in the trash where anyone could pick them up. So if you used a credit card up through the early nineties, you may have already taken bigger risks than you would take now ordering from a secure website. Still, if you are concerned, you can read the security policy of any online vendor you're thinking of ordering from to see what steps it's taken to protect your information.

The best way to find something online is to use a search engine. For example, go to www.yahoo.com, click on "shopping," and fill in the box next to "search" with keywords of what you're looking for, for example, "square dishes." Then click on "search." If you type the words "square dishes" inside quotation marks, you'll get a listing of only those products with the two-word phrase "square dishes" in their descriptions. No quotation marks? You'll get a whole list of products whose descriptions include the words "square" and "dishes," in any order or context, including one that could potentially say something like, "Don't be square; order one of our satellite TV dishes today." Still, you may want to try it both ways, because with the phrase in quotation marks you will not see listings with descriptions that could be phrased like this: "We have thousands of dishes at huge discounts, in round and square." Personally, if I were shopping for square dishes, I'd want to know about that place!

The Yahoo page results will have a small photo, description, and price for about ten products per page. Probably there will be more than one page of results, each with up to ten photos and vendors on it. This is a great function because it allows you to see a lot of options quickly. If one photo displayed looks almost right, but you don't like the color, size, or some other detail, click on "see all matches at this store" to see if they have any variations.

Another excellent shopping search engine is Froogle. Go to www.google.com, click on Froogle (or just go to www.froogle.google.com) and again enter your keyword term (with or without quotation marks) in the search box.

Both Yahoo Shopping and Froogle let you refine your search by narrowing it to a certain price range or category. For me, searching by price range has always been very effective when shopping for multiples of something. You probably already know that you need one hundred of something as a party favor or fifteen of something as a centerpiece, and how much you want to spend, so why waste time or torture yourself looking at much more expensive versions of the same idea? I also don't search by category because, particularly with wackier ideas, you never know where you'll find something and you don't want the search engine looking at too narrow a range of stores. I've sometimes gotten a great new idea because the search engine wandered a little too far afield and ended up presenting an interesting new store or item.

Where Do I Go to See the "Party Ideas Titled . . ."?

In several places in this chapter, you'll see the phrase "see party idea . . ." These are the parties described and photographed in "Eight Complete Parties That Will Leave You *Farklempt!*" So go to that chapter to see them. Otherwise, enjoy this chapter and let your mind roam free. Remember that many themes in the Torah are repeated over and over, so it may be worthwhile to skim the Themes/Ideas for several portions, not just the one your child will be reading.

BERESHIT

In the beginning

NEARBY HOLIDAYS

Rosh Hashanah
Yom Kippur
Sukkot
Simchat Torah

For information on holidays, see pages 153–156.

PORTION OR HOLIDAY THEMES AND IDEAS

Rosh Hashanah is the New Year. Yom Kippur is the Day of Atonement. Sukkot means "booths" and refers to the structures the Israelites erected in the desert during the Exodus and later in their fields to give shade during the harvest. Simchat Torah is "Rejoicing of the Torah." The main theme of this Torah portion is the wonder of God and creation.

Ideas: See party idea "Beginnings." Use fruit topiary centerpieces (see "Crafts for Style and Therapy"), or—really beautiful—put colorful small fruits in the bottom of clear vases holding flowers. Invite everyone to write a brief reply to the question "Am I my brother's keeper?" and post the notes on a corkboard or an easel where all can read them. Let guests design their own new animals (get simple animal pictures from coloring books; make photocopies on card stock, and have the kids cut out heads, arms, legs, wings, bodies, and put on table with markers and brass fasteners). Ask people to name their animals and say where they live, what they eat. Or get animal masks and balloons to play with plus animal-print party favors (small notebooks, snap bracelets, CD holders, etc.). Instead of numbering tables, name each one after something made during Creation.

NOAH

Noah

PORTION OR HOLIDAY THEMES AND IDEAS

Themes: Faith, Covenants, water, two of a kind

Ideas: See party idea "Beginnings." Have your party on a boat. Incorporate floating candles into centerpieces. Use simple boat-shaped baskets (see www.MitzvahChic.com for sources) as "vases" or (filled with candy) weights for balloons and surround with small animals. Get animal masks and balloons to play with plus animal-print party favors (small notebooks, snap bracelets, CD holders, etc.).

LECH LECHA

Go out or go alone

PORTION OR HOLIDAY THEMES AND IDEAS

Themes: Abraham and Sarah, joy of parenthood (Sarah learns she'll have baby; Abraham that he will be the "father of nations")

Ideas: As centerpieces, have gift baskets made up to donate after the party to indigent mothers with new babies. See party idea "Beginnings."

VAYERA

The Holy One of Blessing appeared	PORTION OR HOLIDAY THEMES AND IDEAS
	Themes: God spares Isaac and rewards Abraham for his faith; angels destroy Sodom and Gomorrah but save Isaac
	Ideas: Use angel decorations (see party idea "Saving Grace"). Use star motif, as God promises to make the Jews as numerous as "the stars of heaven." As an activity, set up a table with inexpensive flashlights, thick-sided paper cups, Sharpie markers, and pushpins, plus star maps that show simple constellations—guests can draw a constellation on the bottom of the cup, poke out stars with the pushpin, and tilt the cup over the end of the flashlight to project the stars onto ceiling and walls. Try it first to get the hang of it.

CHAYE SARAH

Sarah's lifetime	PORTION OR HOLIDAY THEMES AND IDEAS
	Themes: Sarah as the great-great-great-grandmother of us all; Rebekah at the well; Isaac reconciles with his half brother Ishmael, father of modern Arabs
	Ideas: At the party, make a toast to all the grandmothers. For tables, buy greeting cards for grandmothers, have color photocopy enlargements made, mount on cardboard, and stand them up in center of table and surround with flowers and candles. Pay a real *bubbe* who needs money to crochet little coasters or other table accents, or order something appropriate from the elderly craftspeople at the Israeli charity Lifeline for the Old. Donate to the charity Yad Sarah for frail elderly, www.yadsarah.org. (For sources, go to www.MitzvahChic.com.)

TOLEDOT

Generations	PORTION OR HOLIDAY THEMES AND IDEAS
	Themes: Joy of parenting; twins/brothers (Jacob and Esau)
	Ideas: Find old photos or take new ones of all the brothers in the family. Get them to say what they like about having a brother and write it on the back. Array the photos on tables or glue them to "table tents" (for source, go to links at www.MitzvahChic.com) and put their comments on the back. Brainstorm famous brothers (the Wrights, the Kennedys, the Jackson Five, the Marx Brothers, the Brothers Grimm) and/or twins. Make up a quiz with clues and put on the tables for people to guess who the brothers are. Award a prize to person or table with the most correct.

VAYETZE

And he went out (Jacob leaves his homeland)	PORTION OR HOLIDAY THEMES AND IDEAS
	Themes: Jacob dreams of a ladder of angels; leaving home and starting a family
	Ideas: See party idea "Dreams." For centerpieces, put little travel cases open on table and place flowers inside, or get a plain silver metal lunch box for each couple or individual guest and put on tables with travel stickers and paint pens for people to decorate a suitcase. Get "Jacob's Ladder" toys or get the instructions on how to make them (see Appendix I); put out the precut materials and let your guests make their own. (See www.MitzvahChic.com links for all resources.)

VAYISHLACH

And sent (Jacob prepared and sent gifts to Esau)	**PORTION OR HOLIDAY THEMES AND IDEAS**
	Themes: Wrestling with God; reconciliation (Jacob and Esau); coming home
	Ideas: Put welcome mats in middle of tables, top with a flower arrangement with a card that says, "Welcome home! All is forgiven." Put on the table all those things you would have missed if you'd been away from home—if the bar mitzvah goes away to camp, put out all those things he yearns for or you have to send him when he's away.

VAYESHEV

And he [Jacob] settled	**NEARBY HOLIDAYS**
	Hanukkah
	PORTION OR HOLIDAY THEMES AND IDEAS
	Themes: Mercy (Reuben keeps brothers from killing Joseph); Joseph and language of dreams
	Ideas: See party idea "Dreams." Incorporate menorahs into centerpieces but use long-burning candles—for the kids' tables, put in candy stix (like candy canes but no hook on top) instead of candles and glue on gelt for the flames, or use InstaLyte no-flame candles. Use as part of centerpieces reproductions of ancient oil lamps (go to links at www.MitzvahChic.com for source); see next entry.

MIKETZ

At the end of [Joseph's prison time]	**NEARBY HOLIDAYS**
	Hanukkah
	PORTION OR HOLIDAY THEMES AND IDEAS
	Themes: Dream interpretation; being prepared/thinking ahead; forgiveness
	Ideas: See party idea "Dreams." Set up a table with a laptop computer with phone line and let internet-savvy extrovert guests take turns wearing a special turban and being the "dream interpreter"—looking up people's dreams in a "dream symbols dictionary" on a popular website (for address, see www.MitzvahChic.com links). Or visit the website yourself ahead of time and print out the symbols dictionary and put it in a three-ring binder for the mystic interpreter. Have art students make up "dream paintings" on large index cards depicting common dream themes—including Joseph's. Make color photocopies on card stock and scatter on the tables or give to mystic interpreter to use in his or her "dream readings."

VAYIGASH

And [he] went up (referring to Judah interceding for Benjamin)	**PORTION OR HOLIDAY THEMES AND IDEAS**
	Themes: Self-sacrifice (Judah); forgiveness; leaving home (Jacob); family reunion (Joseph and family)
	Ideas: See party idea "Saving Grace" (about people who risk themselves to save others, as Judah does here). See "leaving home" ideas under Vayetze. Make a hunger charity the focus of the celebration, since Joseph saved Egypt and his family from starvation. Fashion your party as a big family reunion but include your friends as family of your heart. In Kabbalah, Joseph is "the harvester" who minds the storehouses of grain but also reaps a great harvest in being reunited with his family, so use harvest imagery.

VAYECHI

He [Jacob] lived (meaning Jacob lived seventeen years in Egypt) End of Genesis	**PORTION OR HOLIDAY THEMES AND IDEAS**
	Themes: A parent's blessing; humility (Joseph refusing to judge his brothers); hope (of the Promised Land)
	Ideas: Print copies of the Jewish parents' blessing for their children (see Appendix 1) and have all the parents read it aloud together over their children. Jacob notes the special character of each of his children's tribes and predicts their future—have each family at your party make a "flag" that shows their character and values, and what they want their future to be (see Appendix 1 for directions). Go to www.MitzvahChic.com links to download artwork to use.

SHEMOT

Names; Exodus begins	**PORTION OR HOLIDAY THEMES AND IDEAS**
	Themes: Baby Moses in the bulrushes; combating intolerance (Moses saving the slave); courage (Moses facing Pharoah); meeting God, heroic women
	Ideas: See party idea "Saving Grace." The midwives of ancient Egypt risked death to defy Pharoah's order to kill all male Hebrew babies. Pharoah's daughter saves Moses ("Whoever saves a single life is as if one saves the entire world"—Talmud). Buy invitations from the Jewish Foundation for the Righteous (www.jfr.org); buy party favors from the online store of the Museum of Tolerance (www.museumoftolerance.com); see MOT's website on teaching tolerance and that of the European Commission Against Racism and Intolerance for props/ideas you can use at your party (their striking black-and-white Passport and "all different/all equal" logos would look great paired with MOT's signature b&w shirts and mugs). See www.MitzvahChic.com links for web addresses. Incorporate reeds and cattails in any floral displays.

VA'ERA

I appeared (God reveals Himself to Moses)	**PORTION OR HOLIDAY THEMES AND IDEAS**
	Themes: Determination; courage (Moses and Aaron returning to Pharoah again and again)
	Ideas: See party idea "Saving Grace" (see reason in previous entry). Read stories of determination, courage, and other values worth having at the website of the Foundation for a Better Life (www.forbetterlife.org/).

BO

Go (what God instructed Moses to tell Pharoah)	**PORTION OR HOLIDAY THEMES AND IDEAS**
	Themes: Leaving bondage; the joy of freedom; feeling compassion for those who wrong you
	Ideas: See party ideas "Beginnings" and "Song." Have your child twin with a child who lacks religious or economic freedom to celebrate bar mitzvah (see "Making the Event More of a Mitzvah"). Join Amnesty International as a mitzvah project (www.amnesty.org). Make up a CD of freedom songs to play at the party (see Appendix 1 for suggested playlist) and then give out as a party favor. Forgive someone. Check out www.freethechildren.org to find out how to help end child slavery.

BESHALACH

[Pharoah] sent them out

NEARBY HOLIDAYS

Tu B'Shvat

PORTION OR HOLIDAY THEMES AND IDEAS

Themes: Entering the unknown; God leading as a pillar of smoke by day and fire by night; manna from heaven; celebrating trees

Ideas: See party ideas "Beginnings" and "Song." The first song of the Torah, the "Song at the Sea," happens in this portion. In honor of Tu B'Shvat, plant a tree in Israel in honor of each guest or couple (www.jnf.org). Serve manna at the party (see recipe in Appendix 1). Make seashell candles for tables (see "Crafts for Style and Therapy").

YITRO

Jethro
(Moses' father-in-law)

NEARBY HOLIDAYS

Tu B'Shvat
From this point on, the major theme for all portions is keeping the commandments.

PORTION OR HOLIDAY THEMES AND IDEAS

Themes: Settling arguments; setting rules; getting the chance to become God's "treasure" by embracing His Covenant; Moses receiving the commandments; celebrating trees

Ideas: See party ideas "Gifts" and "Beginnings." In honor of Tu B'Shvat, plant a tree in Israel in honor of each guest or couple (www.jnf.org). Work for or contribute to one of the many environmental charities here and in Israel—the Coalition on the Environment and Jewish Life (www.coejl.org) lists organizations; also check out www.ecojew.com to access the "Eco Kosher Network" and the "Guide to Judaism and the Environment" to read how Jewish philosophy suggests ecoconsciousness.

MISHPATIM

Judgments

PORTION OR HOLIDAY THEMES AND IDEAS

Themes: The first "laws" for humankind; the people accept the Convenant; Moses' forty days and nights on the mount; empathy; being a stranger; laws of kashruth

Ideas: See party ideas "Gifts," "Beginnings," and "Song." Even if you're not kosher, serve a kosher meal and explain its features. Invite a newly arrived immigrant Jewish family. Have guests write on index cards one new law they would propose if they could participate in making a new world and let the kids collect them and post on cork board or read aloud. Buy ritual or party items from the North American Conference on Ethiopian Jewry (NACOEJ.org) (see "Making Your Event More of a Mitzvah" or go to www.MitzvahChic.com and look for links). As a mitzvah project, write to politicians about issues that concern you. Teach English to refugees or collect needed supplies for them.

TERUMAH

Gifts (brought to the tabernacle)

PORTION OR HOLIDAY THEMES AND IDEAS

Themes: This portion is very similar in content to Tezaveh, Vayakhel, and Pekudei, so look at all; building the first house of worship; the ark

Ideas: See party idea "Gifts." Incorporate into centerpieces miniature arks or set out on tables small papier-mâché boxes with paint pens, glue, and flat brass charms in Egyptian and Jewish designs (see www.MitzvahChic.com links for all sources), and let everyone make his or her own ark.

TEZAVEH

Instruct or command (refers to Moses telling people to bring oil for the lamps)

NEARBY HOLIDAYS

Purim

PORTION OR HOLIDAY THEMES AND IDEAS

Themes: This portion is very similar in content to Terumah, Vayakhel, and Pekudei, so look at all; what priests wear and how they are consecrated; oil for the lamp; sacrifice; altar of incense

Ideas: See party idea "Beginnings," as this was the beginning of the priesthood and the house of worship. Use as part of centerpieces reproductions of ancient oil lamps (see links at www.MitzvahChic.com). Give packets of incense with beautiful holders as party favors (see www.MitzvahChic.com links).

KI TISA

When you take up (referring to the census)

NEARBY HOLIDAYS

Purim

PORTION OR HOLIDAY THEMES AND IDEAS

Themes: Figuring out the size of your army and taxing the people ½ shekel per soldier; giving second chances (the people fail but God remakes His Covenant with them)

Ideas: Order enough modern half-shekels through a bank or coin dealer that you can give one to each guest. Buy bezels for them (expensive) or hire a retired handyman (inexpensive) to drill a small hole at the top of each coin. At the party, hand them out and have a supply of neck chains or heavier bracelet chains, jump rings, and beading supplies to let everyone make a piece of jewelry. For bezel source, visit www.MitzvahChic.com links.

VAYAKHEL

To call together

NEARBY HOLIDAYS

Purim

PORTION OR HOLIDAY THEMES AND IDEAS

Themes: This portion is very similar in content to Terumah, Tezaveh, and Pekudei, so look at all. Kehillah, meaning a "Jewish community," comes from the name of this portion; giving loving attention to an effort; honoring religious leaders; building the tabernacle; observing Shabbat; giving generously and from the heart

Ideas: This portion and the other three named above discuss all the artisans and ritual objects needed to create and furnish the tabernacle: Make your own versions of the objects, number them, and pass them around at the party and let people record their guesses on what they are and what they were used for. Have someone who spins her own yarn bring her spinning wheel and demonstrate—let guests try it themselves. See party idea "Tzedakah."

PEKUDEI

The Records (an accounting of metals and other donations to the tabernacle); end of Exodus

NEARBY HOLIDAYS

Purim

PORTION OR HOLIDAY THEMES AND IDEAS

Themes: This portion is very similar in content to Terumah, Tezaveh, and Vayakhel, so look at all. God making His presence and guidance obvious to the people; the cloud covering the tent of meeting; when the tabernacle is completed, God says "Woe is Me" (why?); how the creation of the tabernacle is like God creating the universe; sacred work and how we feel about our own work

Ideas: For centerpieces, get a couple of yards of sparkly organza and bunch and fluff it up to make a poofy cloud for the center of the table. Underneath it, put two strings of battery-operated minilights (see www.MitzvahChic.com links). Make little metal books as party favors (see "Crafts for Style and Therapy"). Rent a fog machine (or have the DJ supply it) to re-create the wonder of the cloud. Pose the questions in your speech: Can we find ways to do sacred work in our daily lives, work that benefits the world and humankind rather than just ourselves? Can our existing jobs be made in some way sacred?

VAYIKRA

And He called (God calls Moses) Beginning of Leviticus, which has half the 613 mitzvot in it. Leviticus is about the giving of the laws.

NEARBY HOLIDAYS

Purim

PORTION OR HOLIDAY THEMES AND IDEAS

Themes: This portion is very similar to Tzav, so look at both. Making sacrifices to honor God—in modern times we offer prayer instead; how individuals are held responsible for sins of the community; sacrifice as an expression of the desire to be purified; home as a tabernacle with women as the priests; in ancient times, it was vital that all sinners—even wealthy and important people—atone *publicly* (now they're allowed to settle lawsuits for wrongdoing without admitting guilt—progress or no? Talk amongst yourselves); two sins discussed—failing to fulfill an oath and failing to testify—are known only to the sinner, hence they are akin to modern honor systems

Ideas: Give packets of incense with beautiful holders as party favors (see MitzvahChic.com links). In warm weather, have some little goats as special guests at your party and pen them where people can pet them and reflect on how in ancient times they'd have been used as "scapegoats." Have your child make a list of duties performed by the ancient priests and, next to it, a list of jobs performed in the home, and look for "matches." Talk about situations where having knowledge and not speaking up could change the outcome. Apologize to someone in front of other people and note how it feels. Talk about that in your speech.

TZAV

Command (God tells Moses to command Aaron)

NEARBY HOLIDAYS

Purim
Pesach

PORTION OR HOLIDAY THEMES AND IDEAS

Themes: This portion is very similar to Vayikra, so look at both. God speaks to His priests; keeping the light burning on the altar; priests perform rituals that influence other people—can we use our behavior to influence others?; wearing special clothes as a sign of respect; no worthy task is beneath our dignity to perform; should community leaders be held to a higher standard of behavior?; the sacrifice and prayer of well-being or thanksgiving—what are we thankful for?

Ideas: As a family, decide to make a regular sacrifice or gift—volunteer work or a donation—in gratitude for your well-being; choose an idea that most reminds you of your good fortune. Ask your rabbi to show you *Birchot HaNehenin*—blessings for the pleasures we receive through our senses. However many tables you have at your party, think of that many "pleasures we receive through our senses" (food, music, the human voice, art, beautiful scenery, etc.) and incorporate into the centerpiece at each table a symbol of that pleasure. Instead of numbering tables, indicate on the place cards that guests are at the "music" table, "paintings" table, and so on.

SHEMINI

Eighth (referring to the final day of ordination for the priests)

NEARBY HOLIDAYS

Pesach
Yom ha-Shoah (Holocaust Memorial Day)

PORTION OR HOLIDAY THEMES AND IDEAS

Themes: The importance of following instructions, especially the commandments; *Pirkei Avot:* "One who grabs too much loses all"; we should be holy because God is holy—what we consider holy; laws of kashruth

Ideas: For Holocaust Memorial Day, see party idea titled "Saving Grace." Do a simple murder mystery on deaths of Nadab and Abihu. Make up a flyer that tells the who, what, when, where, why, how of their deaths. Have it copied onto several different colors of card stock (one color for each team at the party). Cut each sheet into six large puzzle pieces and hide them all over the party hall. Divide kids into teams and have them look for the puzzle pieces in their team's color, then assemble them to solve the murder mystery. Serve a kosher meal and/or as an educational tool make up a *not* kashruth menu and explain what's awry with each dish. Put on kooky things people routinely eat today, like shark, octopus, and ostrich, that ancient people would not have been confronted with. Would the ancients have been allowed to eat sushi? Talk amongst yourselves!

TAZRIA

She gives birth

NEARBY HOLIDAYS

Pesach
Yom ha-Shoah (Holocaust Memorial Day)
Yom ha-Zikaron (Remembrance Day)
Yom ha-Atzma'ut (Israel Independence Day)

PORTION OR HOLIDAY THEMES AND IDEAS

Themes: Tazria and Metzorah are usually read as a double portion, so look at both. How people and things become impure; childbirth; caring for the sick; blood as symbolic of the holiness of both life and death and rituals for those touched by it (the Torah calls the blood of childbirth a "source" or "fountain"); rabbis connect the Hebrew for "leper" to the words for "slander" and bad behavior—do bad deeds lead to affliction or make us impure?; slander as an injury to the speaker, the listener, and the one spoken about

Ideas: As a mitzvah project, collect medical supplies to be sent overseas; donate to the ARMDI: American Red Magen David for Israel (Israel's "Red Cross," www.armdi.org). Or help www.birthdayfoundation.org, a charity that throws birthday parties for kids in homeless shelters. Buy party favors from the Museum of Tolerance (www.wiesenthal.com/store). Use as centerpieces gift baskets for new mothers, then donate them after the party.

METZORAH

Leper

Pesach
Yom ha-Shoah (Holocaust Memorial Day)
Yom ha-Zikaron (Remembrance Day)
Yom ha-Atzma'ut (Israel Independence Day)

PORTION OR HOLIDAY THEMES AND IDEAS

Themes: Metzorah and Tazria are usually read as a double portion, so look at both. Purification rituals; understanding the plight of the outcast; if illness is caused by God, should human physicians try to heal it?; immersion in water as a means to purify; objects can also be impure; a house becoming infected because its owner is a miser or guilty of other improper behavior; how those afflicted or different are treated by society

Ideas: See party idea "Beginnings." Work for an AIDS charity or contribute to one of these providing meals to people with AIDS:

New York: God's Love We Deliver (www.godslovewedeliver.org)
Philadelphia: Manna (www.mannapa.org)
Minneapolis: Aliveness Project (www.aliveness.org)
Vancouver: A Loving Spoonful (www.alovingspoonful.org)
Washington, DC: Food & Friends (www.foodandfriends.org)
Columbus, OH: Project OpenHand (www.outincolumbus.com/pohc/)
Los Angeles: Project Angel Food (www.angelfood.org)

Make a list of things that are impure physically (toxic substances) or ethically (biological weapons) and write to world leaders urging their elimination. For a leper declared "clean," one bird is sacrificed and another is set free, so hire a bird handler to loose birds outside at the beginning of your party and explain to your guests that this was an act of purification for the ancients and marks a new beginning for your child. Use all-white flower centerpieces. Incorporate water into centerpieces (floating candles, large clear vases with fruits in the bottom and simple flowers above, etc).

ACHARI MOT

After the death
(of Aaron's sons Nadab
and Abihu)

NEARBY HOLIDAYS

Pesach
Yom ha-Shoah (Holocaust Memorial Day)
Yom ha-Zikaron (Remembrance Day)
Yom ha-Atzma'ut (Israel Independence Day)

PORTION OR HOLIDAY THEMES AND IDEAS

Themes: This portion is often read with Kedoshim, so look at both. Preserving what is holy; praying with sincerity and being truly repentant when asking forgiveness; scapegoating; attitudes and rules that protect family life; God cannot forgive sins we commit against others—we must gain the person's forgiveness first; how we can right our wrongs against others; Yom Kippur; introspection; prohibitions against marrying relatives; what is the Holy of Holies as described in the Torah and how it compares with this thought from *The Dybbuk* by S. Ansky: "Every spot whereon a man may stand and lift his eyes to heaven becomes a Holy of Holies . . ."

Ideas: Donate to the Eldridge Street Project, which is working to preserve one of New York's oldest and most beautiful synagogues. Wear simple white garments to the service or party. In warm weather, have some little goats as special guests at your party and pen them where people can pet them and reflect on how in ancient times they'd have been used as "scapegoats."

KEDOSHIM

Plural of the word "holy"
(refers to the laws that
make us holy)

NEARBY HOLIDAYS

Pesach
Yom ha-Shoah (Holocaust Memorial Day)
Yom ha-Zikaron (Remembrance Day)
Yom ha-Atzma'ut (Israel Independence Day)

PORTION OR HOLIDAY THEMES AND IDEAS

Themes: This portion is often read with Achari Mot, so look at both. The "heart" of the Torah, the Golden Rule ("love thy neighbor as thyself"); life is sacred; love the stranger as we were strangers once in Egypt; being holy and moral while participating in daily life; we're a separate people but should not separate ourselves from the world; holy times, places, and things; leave the gleanings and the edges of the fields for the poor

Ideas: See party ideas "Saving Grace" and "Heart." Sing the *Ve'ahavta* (check out the recording by singer/cantor Debbie Friedman). Serve a vegetarian meal. Buy ritual objects or partyware from refugee Ethiopian Jews in Israel (see www.MitzvahChic.com links for North American Conference on Ethiopian Jewry). For centerpieces, get large square dishes, grow wheatgrass on the edges (soak wheat berries in water to cover overnight, put on moist dirt, pat around edge of dish and keep in dark cool place to sprout; then give light and keep moist to grow). Experiment well ahead of the party to see how many days the grass needs to grow, so you'll know how far ahead of the actual party date you need to start the seeds. Put pillar candles or a low vase of flowers in the middle.

EMOR

Speak (Moses speaks laws of holiness to the priests)

NEARBY HOLIDAYS

Yom ha-Zikaron (Remembrance Day)
Yom ha-Atzma'ut (Israel Independence Day)
Lag Ba'Omer (the 33rd day of counting the Omer)

PORTION OR HOLIDAY THEMES AND IDEAS

Themes: The holiness of time—Shabbat and the holidays; honorable conduct; dealing with imperfection; kindness to animals; keeping the experiences of our ancestors alive today; the responsibility of Jewish people to preserve God's reputation by being moral and ethical

Ideas: Work together as a family to write an "oath" of right behavior. Create a grouping of remarkable "family archaeology" clocks to work into the decorating scheme by drilling a hole in the front of a number of metal or wooden household items (coffeepot, lunch box, old signs, old license plates, etc.) and threading through the simple clockworks sold at all large craft stores. Create a family history video. Give small travel clocks as party favors. Find a mitzvah project having to do with animals (most shelters will not allow youngsters to work in them, but you can find other jobs by going to www.volunteer match.org and searching under "animals" and "virtual" for projects—like crafting animal-themed items to sell at craft fairs—that benefit groups serving animals), or raise money to adopt a raptor through the Birds of Prey Foundation (www.birds-of-prey.org), a whale (www.whalecenter.org), or an animal you can visit regularly at your local zoo. Kids can raise money by selling old video games and such on auction sites.

BEHAR

On the mount

NEARBY HOLIDAYS

Lag Ba'Omer

PORTION OR HOLIDAY THEMES AND IDEAS

Themes: This portion is often read with Bechukotai, so look at both. Importance of balancing work and rest to keep a system healthy; giving freedom; preventing poverty; making a fresh start; sevens; freeing slaves; "the earth is the Lord's, and the fullness thereof; the world and they that dwell in it" (Psalms 24:1); the idea that we can't "own" anything—we pass through life, the land stays; the words on the Liberty Bell ("Proclaim liberty throughout all the land unto all the inhabitants thereof") come from this portion

Ideas: See party idea "Beginnings." Make your celebration as environmentally correct as possible by using recycled items and conserving resources. Volunteer or support an environmental charity—check out Kids for a Clean Environment (www.kidsface.org) and Youth for Environmental Sanity (www.yesworld.org). Visit as a family the Eco-Center at the Lotan Kibbutz in Israel (www.birdingisrael.com); see Yitro for other environmental charities. Go to www.freethechildren.org for ideas on helping to end child slavery. Have on the tables big colorful buckets of sidewalk chalk and array around the room small blackboards with inscriptions on the frame: "Things to clean from the world," "Things to clean from my life," "Things to clean from a stream," "Things to clean from the air," "Things to clean," "Things we hate to clean." Have erasers around so people can *wipe the slates clean* (to share the experience more, have someone walk around and note people's responses and read them aloud later in the party). If you don't want to use chalkboards, you can make any flat solid thing into a chalkboard by spraying it with chalkboard paint.

BECHUKOTAI

My Laws
End of Leviticus

NEARBY HOLIDAYS

Lag B'Omer

PORTION OR HOLIDAY THEMES AND IDEAS

Themes: This portion is often read with Behar, so look at both. The blessed life that comes with faith; the merit of the patriarchs (how God's love for Abraham, Isaac, and Jacob causes him to forgive Israel); how the merits of one person can redeem the Jewish people; gifts to the sanctuary; blessings and curses—is it better to reward good behavior or to punish bad?

Ideas: See party idea "Gifts." Find out what "gifts" have been made to your sanctuary—including volunteer work—and recognize them. Contribute a gift of your own. See party "Saving Grace" for how one person can make a difference. Celebrate fathers in your decorating: use photos of fathers with their children or "famous fathers," quotes from fathers (see Bill Cosby and Paul Reiser books on parenting), or classic father gifts like neckties in the centerpieces. Give kids a chance to come up and say what they love about their dads, and at the end of the evening have the kids who participated award the classic dad gifts from the centerpieces to their dads.

BAMIDBAR

In the desert
Beginning of Numbers, consisting largely of lists and accounts: the census, order of the march, gifts to the Temple, etc.

NEARBY HOLIDAYS

Shavuot

PORTION OR HOLIDAY THEMES AND IDEAS

Themes: Assessing strength; being organized; "wilderness experiences"—which life passages are wilderness experiences; times of personal wandering and searching; the value of the individual; knowing your family history; "parenting" children other than your own; redeeming the firstborn

Ideas: See party idea "Heart" (due to family focus of this portion, plus heart in the sense of courage in the wilderness). Go camping as a family before the bar/bat mitzvah and have your own wilderness experience, or check out www.torahtrek.com and go on a Jewish "visionquest." Help redeem the Jews of Ethiopia who now live in Israel by buying ritual and party items from the North American Conference on Ethiopian Jewry (see "Making the Event More of a Mitzvah" or go to www.MitzvahChic.com links). "Adopt" a poor child by taking responsibility for his or her financial support or get matched with a child through the Big Brothers/Big Sisters organization. At the party, make "family flags" that show the family's history and values (see Appendix 1 of this book for directions or go to www.MitzvahChic.com to download the artwork). Make a well-researched family history video and show it at the party.

NASO

Lift up (refers to Moses counting the Levite census)	**NEARBY HOLIDAYS** Shavuot

PORTION OR HOLIDAY THEMES AND IDEAS

Themes: The priestly blessing; gifts offered in dedication of the altar; Nazirite vows and other ways of separating from the world to be closer to God; blessings—with what do we wish to be blessed?

Ideas: See party ideas "Shine" and "Gifts." Get a recording of Debbie Friedman singing "Y'varech'cha" from the album *If Not Now, When?* (this is the priestly blessing). Write your own blessing for your family and friends and read it at your party. Ask several friends and family to think of what they wish to be blessed with and, at the end of your reading, gesture to each of them in turn, saying, "May we be blessed with _____," and let them fill in the last word. Learn to meditate as a way of separating from the world and being closer to God.

BEHAALOTECHA

Refers to Aaron lighting the menorah	**NEARBY HOLIDAYS** Shavuot

PORTION OR HOLIDAY THEMES AND IDEAS

Themes: Being steadfast in the face of unfair criticism; believing in yourself; being strong enough to ask for help; resolving sibling conflict; being satisfied with what God gives you; how God communicates with us; Miriam becomes a leper; hearing the shofar; the new moon

Ideas: See party idea "Shine." Incorporate menorahs or ancient oil lamps into your centerpiece (for oil lamp source see www.MitzvahChic.com links). Research why and when the shofar was blown in ancient times and have a *ba'al tekiah* come to the party and demonstrate the various ways to blow the shofar. Let a few people from the audience try it and receive pointers. Decorate using moon and star imagery.

SHELACH-LECHA

You may send
(God lets Moses decide whether or not to send spies into Canaan)

PORTION OR HOLIDAY THEMES AND IDEAS

Themes: Courage; having faith; trying fringes on garments as a reminder of God and the commandments; worthiness; when God said the Israelites will not see the land, it was on Tisha B'av; the significance of numbers in the Torah (ten spies, ten in a minyan, ten commandments, ten righteous men needed to save Sodom; forty days the spies were gone, forty years Israelites wandered in desert, forty days and nights Moses spent on Mt. Sinai, forty days and nights it rained in Noah's flood); spies report the people in the land were "giants"; rules for making challah

Ideas: Make your own tallit (see "Crafts for Style and Therapy"). Create a travel brochure showing the Promised Land as Joshua and the spies described it; decorate the room with oversized items that the "giants" of the Promised Land would have used. Set aside a table, overseen by an expert, where guests can go to make challah or get precut and hemmed tallit fabric and strings and learn to tie the fringes. (*The First Jewish Catalog* by Michael Strassfeld et al. has fringe-tying instructions, but it's a complicated procedure, so have a knowledgeable person there to instruct. You might also want to have some practice pieces made out of rope so it will be easier to demonstrate and follow; provide printed instructions so people can take their tallit home and work on the fringes in a quieter atmosphere. See www.MitzvahChic.com for all resources). Give spy gear to the kids as party favors.

KORACH

Korach (a Levite who rebelled against Moses and Aaron)

PORTION OR HOLIDAY THEMES AND IDEAS

Themes: Being a peacemaker; finding paths to peace; trying to reconcile; monuments as reminders and deterrents to wrong behavior; arguments "for the sake of heaven" (moral arguments) vs. troublemaking; Aaron's rod; redeeming the firstborn

Ideas: Find a mitzvah project by visiting the website of Interfaith Voices for Peace and Justice (www.interfaithvoices.org); see other peace website addresses in Torah portion Pinchas. Collect photos of various monuments—some very famous and others less so. Arrange on posterboard and number them. Have guests write their guesses of monument's name and what behavior it seeks to encourage or deter. Visit website of Yad Vashem (www.yadvashem.org) to see how they keep the memory of heroism alive. Incorporate into centerpieces modern "sticks," like Aaron's flowering rod, that are symbols of authority: a judge's mallet, conductor's baton, shepherd's rod, king's scepter, police officer's baton, etc.

CHUKAT

A law whose origin and purpose are unclear

PORTION OR HOLIDAY THEMES AND IDEAS

Themes: Preparing for the final journey; water from the rock; following rules even when they don't make sense; celebrating Miriam's accomplishments (as a seer, baby Moses' protector, midwife, leader of the "Song at the Sea"); people giving their special gifts to society; should leaders have more self-control than ordinary people?

Ideas: See party idea "Song." Adopt a stream. Contribute to charities that foster water quality and quantity here or in Israel. Look on www.idealist.org for volunteer opportunities for kids and families to help the environment, and see Torah portions Yitro and Behar for more environmental websites and party ideas. Check out a company offering spiritual wilderness adventures at www.torahtrek.com. Use water in centerpieces (floating candles or big clear vases with fruits in bottom and simple flowers on top). Ask guests ahead of time to give their special gifts to society by donating an hour of their professional or personal time performing some kind of errand to be auctioned at your party—have a silent auction at the party and donate the proceeds to the bar/bat mitzvah's favorite charity.

BALAK

Balak
(king of Moab)

PORTION OR HOLIDAY THEMES AND IDEAS

Themes: Talking donkey; "how goodly are thy tents, O Jacob"; speaking only blessings instead of curses; seeing angels; finding your own space; Balaam (prophet or sorcerer?); Pinchas as an Egyptian name that means "black-skinned"; "Israel will perish when her children cease to study"

Ideas: Balaam's blessing contributes the beginning of the *Mah Tovu* prayer (said silently upon entering the synagogue). It has been set to various tunes—ask your cantor if the congregation can sing this at your service and ask to hear the tunes he or she knows. Help the Jews of Ethiopia who now live in Israel by buying ritual and party items from the North American Conference on Ethiopian Jewry and/or twin with an Ethiopian or other Jewish child (see "Making the Event More of a Mitzvah"; for NACOEJ go to www.Mitzvah Chic.com and look under links). Use angel motif in your decorating or see party idea "Saving Grace." Set up a simple tent—Jacob's tents were likely black and made from goat hair, but you can do a simple version—(see Appendix 1 for instructions). Furnish with a rug and big pillows, have some dress-up stuff there, and have a photographer to take instant pictures of guests posing in Jacob's famous tent.

PINCHAS	
Pinchas (a priest, son of the priest Eleazer)	**PORTION OR HOLIDAY THEMES AND IDEAS**
	Themes: The birth of women's rights (daughters of Zelaphchad asking to inherit); passing the torch (Moses to Joshua); peace maintains the world; the new moon and festivals/the Jewish calendar; Pinchas as an Egyptian name that means "black-skinned"
	Ideas: See party idea "Shine." Help the Jews of Ethiopia who now live in Israel by buying ritual and party items from the North American Conference on Ethiopian Jewry (see "Making the Event More of a Mitzvah" or go to www.MitzvahChic.com and look at links). Use moon imagery in your decorating: Look for a "peace" charity for a mitzvah project and ongoing—check out some of these sites:
	Interfaith Voices for Peace and Justice (www.interfaithvoices.org) for comprehensive listing of opportunities to work for peace
	Idealist.org for huge listings of volunteer opportunities, organizations that match people with volunteer opportunities, and under "kids and teens/volunteering with your family," chances to do just that, here and overseas
	International Peace Bureau (www.ipb.org) for peace ideas and links
	Volunteers for Peace (www.vfp.org) to find work camps families can join here or abroad for a couple of weeks

MATOT	
Tribes	**PORTION OR HOLIDAY THEMES AND IDEAS**
	Themes: This portion is often read with Masee, so look at both. Working together for a common goal; being accountable to God and your fellow man; showing loyalty and true feelings (Israel's love for Moses); choosing between working for personal gain or a divine mission (tribes wanting to settle east of the Jordan River and not fight to gain the Promised Land); do Jews today have a divine mission to help secure the Promised Land?; putting your children before your possessions; rules of kashruth; annulling vows; being "clear before the Lord"—have a clear conscience and faultless behavior
	Ideas: See party idea "Tzedakah." Serve a kosher meal. Have guests experience working together for a common goal by having a scavenger hunt. Buy whatever you can for your service and party from Israel. Be sure to make your loyalty to and feelings about your friends and family clear in your speech welcoming them. See "Writing a Great Speech and Finding the Courage to Give It" for suitable quotations on friendship.

MASEE

Marches; the end of Numbers	**PORTION OR HOLIDAY THEMES AND IDEAS**

Themes: This portion is often read with Matot, so look at both. Remembering where you came from; creating sanctuaries; places of refuge; can religion thrive within secular society?; mercy to unintentional lawbreakers; Shabbat walking limits of 2,000 cubits (½ mile) around your home; Moses as the wise judge

Ideas: See party idea "Song." Create a "travel diary" of all the places Israelites went in their wanderings; illustrate with photos off the internet and share it at the party: Contribute to or volunteer at a shelter for battered women (a place of refuge) or work with refugees. Seek mercy for others by joining Amnesty International. Create a family history video as a way of remembering where you came from and show it at the party: Take all your guests on a 2,000-cubit walk. Before you set out, ask them to guess what landmark they think is 2,000 cubits away and record the guesses. Award a prize to the person who comes closest without exceeding 2,000 cubits.

DEVARIM

Words or *Discourse;* Deuteronomy begins	**NEARBY HOLIDAYS**
	Tisha B'av

PORTION OR HOLIDAY THEMES AND IDEAS

Themes: Knowing your history; parting words/saying good-bye; a hymn to Israel; taking Jewish history to heart as if it had actually happened to us today; spies; warriors/pioneers; Moses: "God has made you numerous as the stars"

Ideas: See party idea "Song." Decorate with star imagery (see "star" activity under Vayera and check www.MitzvahChic.com). Find interesting quotes/passages from the farewell speeches of various leaders (Martin Luther King, Gandhi, presidents, prime ministers, etc.) and computer-print them onto table tents and array on tables (see www.MitzvahChic.com links for source for table tents). Ask your cantor how to find "warrior songs" (songs that were sung by chalutzim of old, songs sung by today's Israeli army, or songs with the word *chalutzim* in them) for the kids to sing. Buy gift parcels for actual Israeli soldiers (www.apackagefromhome.org). Give away spy gear like ultraviolet ink pens or door alarms as party favors (see www.MitzvahChic.com under links; search the web under keywords "Spy Toys" for other options). Have a table where kids can write with "disappearing ink" (fresh-squeezed lemon juice) using Q-tips; have a lamp on the table to show them that, once the juice is dry, holding the paper over a warm lightbulb reveals the message. Create a family history video to show at the party.

VAETCHANAN

And I pleaded
(refers to Moses pleading to be allowed to enter the Holy Land)

NEARBY HOLIDAYS

Tisha B'av

PORTION OR HOLIDAY THEMES AND IDEAS

Themes: Great people should be held to a higher standard; being just and moral; the Shema; the *Ve'ahavta,* "put these words on your heart"; being responsible for your actions; significant moments in Jewish history; love of the mountains (Moses goes up Mt. Pisgah to view the whole of the Promised Land); all Jews stand at Sinai; cities of refuge; this is the "Shabbat of Comfort" or "Consolation," as the portion begins, "Oh be comforted, my people" (because of the destruction of the Temple and other ills that have befallen the Jewish people)

Ideas: See party idea "Heart." In your speech, reveal the most significant Jewish moments in your family's history. Before the bar/bat mitzvah, take a family trip to the top of a mountain. Print out song sheets (see www.MitzvahChic.com links to download) so everyone can sing the *Ve'ahavta* "you shall love" (try cantor/singer Debbie Friedman's version) together. Set aside a table for mezuzah making (the strip of paper inside a mezuzah has the Shema and *Ve'ahavta* written on it). The simplest "container" to make is felt fabric that's decorated, then rolled or folded and glued, but your young guests would doubtless also enjoy it if you had a bunch of bright-colored fimo clay, rolling pins, and boards, and an adult posted there with a toaster oven to bake the finished products. (Tip: Get 4" lengths of copper pipe that the kids can press the rolled-out clay onto and use more clay to plug one end.)

EKEV

Heel (refers to the Messiah's approaching footsteps)

PORTION OR HOLIDAY THEMES AND IDEAS

Themes: "Man doth not live by bread only but by everything that proceedeth out of the mouth of the Lord . . ."; what God wants us to do; interceding on behalf of others (Moses frequently interceded with God on behalf of the people; when God punishes Moses by not letting him enter the Promised Land, Moses wishes the people would intercede for him); hardships and blessings; tests by hardship; befriending strangers

Ideas: See party ideas "Dreams" and "Saving Grace." Serve manna at the party (see recipe in Appendix 1). We don't live by bread alone: Decorate each table with centerpieces that evoke the other things we need in order to live fully, according to your family (suggestions: love, friendship, faith, music, books). Donate 3 percent of the cost of your party to Mazon, a Jewish Response to Hunger (www.mazon.org). Donate leftover unserved food through Rachel's Table (www.rachelstable.org); or contribute to another hunger charity (search the web under keyword "hunger"). Attach to party favors a card with web addresses of sites that have a free "click and donate food" button (www.thehungersite.com, www.stopthehunger.com, www.againsthunger.org) with a request that people visit these sites daily.

RE'EH

See	**PORTION OR HOLIDAY THEMES AND IDEAS**

Themes: Making choices ("behold, I set before you this day a blessing and a curse"); free will; false prophets; tzedakah is obligatory, not a choice

Ideas: See party idea "Tzedakah." Check "Making Your Event More of a Mitzvah" for additional mitzvah ideas. The portion talks about a tel—tel, as in Tel Aviv and many other place names, means "mound" and is often the site of archaeological findings. Have at the party one or two rigid plastic kiddie pools filled with sand; mix in inexpensive "artifacts" and colored rocks that the kids can dig for (see www.MitzvahChic.com for sources of stampings of old Roman coins, pieces that look like ancient jewelry, bows and arrows, sphinxes, etc.). Limit the number of "treasures" each child is allowed to keep so you don't run out. Have plain white canister tzedakah boxes there for the children to glue on their "finds."

SHOFTIM

Judges	**PORTION OR HOLIDAY THEMES AND IDEAS**

Themes: Creating government; preserving the land in recognition that we pass through but the land stays; "justice, justice you shall pursue"; preserving fruit-bearing trees; "when you approach a town to attack it, you shall offer terms of peace"; God owns the earth and we care for it; it's forbidden to destroy anything that can still be useful to people; two witnesses are required for a conviction

Ideas: See party ideas "Gifts" and "Tzedakah." Make your celebration as environmentally correct as possible by using recycled items and conserving resources; volunteer or support an environmental charity—check out Kids for a Clean Environment (www.kids face.org) and Youth for Environmental Sanity (www.yesworld.org). Visit as a family the Eco-Center at the Lotan Kibbutz in Israel (www.birdingisrael.com). Pursue justice by joining Amnesty International (www.amnesty.org) or Interfaith Voices for Peace and Justice (www.interfaithvoices.org). Plant a fruit tree in your yard (use its branches as part of the chuppah when the bar/bat mitzvah marries). Check local nurseries to see if they sell dwarf fruit trees in containers that can be used as centerpieces. Write to a politician about an injustice.

KI TEZE	
When you go out (to battle your enemies)	**PORTION OR HOLIDAY THEMES AND IDEAS**
	Themes: Laws having to do with humanity, marriage, and equity; rejecting cowardice; the community is responsible for the stranger, orphan, and widow; this portion has 72 of the 613 mitzvot: prohibition against mixing linen and wool in the same garment and yoking an ox and an ass to the same plough; the traditions and shared interests in families; how behaviors of parents are passed down to children; kindness to animals
	Ideas: See party idea "Heart." If your family members don't share any interests, pick one and participate in it together; talk about the experience in your speech. If the family likes to do crafts or to garden, for example, see if you can make or grow something to go on the tables at the party. Talk also in your speech about any family traditions you follow. Find a mitzvah project having to do with animals (most shelters will not allow youngsters to work in them, but you can find other jobs by going to www.volunteermatch.org and searching under "animals" and "virtual" for projects—like crafting animal-themed items to sell at craft fairs—that benefit groups serving animals), or raise money to adopt a raptor through the Birds of Prey Foundation (www.birds-of-prey.org), a whale (www.whale center.org) or an animal you can visit regularly at your local zoo. Even if they're too young to work, kids can raise money by selling off their old toys and video games on auction sites.
KI TAVO	
When you enter (the Promised Land)	**PORTION OR HOLIDAY THEMES AND IDEAS**
	Themes: First fruits, tithing to the poor, having ceremonies to mark occasions (in this case, entering the Promised Land); acting with intent; Jews as a people with a spiritual purpose; carving laws onto rocks; a spirit of joy and gladness; the importance of belonging to a community/synagogue
	Ideas: See party idea "Beginnings." Make carved stones as part of the centerpieces or as party favors by sculpting "stones" out of oven-baked clay and using rubber word stamps to press words in before baking (see "Crafts for Style and Therapy" for complete instructions). Use as centerpieces large clear vases or pitchers filled on the bottom with fruits and topped with large simple white flowers. Tithe by giving 3 percent of your event's cost to Mazon, a Jewish Response to Hunger (www.mazon.org). Create a ceremony specifically for your event—see "The Little Party Details That Really Matter" for ideas on changing the candlelighting ceremony.

NITZAVIM

You are standing

NEARBY HOLIDAYS

Rosh Hashanah

PORTION OR HOLIDAY THEMES AND IDEAS

Themes: This portion is often read with Vayelech, so look at both. "The things that are revealed belong unto us and to our children forever"; the power of repentance; "choose life"; children as the guarantors of the Torah forever; the hardest part of a long journey is the first step (reading and using God's law); traditions that maintain us

Ideas: See party idea "Heart." Have as much "tradition" at your party as possible—ask the rabbi to suggest any you may not be familiar with and choose the ones that appeal to you most. Place on the table lists of the most enjoyable Jewish traditions and ask guests to think about adopting at least one in their family. Have traditional Jewish/Israeli dancing at your party; buy 8"-high Torahs with embroidered velvet covers as the basis for your centerpieces—give them away at the end of the night to children.

VAYELECH

And he went

NEARBY HOLIDAYS

Rosh Hashanah
Yom Kippur

PORTION OR HOLIDAY THEMES AND IDEAS

Themes: This portion is often read with Nitzavim, so look at both. The Song of Moses; how to make sure Judaism continues; assuring the future—our responsibility to future generations; is God still there when He cannot be seen or felt?

Ideas: See party idea "Song." Attach to every place card one or two blank index cards and an envelope with each guest's name. Ask everyone to write on the card what they wish ultimately to have accomplished in their lives and what they can do in the next two weeks to begin it. Have them place the card in the envelope and seal it—let the bar/bat mitzvah or some younger children go around with a basket to collect the envelopes. At home, put a complete address label over the name, stamp, and mail envelopes a week after the party. This portion discusses every Jew's obligation to write a Torah—your family can pay to have an existing Torah examined, repaired, and donated to a group that needs it. (Go to www.sefer-torah.com.)

HAAZINU

Give ear
(Moses calling on
heaven and earth)

Rosh Hashanah
Yom Kippur
Sukkot

PORTION OR HOLIDAY THEMES AND IDEAS

Themes: Upon Exodus, Moses began his ministry with a song of praise. He ends now with a song that recounts Israel's history and calls on all nations to join Israel in its song of deliverance; God's laws as the center of our lives; the expressive power of poetry and song; God as the "Rock"; God creating Israel out of chaos as He first created the world out of chaos; the responsibility of Jewish parents to teach their children; Moses heeds Jewish laws of testimony by calling upon two witnesses—heaven and earth—to hear him

Ideas: See party idea "Song." Serve at your party foods detailed in Deuteronomy 32:13–14 (honey, oil, cow's milk cheese, sheep's milk, lamb, wheat, and grapes/wine). Help "give ear" by contributing to buy amplifying headsets for your synagogue or another. Decorate the tables like Creation with a sun and moon (painted on a flowerpot), star confetti, flowers, or a dwarf apple tree in the pot (check availability with a local nursery), little people and animals; or make topiaries with the apples and toys. Another beautiful centerpiece idea: Use large clear vases and fill the bottom with water and small fruits (crab apples or small green apples would fulfill the apple theme, but also kumquats, orange slices, cranberries, etc.) and have simple flowers on top.

VE-ZOT HA-BRACHA

This is the blessing
This portion is read only
on Simchat Torah.

PORTION OR HOLIDAY THEMES AND IDEAS

Themes: Blessings, a spiritual heritage that will endure forever, remembering Moses, parting words/saying good-bye.

Ideas: See party idea "Song." Find interesting quotes/passages from the farewell speeches of various leaders (Martin Luther King, Gandhi, presidents, prime ministers, etc.) and computer-print them onto table tents and array on tables. See party idea "Saving Grace" to remember the effort made to extinguish Judaism from the earth and the brave people who defeated it.

Jewish Holiday Summaries and Symbols

If your bar or bat mitzvah coincides with a holiday, you may choose to incorporate symbols or themes from the holiday into your celebration. This overview is presented to help you do that.

Rosh Hashanah

Rosh Hashanah is the New Year. An important symbol is the shofar, or ram's horn, drawn from the story of Abraham and Isaac. In ancient days, the shofar was blown to announce the beginning of the month, to proclaim a new king, or to warn of danger. The shofar is blown during Rosh Hashanah, and when the sound reaches God's ears, He opens the Book of Life. One tradition of Rosh Hashanah is *tashlick:* going to "live water" on the first day and emptying your pockets while praying that the water will also carry away your sins. Ten days after the beginning of Rosh Hashanah comes Yom Kippur. Apples and honey are also symbols of Rosh Hashanah—they express the hope of sweetness in the coming year.

Yom Kippur

Yom Kippur is the Day of Atonement, a day of fasting and prayer. It begins at sundown with the Kol Nidre ("all vows") service and ends the following sundown with the blowing of the shofar to close the Book of Life. From Rosh Hashanah until the end of Yom Kippur, Jews ask forgiveness from those they've wronged during the previous year and repent with sincerity in hopes of having their names inscribed in the Book of Life for another year. The story of Jonah and the whale is also associated with Yom Kippur.

Sukkot

Sukkot means "booths" and refers to those built as portable shelters during the Exodus. Later, after the people were settled in the Promised Land, they continued to erect sukkot beside their cultivated fields to serve as shelters for the workers. Today, we build simple structures and decorate them with fruits, fronds, and gourds. In addition to the structures themselves, symbols of Sukkot are the etrog (a lemonlike fruit), the lulav (a palm frond), myrtle twigs, and willow branches of the stream. Sukkot comes during the secular autumn season, so it is often celebrated with harvest symbols.

Simchat Torah

This is the "rejoicing of the Torah," when the cycle of reading the entire Torah is completed and begun anew. Symbols include the Torah, flags, the Star of David, the Ten Commandments, and the lions of Judah.

Hanukkah

The symbol of Hanukkah is the nine-place candleholder called the menorah. The story of Hanukkah is this:

In 165 B.C.E., King Antiochus, the Greek king of Syria, conquered the Jews and ordered them to follow the Greek religion. Most resisted. One day the king's soldiers came to a small village and ordered all Jews to perform a ritual that involved bowing to an idol and eating pork. The Greek officer asked Mattathias, a village leader, to come forward and be the first to comply in order to set an example. When he refused, another man stepped forward, offering to be the first. Mattathias slew him on the spot and, with his five sons, killed the Greeks and went to hide in the mountains, staging raids from there. A year later, Mattathias died, but not before putting his son Judah Maccabee in charge of the army. Though the Greeks vastly outnumbered the Jews and had superior equipment, including trained elephants, the Jews finally drove them out. When the Jews returned to their beloved Temple in Jerusalem, they found a statue of Zeus in their holiest place and all the Jewish ritual implements broken. They cleaned and repaired what they could, but when it was time to light the lamp, they could find only one small sealed bottle of oil—enough for one day. Miraculously, it burned for eight days.

Also associated with this period and this holiday is the story of Judith. A warlord named Holofernes crossed Judaea on his way to invade Egypt. His army came to Judith's city and stormed it. As the people trapped inside the city grew hungry and thirsty, Judith took matters into her own hands. A legendary beauty, she went to Holofernes, who quickly fell in love with her. Judith then fed him "salty cheese," and when he fell into a stupor, she killed him. Leaderless and confused, his army ran away.

Tu B'Shvat

Tu B'Shvat is the new year of the trees. To a region that is mostly desert, trees had such importance that in the Torah there is a prohibition against harming fruit trees unless it is strictly necessary. The Torah itself is called the "Tree of Life."

Purim

Purim is the holiday that recounts the biblical story of Esther. In ancient Persia, Esther was the only Jewish wife of King Achashverosh. Her uncle Mordechai, an adviser to the king, had advised her to keep her Jewish identity a secret. The king's prime minister, Haman, hated Mordechai because Mordechai refused to bow down to him. As punishment for Mordechai's disrespect, Haman vowed to kill all the Jews of Persia. Esther visited the king and cleverly asked what fate would befall anyone who wished her dead. When the king replied that he would kill such a person, Esther revealed Haman's plan for the Jews, and it was Haman who ended up on the gallows.

Pesach (Passover)

The command to hold a Passover seder as a remembrance of the liberation of the Jews from Egypt appears in the Torah. The actual service booklet is the Haggadah. The story of the Jews in Egypt actually begins when Joseph, the next-to-youngest of Jacob's thirteen children, is sold into slavery by his brothers. Through his gifts of reading prophecies in dreams, Joseph rises to power in Egypt, ultimately being put in charge of the grain storehouses. When a seven-year famine grips the land, Joseph's brothers come to Egypt, where they've heard there is food. Although they don't at first recognize him, and then are fearful of his anger, the brothers receive Joseph's forgiveness and an invitation to dwell in Egypt where Joseph can watch over them.

Many years later, the Jews in Egypt, now numbering more than a half million, are enslaved. Moses, born a Jew but adopted in infancy by Pharoah's daughter, is called by God to win the people's freedom and lead them out of Egypt. After nine attempts to persuade Pharoah to "let my people go"—each accompanied by a show of God's power in the form of plagues of frogs, locusts, boils, gnats, etc.—the tenth and final plague is death of the firstborn. Moses instructs the Jews to paint the frames around their doors with lamb's blood as a sign to the angel of death to "pass over" those houses. After this plague, Pharoah lets the people go, but he soon changes his mind and chases them, only to have his soldiers killed when the Red Sea—parted by God to let the Jews cross—closes back over them.

Yom ha-Shoah (Holocaust Memorial Day)

Day to remember and honor those who perished in the Nazi Holocaust.

Yom ha-Zikaron (Remembrance Day)

Always the day before Israel Independence Day. Remembers all the heroes who have died to defend or preserve Israel.

Yom ha-Atzma'ut (Israel Independence Day)

Anniversary of the 1948 establishment of Israel as an independent nation.

Lag Ba'Omer

The Omer is counted from the second day of Pesach until Shavuot. Lag Ba'Omer is the thirty-third day of the Omer, and it's the only festive day during the counting of the Omer. This "break" takes place in commemoration of a soldier, Bar Kokhba, who won victory against the Romans.

Shavuot

Shavuot means "weeks," a reference to Shavuot occurring seven weeks after Pesach. The holiday celebrates Moses receiving the commandments on Mt. Sinai. Many synagogues hold confirmation ceremonies on Shavuot. Symbols of Shavuot, in addition to the tablets of the commandments, include greens and flowers, particularly roses. One legend holds that Mt. Sinai was covered with roses at the time that Moses was there. Persian Jews called Shavuot the "Feast of Flowers" and Italian Jews called it "Feast of the Roses." The biblical story of Ruth is also associated with Shavuot.

Tisha B'av

The First Temple, a grand structure covered in gold and built by King Solomon around 960 B.C.E., was destroyed in 586 B.C.E. by the King of Babylon. Rebuilt seventy years later out of marble, it was destroyed again in 70 C.E. by the Romans. Legend holds that on both occasions, the Temple was destroyed on the same day—the ninth day of the month of Av. All that's left today is one of the walls that once surrounded the Temple. We know this as the Western Wall in Jerusalem.

twelve Eight Complete Parties That Will
Leave You *FARKLEMPT*!

beginnings

Bar/Bat Mitzvah and adolescence

mark the beginning

of a new life.

But beginnings happen

throughout life.

This party is

a contemplation and celebration of that.

What's on the Table

A tree decorated with twinkly lights and hanging candles. The pot has a soft Tuscan finish and features cartouches of baby footprints. Other symbols suggesting new life are the pastel favor dishes in the shape of leaves, a nest with eggs and a bird at the base of the tree, and the wire brass baby bassinet holding photos. You can also make a baby album depicting this first phase of your child's life and place that on the table. Also, find some beautiful seeds and scatter them around the center of the table.

Elsewhere in the Room

Place an ornate frame filled with smooth white fabric on a table in a quiet spot and use a slide projector behind it to project a changing array of framed photos, a review of your child's life up to now.

Hot Party Favors and Crafts

Desktop Garden in a Tin

Toddler Sock Change Purses

See "Crafts for Style and Therapy" for instructions on making the Tuscan Pot, Baby Album, Changing Masterpiece Frame, and Toddler Sock Change Purses.

Credits, Sources, and Tips

Pastel Favor Leaf Dishes—Beaucoup (www.beaucoup. com). For all others, see Appendix 2. Visit www.Mitzvah Chic.com links to download round label artwork for Desktop Garden in a Tin.

song

The Torah has several songs
and ends with the song of Moses,
a hymn and a history designed to be
a remembrance and inspiration.

This party is a celebration of
how we've all learned from
and been inspired by song.

What's on the Table

A big candle with sheet music wrapped around. Wide, sparkly table ribbons arranged in "spoke" fashion. Ribbons have felt diamonds with your favorite song lyrics printed on them. The lyrics are numbered so guests can have fun guessing the song title and artist. If you want to make it harder, ask the year as well.

What Happens

On arrival, guests receive place cards attached to kalimbas, African thumb pianos. The pianos have been tuned (by a music student) to a particular set of notes, and the tips of the keys are painted different colors. On the back of the place card is the song "Happy Birthday" shown as colored dots. Just before dessert is served, have everyone play "Happy Birthday" to your child.

Also, give out answer blanks and pens for people to write their guesses of the song titles and artists from the lyrics on the table ribbons. Have some kids collect and grade the answers. If there's a tie, have the band play a game of Name That Tune with the know-it-alls to eliminate the extra people. Give guests an opportunity to come up and recite their favorite song lyrics and try to stump the audience.

Set up a table where anyone can go and make a rain stick.

A very cool idea: Hand out drumsticks and have the band's drummer beat out wild rhythms for the audience to repeat (drumming on the edge of their table). If you have a DJ, ask him to record a drummer doing this to play back at the party. Warning: This is a highly energizing activity, so consider your timing carefully.

Hot Party Favors and Crafts

Kalimbas for adults

Imprinted drumsticks for the kids

See "Crafts for Style and Therapy" for instructions on making the Singing Table Ribbons and Forest Rain Sticks.

Credits, Sources, and Tips

See Appendix 2 for all resources. See www.MitzvahChic.com links for downloadable colored-dot place cards and other art. Flowers by Nancy Rackow.

saving grace

Recalling and honoring those who risked or gave their lives to save others.

What's on the Table

Angel candleholders with beautiful candles. Small frames that hold the stories of Righteous Gentiles who rescued Jews during World War II with small photos that show rescuers then and now. Candles with framed portraits of other rescuers tied on with ribbon.

What Happens

This is a very profound, inspirational theme—one that invites all to consider where courage comes from and how often bravery is a decision, not a trait.

If you are interested in using this theme, you and your child have a real opportunity to do life-affirming research that could include not only studying rescuers in the Holocaust, but also 9/11 heroes and the everyday heroes in your own community. Your child could also twin with a Righteous Gentile through the Jewish Foundation for the Righteous (see "Making the Event More of a Mitzvah" and www.MitzvahChic.com, "Great Ideas" and "Invitations," to buy JFR invitations).

Hot Party Favors and Crafts

Most appropriate would be donations that support those with "saving grace"—Righteous Gentiles through the Jewish Foundation for the Righteous, or anyone else you find heroic and worthy.

If you wish to also give out something tangible at the party, you could create the stones described in the party "Dreams" and stamp "Courage" or another appropriate word on them instead of "Dream." See www.MitzvahChic.com for more ideas.

Credits, Sources, and Tips

Gold Leaves Organza tablecloth—Cloth Connection (www.weddinglinens.com)
For all others, see Appendix 2

gifts

*The Torah is God's gift
to the Jews
and to humanity.*

*The party is an invitation
to reflect on the gifts
in our lives.*

What's on the Table

A wonderful cake that looks like a stack of three wrapped gifts sits high atop a layer of ribbons with keys or charms attached, arrayed in key-charm-key-charm order. After dinner, ask everyone to pull two adjoining ribbons (they will get a key and a charm). Then have them eat the cake for dessert. The table also has square votive candle holders decorated with family photos.

Elsewhere in the Room

Before the party, prepare a treasure chest, decorated or left plain. Inside, place whatever "gifts" your family members can give of themselves to friends and family. It could be an invitation to join you for an evening at a later date, or a DVD rental gift card, but with the condition that the recipient bring the video/DVD to your house to watch together. The treasure chest is padlocked. You can purchase any number of working and non-working keys to give out at the party; the number of working keys must match the number of prizes inside. Be sure to give out all the working keys!

What Happens

On arrival, guests find that their place cards have a hole punched in them and a ball chain necklace threaded through. Throughout the evening, they wear the necklace and can earn keys for any reason you devise— being the first to dance, answering questions about the hosts or the guest of honor, etc. After dessert, roll out the treasure chest on a table and allow everyone to try his or her key to see who the winners are. It's Cinderella and the glass slipper all over again!

Sending an invitation with a key previews the party to come

Hot Party Favors and Crafts

Give out wood boxes that look like stacked gifts for everyone to take home their charm necklaces.

See "Crafts for Style and Therapy" for instructions on making Ribbon & Charm Invitations.

Credits, Sources, and Tips

Cake—Weinrich's Bakery (www.weinrichbakery.com)

Treasure Chest—Rainbow Keys (www.rainbowkeys.com)

For all others, see Appendix 2

What the Charms Mean

Treasure Chest	Gain Wealth
Castle	Add or Change Homes
Crown	Gain Power & Influence
Shell	You'll Make a Discovery
Unicorn	Magic Will Come
Trophy	You Will Achieve
Hand	You'll Help Another
Key	You'll Find

shine

From the priestly blessing in Naso:
May "The Lord bless thee and keep thee;
the Lord make his face shine upon thee
and be gracious unto thee;
the Lord lift up his countenance upon thee
and give thee peace . . ."

What's on the Table

This party is about light shining forth on us and on our children. The center-piece is a bowl of water with floating candles and a spray of flowers standing up in the center. Surrounding it is a castle of photos of the guest of honor, the light pouring through his or her image, and the golden windows. Tiny chair place card holders display cards printed with the blessing above.

Elsewhere in the Room

Place beautiful lanterns or luminaria around the room. Rent spotlights and shoot them up the walls to make brilliant patterns.

Hot Party Favors and Crafts

Wearable ravewear lights for kids (give out during the party); candles for adults

See "Crafts for Style and Therapy" for instructions on making the Shining Castle and Copper Luminaria.

Credits, Sources, and Tips

Copper lamé tablecloth—Cloth Connection (www.weddinglinens.com)
Flowers by Nancy Rackow
For all others, see Appendix 2

heart

From the first discourse of Moses in Vaetchanan
the same parashah/sidra that gives us the Shema,
comes the exhortation to "Put these words
on your heart, teach them to your children,
talk of them at home and on your way,
when you lie down and when you rise up."

What's on the Table

A topiary of a lit-from-within heart balloon decorated with glimmering ribbons in a calligraphy pot. Glowing words to "put upon your heart" are etched on the votive holders. Heart-shaped place card holders display family photos. Transparent heart-shaped boxes hold gold-wrapped candies and are finished with organza ribbon.

What Happens

A tin of word tattoos left casually on the table gives guests a chance to play with words and consider which ones they would place on their hearts . . . their arms, their cheeks, and their hands.

Hot Party Favors and Crafts

Glass vials of lavender and white heart-shaped sugar or Japanese drop tea

A heart of handmade paper embedded with wildflower seeds to plant at home

See "Crafts for style and therapy" for instructions on making the Words on Your Heart Votives

Credits, Sources, and Tips

Celadon and gold swirl damask tablecloth and napkins— Cloth Connection (www.weddinglinens.com)

Heart-shaped sugar or Japanese drop tea in glass tubes—Beaucoup (www.beau-coup.com)

For all others, see Appendix 2

dreams

Jacob and his son Joseph

both had dreams

that changed the course

of their lives

and of history.

What do we dream of,

and how do we make

dreams into reality.

What's on the Table

A giant crystal ball with flowers inside glows at the center. Fortune cookie place card holders display quotes about dreams. Little armoires are decoupaged with dreamscape artwork. "Dream stones" go home with guests and remind them to dream long after the party is over. A chest with cloud paper collects the "What do you dream of doing?" cards.

What Happens

The place cards are actually envelopes with the guest's name and table number. Inside is a card that says, "What do you dream of doing?" and "What could you do in the next two weeks to begin to live your dream?" When everyone is seated, ask them to answer the questions and put the card in the envelope. Then, if they will allow their response to be read without identifying the author, ask them to leave the envelope unsealed. Otherwise, instruct them to seal it. Have kids go around with cloud chests and collect the envelopes. After dinner, read the responses aloud. Take all the envelopes home, seal them, and put a label with the guest's complete home address over the original printed name on the envelope. Two weeks after the party, mail them.

Or type up several wishes, prayers, fortunes, and dreams on small pieces of paper. Rent a "wind booth" used for "catch-the-money" promotions and let people take turns catching as many of your slips as they can.

Hot Party Favors and Crafts

Dream stones in beautiful metallic organza bags

The silk fortune cookies and any other theme decor from the table

Custom edible fortune cookies—with up to four different fortunes *you* write

See "Crafts for Style and Therapy" for instructions on making the Crystal Ball Centerpiece and Dream Stones

Credits, Sources, and Tips

Napkins and brown velvet tablecloth—Cloth Connection (www.weddinglinens .com). Go to www.MitzvahChic.com links to download "What do you dream of?" cards. For all others, see Appendix 2.

WHEN WE CEASE TO
DREAM
WE CEASE TO LIVE.

—William S. FORBES

WHAT DO YOU DREAM OF DOING?

WHAT COULD YOU DO IN THE NEXT
TWO WEEKS TO BEGIN LIVING YOUR
DREAM?

DREAMS

OF
DREAMS

DREAM

DREAM

Dream

tzedakah

All Jews are obligated to pursue justice

through charitable deeds.

This party uses as many

charitable ideas as possible.

What's on the Table

A French tiered and jeweled box full of books and toys to be donated to shelters or hospitals after the party. At each place is a painted silk tallit bag or spice bag and mezuzah purchased from the elderly artisans at Lifeline for the Old in Jerusalem. Chocolate coins to remind everyone that money also makes a nice charitable gift.

What Happens

When the invitations go out, ask all your invited guests to donate an hour of their personal or professional time to be sold at a silent auction at the party. Select one very desirable item to be a grand prize and sell a limited number of chances to win it.

Read "Making the Event More of a Mitzvah" for additional ways to serve the cause of tzedakah.

Hot Party Favors and Crafts

Silk purses, mezuzot, and other small items from Lifeline for the Old

Pens and scented votive candles that contribute to breast cancer research, from Avon

Buy each guest a tree in Israel, from the Jewish National Fund

See "Crafts for Style and Therapy" for instructions on making the Jeweled French Toy Box and Scratch-Off Tickets

Credits, Sources, and Tips

Lime and turquoise satin napkins—Cloth Connection (www.weddinglinens.com)

For all others, see Appendix 2

thirteen Crafts for Style and Therapy

I'm just going to say this straight out—I'm not Martha Stewart. I don't have the house in the Hamptons, the staff of eighty, the budget, the insomnia—any of the things apparently required to achieve her vision. This is actually very good news for you, because if you don't have any of those things either, you can probably do my projects.

There's something else I want to say about crafting that will make it really clear I'm not Martha: Making things should be easy and fun! Fun because you either enjoy the work itself, enjoy anticipating your guests' delighted reaction, or simply get a kick out of being able to present a really wonderful, unique decoration or gift. If you don't feel any of these joys of crafting—I'm serious—don't do it! And if you don't want to do it but still want to have the craft items at your party, the solution is very simple. There are legions of unemployed and underemployed all around you: students, artists, retirees, stay-at-home moms, handymen. Giving them a chance to earn a little extra money will make your event even more of a mitzvah.

Still reading? Great! If you decide to try crafting something, I'll promise this: Most of my projects will turn out well even if you're a novice or you mess up a bit. You should also know you're probably going to need some help even if you're determined to do much of the work yourself, purely because of the volume. If you're doing a table decoration, you could need one or several per table; party favors could number in the hundreds. It's great that you won't be able to do it all yourself, and to explain this provocative statement, let me tell you a story.

When I was designing and crafting for my second son's bar mitzvah, something very lucky happened to me: I ran out of time to finish all my projects and I had to ask my friends to help me. I hated asking—it felt so incompetent—but we ended up having so much fun! I stopped feeling stressed out and actually started to relax and enjoy myself. After the bar mitzvah, I had them over for a little party to thank them . . . and we had fun all over again! This isn't the way it's supposed to be.

I realized that my shameful time-management lapse was an inadvertent stroke of genius. Most of us—and I do blame Martha for *this!*—treat an event like this as if it were a geometry exam. We're being tested; we're supposed to toil away alone, do all the problem solving ourselves, and then, with little help from the friends we regularly turn to on lesser matters, emerge from isolation with everything perfectly worked out.

My credo now when planning a big party is: Do *nothing alone!* In the old country, preparations for a big event—like a wedding—would naturally have been a group activity, with the whole village cooking food, making wine, and dressing the tables. By carefully choosing your most upbeat family and friends to help you, you'll slash your workload and luxuriate in weeks of camaraderie instead of shrinking it down to one weekend. It's like starting the party a month early! One mom I heard about hosted four Sunday open houses leading up to her son's bar mitzvah. People could drop in, have some food, and do some crafting. She got all her work done *and* had far more time to visit with her friends than the one chaotic afternoon of the party.

The whole feeling of the event changes then too. It's no longer your Broadway opening with your guests as dreaded critics. You did it together, and now they can't wait to come and see "their stuff" in the spotlight. So without further ado, let's lift the curtain on projects you can do with your friends. Remember, you can find links to almost everything you'll need by going to www.MitzvahChic.com and looking for the links section.

JUST-FOR-FUN PARTY ITEMS

Soap with a Purpose

Some preteens need help to build their zeal for regular bathing. This may just be it. To make this soap exciting to boys, plant a Sacajawea dollar in it instead of the lip gloss and body glitter I'm showing and package in a manly burlap or suede bag.

Materials
Clear glycerin melt-and-pour soap base
Soap fragrance, if desired
Soap molds
Implantable prizes: cosmetics, coins (nothing glass)
Organza, burlap, or suede gift bags

Directions
1. Place "prize" in mold just to see how deep it needs to sit in the mold to be covered on top when mold is filled.
2. Melt soap according to package directions, add any desired fragrance, and pour just enough into mold to make the surface rise to where the bottom edge of prize should go. Let cool until soap starts to firm.
3. Put the prize into the mold, pushing it slightly into the cooling soap. This will anchor it and keep it from floating up when you pour more soap in.
4. Fill rest of mold with melted soap, tapping mold briefly to bring bubbles to surface (you'll always have some bubbles, but they look nice). If you don't fill completely to the top, you'll have an easier time unmolding soap.
5. When completely cool, unmold soap according to directions.

Scratch-off Tickets

This project introduces you to a fun material with many uses—the scratch-off coating. It comes in many colors and is easy to cut, peel, and stick onto whatever you like. To download the card that decides who drinks and who drives, go to www.MitzvahChic.com.

Materials
Scratch-off coating   Decorated cards

Directions
1. Download my drinking-or-driving card or make up your own card. (I put four cards on one sheet of paper.) Visit your local crafts store for colorful scrapbooking papers you can print your message onto. Once you've created an original, have it photocopied onto card stock.
2. Cut scratch-off coating to size, peel off the backing, and stick it over the mystery information on your cards. Cut your sheets into individual cards.

Gem Photo Magnets

A great craft for kids (the decoupage part) or to do with friends. No matter how much wine you consume, you can't do a bad job, and the finished magnets are great! Mix pictures and words by downloading word art from www.MitzvahChic.com.

Materials

Clear glass "jewels"
Color photocopies of your
    favorite snapshots
Mod Podge decoupage medium
    matte or gloss
Small foam brush

Small strong magnets
Hot-glue gun with gluesticks
Iron or rusted metal squares
    (for presentation)
Clear cellophane candy bags
Ribbon

Directions

1. Hold a clear glass jewel over the parts of the photocopied pictures you want to use to ensure that the images are small enough to fit. Place the jewel with the flat side over the face or image you want and draw around it with a pencil. Cut out the shape, cutting a bit *within* the pencil line.
2. On the printed side of the paper, brush a thin coat of Mod Podge with the foam brush and smooth it onto the flat side of the jewel. Use your finger to flatten the paper against the glass and wipe away any extra glue that oozes out.
3. When dry, hot-glue a magnet to the flat side of the jewel.
4. Arrange magnets on iron squares (these can be spray-painted any color) or small rusted metal sheets. Place in crackly cellophane bags and finish by gathering top with ribbon.

Homemade Invitations That Look Custom

Using a star theme for your event? Or no theme, but you just want something beautiful you can do by yourself? Anyone with basic word-processing skills can turn out exquisite invitations on a home computer and put the savings into the party, a charitable donation, or the college fund.

Materials

Ready to print invitation blanks
Your computer and printer
Mailing envelopes if they're not included
Blank enclosure cards

Directions

1. Make sure to choose an invitation that can be printed on your type of printer (laser or ink-jet). Otherwise, you may have to buy a new printer, which could still end up being cheaper than having invitations professionally printed, *and* you get to keep the printer.

2. On your computer, set up the page to match the size and printable area of the blank invitation. If the invitation, for example, gives you a 6" square as the sheet to print on, you need to tell the computer that the page is 6" by 6" and adjust the margins to be smaller than they'd be on a full-sized sheet of paper. Some invitations give you a full-sized sheet for printer purposes, but the actual invitation is a smaller punch-out portion of the paper.

3. Decide on your wording and type it out on the computer, experimenting with different sizes and styles of type. When you think it's right, print it out on plain paper to see if it will print correctly on the good stuff. Adjust the margins and type size and keep printing on plain paper until you're satisfied. Once it's perfect, print the whole batch on the invitation paper.

Party or Sleepover in a Can

Kids just wanna have fun, and at this age that means herding in ever larger numbers to parties and sleepovers. This party favor guarantees that at the end of *your* bar or bat mitzvah, they're just getting started.

Materials
Decorated stationery for the label

Full-sheet white printable
   peel-and-stick labels
   (make sure they're copier compatible)

Paint cans

Rubber mallet

Ribbons to decorate cans

Suggested can contents
Girls: Glitter body gel, facial masks, nail polish, manicure and pedicure tools, temporary tattoos, gel jewelry, hairwrap supplies and beads, truth or dare cards, appropriate add-ons from boys' list below

Boys: Sunglasses, disposable cameras, card games, magic tricks, hackey-sacks, gum, CDs, colored hair gel, small flashlights, skateboard stickers, food, socks

Directions
1. The hardest parts of this party favor are making the label and deciding which great gifts to put inside.
2. For the label, get some decorated stationery with a party theme or theme that reflects your child's interest. Type out on your computer your label message (see mine for one idea). If you're really computer-shy, you can go to a Kinko's or other copy shop for help. Once you've got a label design you like on the stationery, have it copied onto full-sheet peel-and-stick label paper, one copy for each can you're making.
3. Cut out labels and stick onto the cans. Fill the cans with loot and seal them with the rubber mallet. Decorate with curly ribbon.

CRAFTS FROM "EIGHT COMPLETE PARTIES THAT WILL LEAVE YOU *FARKLEMPT*!"

Charm and Ribbon Invitations

Materials

Prepackaged card sets (card with envelope—get a type that has
  matching enclosure cards you can purchase separately)
Beautiful card liner paper in contrasting color to print message on
Double-sided tape
Hot-glue gun with gluesticks
Heart Invitation: heart charms, large jump rings, and organza ribbon (for
a puffy heart, you will need to buy plastic boxes for mailing)
Key Invitation: key charms, metallic thread, organza ribbon, small coin
envelopes, sealing wax, wax stamp, inked stamping pad

Heart Invitation

Directions

1. Fold the card in half and cut a window where you want charm to be. To make this go faster, cut a piece of cardboard the size and shape of your "window" and trace it on the inside of each card front as a cutting guide. Cut with an X-Acto knife and straightedge.
2. Cut slits by the top corners of window, as shown.
3. Place jump ring through hole in charm. Cut organza ribbon the length you need to hang the charm in the right position, then go through the slits and extend about ½" beyond them. You may want to double or triple the ribbon to make the color richer. Thread charm on ribbon. Place ribbon ends through slits and tape ends to back of card front.
4. Print message on liner paper; cut it so it's slightly smaller than card, crease in middle and affix it to card inside with double-sided tape (one small piece on each edge) working from fold outward.

Key Invitation

1. Glue coin envelope to card front. Cut slits on either side of envelope to thread ribbon through.
2. Cut a piece of ribbon long enough to start at envelope center, go through slit, across inside of card front, out through other slit to meet back on envelope front. Gather two ribbon ends slightly and hot-glue to front of envelope.
3. Melt sealing wax and drip all over ribbon ends. When you have enough melted wax (experiment ahead of time to be able to judge this), press your wax stamp onto inked pad and then into the soft wax for a painted wax impression.
4. Install paper liner as in Heart Invitation and place key charm in envelope.

Singing Table Ribbons

Materials

1½ yards fabric, at least 48" wide, cut into eight 6" x 54" strips
½"-wide Stitch Witchery fusible webbing or iron-on adhesive
Cool peel transfer paper
Fineline fabric paint
Four 12" squares white felt

Directions

1. "Hem" the strips on long sides by turning over ½" and securing with iron-on adhesive or fusible webbing. If you like, cut one end of each into a point and hem it.
2. Download my "song lyric diamonds," fill in your own lyrics, and print them out using an ink-jet printer on cool peel transfer paper MIRRORED so, when pressed onto felt, they'll read correctly. If you don't know how to print a mirror image (selection is usually in "print" dialog box, but this function cannot be performed by several Epson Stylus printers), consult a computer-savvy friend. Worst case scenario: You'll have to go to a local quick-print place to have these copies made on their transfer paper.
3. Fuse lyrics onto felt, following transfer paper instructions. Cut out the diamonds.
4. Glue diamonds onto fabric strips, about 7" from the unfinished ends. Make sure numbers on diamonds are closest to the unfinished ends.
5. Decorate by squeezing fabric paint in swirls along diamond edges. When all are dry, overlap and glue the unfinished ends of each pair of strips together to make four long strips. (Glue #1 to #5, #2 to #6, #3 to #7, and #4 to #8.) To set up table, lay them in order spoke fashion over tablecloth, piling the seams where joined on top of each other and place candle base on top.

Forest Rain Sticks

Kids (and frustrated adults) love wailing away with their hammers on this project, and it's so easy to get great results.

Materials

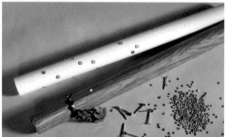

2"-wide cardboard mailing tubes with plastic end caps, any length
1½" roofing nails (with big heads)
Small hammers
Variety of dried peas, beans, rice, unpopped popcorn
Wood-grain or other decorative contact adhesive paper
Yarn for garnish

Directions

1. Precut contact paper so it's the same length as the tubes and will go all the way around and overlap somewhat. Precut 3"–4" circles to go over ends.
2. Let kids hammer as many nails as they want into the tube (have adult supervision at the craft table to keep nails from very small children and to maintain a safe environment). Emphasize that the more erratic the placement of nails, the better.
3. When they've had enough nailing, cap one end and let them put any combination of grains into the tube. Cap other end and have them turn over rain stick and listen, adding more nails and more grains if they wish.
4. When the kids are satisfied, put contact circles over ends. Lay long pieces of contact down, adhesive side up and let them roll up their tubes in it.

Shining Castle

A very inexpensive project that requires just foamcore, an X-Acto knife, color photocopies, and time. But what a beautiful and moving showstopper!

Materials

20" x 30" sheet of ³⁄₁₆" white foamcore
Extra foamcore and white cardboard
   for 3-D architectural effects
X-Acto knife
Straightedge
2 Castle patterns (See Appendix 3)
Large sheets of graphite paper
Masking tape

White Sculpey (for fancy architectural ornaments)
Rolling pin
White tacky glue
Color copies of photos featuring your little
   sweetie, the bar/bat mitzvah
Colored tissue for plain windows

Directions

1. Cut foamcore in half lengthwise into two 10" x 30" pieces. Use a very sharp X-Acto knife and a straightedge. You will need to use very little pressure and score a minimum of 2–3 times. If you use too much pressure, you'll crush the foam and get a very raggedy cutline.

2. Lay the two castle patterns on top of foamcore with graphite paper in between (shiny side against foamcore). Use a few pieces of masking tape to hold pattern in place. Transfer all lines and mark the dividing lines between panels.

3. Cut out all windows and doors. Where panels meet, cut once with a straightedge, being careful not to cut all the way through! You want them to *angle* here, not separate.

4. If you want to add dimension, cut out the extra foamcore pieces and cardboard details. To make ornaments, roll out Sculpey with rolling pin about ¼"–½" thick and make an impression in it with any object or raised design (our angel came from a lamp; you can get pillars from cake-decorating shop). Bake Sculpey until it's hard. Roll out more Sculpey and press it into your "mold." Pull gently out of mold and lay on a flat surface; cut excess Sculpey away with X-Acto knife and bake ornament till hard.

5. To assemble, glue foamcore pieces, cardboard details, and ornaments to basic 10" x 30" castle strips. Cut each photo at least ½" bigger all around than opening it goes in and glue to the castle back. You'll need votive candles on table inside the castle to light the whole thing up properly. Be sure to put them in glass holders to avoid risk of fire!

Copper Luminaria

Materials
Any size food can 20 oz. or more (keep the lid)
36-gauge copper tooling foil
Work or white cotton gloves
X-Acto knife
Straightedge
Caulk adhesive (Home Solutions Crystal Clear Glue)
Masking tape or rubber bands
Artwork (download at www.MitzvahChic.com links)
Hammer
Large nail

Directions
1. Always wear gloves when handling copper foil, as the oil in your skin will stain the metal. Be very careful of sharp edges as well.
2. With X-Acto knife and straightedge, cut a piece of copper foil (by scoring 3–4 times) the height of your can and long enough to go around it and overlap by 1". If needed, flatten bumps in copper by covering with paper (to protect surface) and rolling gently with rolling pin.

3. Squeeze fat lines of adhesive in a zigzag around the whole can. Put a line of adhesive along the seam where the metal overlaps itself. Wrap copper around and tape edge down to hold all in place. Let adhesive cure for several days.
4. Fill can with water up to ¼" from top and place in freezer. When frozen solid, take it out, put lid on top of the ice. If lid is not level with top of can, pack some crumpled newspaper in. Use tape or rubber band around can top-to-bottom to hold can top in place. This keeps ice from shattering and falling out when you're punching holes near the can top.
5. Choose simple artwork and tape it in place on the can. Lay can on a towel between two books to keep it from rolling. Hammer the nail in and pull out wherever you want the light to show through. When you're happy with the design, undo tape or rubber bands, remove top, and set the can upside down on a rack over a pan to thaw. Place inside luminaria (watch out for sharp edges where the nail went in!) candles in glass holders.

Dream Stones

Sometimes all it takes to keep a dream alive is a beautiful little stone on your desk or nightstand to remind you.

Materials

Sculpey in beautiful colors
Rubber stamp with the word "Dream"
For stones with faces, a large sun-face brass charm
    to use as a mold
Acrylic paint for word
Organza bags for presentation

Directions

1. I used Sculpey in gold, red pearl, and teal pearl. Break off a piece of each of two colors and squeeze together so the overall size is that of a walnut. Massage the clay lightly, pushing the two colors together, twisting and folding a couple times. Don't do it too much or the colors will start to blend rather than just marbleizing.
2. Roll into a ball and then flatten into a thick stone. (If you want your stones to have the weight of real stones, stick a nickel into each ball before flattening, then make sure coin is completely covered.)
3. Center rubber stamp and press into clay, wobbling *slightly* up and down and back and forth to make a complete impression. If you go too deep and you see the square outline of the stamp, just smooth those lines out of your stone.
4. Bake according to package directions. When hard and cool, brush over word with acrylic paint and immediately wipe off. This will leave paint only in the letter depressions.
5. To add "face" (do this at the flattened ball stage), press a separate small piece of Sculpey into back of large sun-face charm and pull out. Lay your clay face on the shaped stone and use your fingers to blend the edges into existing stone. Stamp if you wish and bake as instructed.

Crystal Ball Centerpiece

Materials

10 x 8 reducer—a piece of aluminum ductwork available at home
    centers
12" wide fabric (that matches or looks good with your tablecloth) long
    enough to go around reducer
Hot-glue gun and gluesticks, or caulk adhesive
Flower "frog" and flowers
10" bubble ball
Light source for underneath crystal ball

Directions

1. Wrap fabric around reducer, pinning where the fabric overlaps. When you like the way it looks, turn under the edge of the top layer of fabric and hot-glue or sew to the bottom layer. Tuck the top and bottom of the fabric over top and bottom edges of the reducer and glue or hot-glue in place.
2. Experiment ahead of time to see how you like the flowers—floating or stuck onto the frog that will hold them on the bottom—and the water level.

Changing Masterpiece Frame

You can use a high-tech digital photo "receiver" to do the same job, but it won't have the charm of a lovely ornate frame. Place it in a quiet area at your reception on a table where the projector can sit undisturbed about five feet behind it.

Materials

Ornate picture frame
Heavy, smooth white cotton fabric, same shape and 4" larger in length and width than frame opening
Staple gun
2 L-shaped shelf supports
Short screws that fit through holes in supports
Drill
Weights (brick, small bag of sand) wrapped in a napkin to match tablecloth
Projector and slides (can be made by photo store from photo prints)

Directions

1. Lay frame facedown on some padding (folded beach towel) on table. Position fabric so it extends 2" past opening on all sides. Staple to the frame about 1" in from opening in middle of top edge. Stretch fabric slightly and staple in middle of bottom. Next, stretch fabric and staple in center of right side of frame, then go across and staple on left. Keep stapling, stretching, and stapling the matching position on the other side of the frame until fabric is smooth and well anchored.
2. Make sure screws are short enough that they won't come out front of frame. Hold shelf supports against the back of frame so that the bottom of the L is even with the bottom edge of frame. Mark the frame with pencil where the screw holes are. Drill guide holes where the screws go in, being careful not to come out front of frame. Screw supports to frame.
3. Set up the frame at the party, decorate with flowers, and put weights on the supports to keep bumps to the table from knocking it forward.

Words on Your Heart Votives

Materials

Large smooth glass candle cups
Chartpak peel-and-stick vinyl lettering
Narrow painter's tape
Kilz primer/sealer spray paint
Spray paint in your choice of finish coat

Directions

1. Stick the vinyl letters onto the sides of the candle cups. Press down well. If you wish to leave an unpainted rim around the bottom or top of cup, mask off with painter's tape.
2. Turn the cups upside down (so paint doesn't go inside) and place on newspaper. Spray-paint the cups lightly with Kilz. (Do all spray-painting outside with recommended breathing protection.)
3. When dry, spray the finish coat.
4. When the cups are completely dry, remove the tape and letters, using the tip of an X-Acto knife to help you peel up a corner of each letter if necessary.

Jeweled French Toy Box

Materials

Hatbox
24" length of 1¼" wooden dowel
Plastic fluted urn-style pedestal planter
   (use top only), about 14½" across top
Half-gallon plastic container
Closet pole socket
Sixteen 2" teardrop chandelier crystals
Seven dozen plastic crystal beads
Thin brass wire
Plaster of paris
Adhesive caulk
Kilz primer/sealer paint in spray or liquid form
Wide blue painter's masking tape and two colors paint (you'll need
   about 6 oz. of base color and 2–4 oz. of contrast color)
Drill
Screwdriver
Screws that come with closet pole sockets
Nuts to fit screws

Directions

1. Prime the hatbox, dowel, planter, and "full flange" piece of closet pole socket with Kilz (do painting outside and follow all breathing precautions).
2. Paint all pieces with base color. When completely dry, use tape to mask off stripes on hatbox and to wrap around dowel in a spiral, leaving a narrow strip of painted wood showing. Paint second color in unmasked areas; paint second color onto urn freehand, following the contours.
3. Install closet pole socket in urn by centering the "partial circle" piece inside urn on bottom. Mark and drill screw holes. Line up other socket piece on outside, flange down so the urn bottom is sandwiched between the two socket pieces. Thread screws through the three pieces from the outside and secure with nuts inside the urn. Drill holes in rim about 3" apart to later thread wire holding crystals through.
4. File down one end of dowel so it will fit tightly into closet pole socket. Squeeze caulk adhesive into socket and push dowel in, leveling urn.
5. Fill half-gallon plastic container ¾ with warm water. Pour in plaster of paris until the powder stops disappearing and begins to stick up in a mound out of the water. Mix gently until you start to feel mixture thicken. Stick the bottom of the dowel in and hold it straight until the plaster sets.
6. Thread wire through the hole atop the little crystal that comes with each teardrop and twist. Add crystal beads to wire to whatever length you wish. Stick wire through hole in rim from underside. Thread one bead on above rim and feed wire back to underside of rim. Tighten to take up slack and twist wire around beads to secure.

CRAFTS FROM "PARTY IDEAS FOR EACH TORAH PORTION"

Metal Books

Materials

2 metal squares per book: shown here are 4" iron and 6" copper or brass

Coarse Scotchbrite pads

Sticky notepads

Leather lace or ribbon (or you can "bind" these with loose-leaf rings)

For Rusted Iron Book: Rust patina solution, sponge applicator, brass charm, leather lacing, adhesive caulk, rubber cement

For Copper Initial Book: Metal tongs, narrow masking tape, adhesive contact paper, a Sizzix die to cut initial letter (you will need a vise to use this) or a paper punch to cut a shape for book center, gold spray paint, leather laces, 2 gold beads, hot-glue gun

For Brass Stripe Book: Rub 'n Buff in turquoise, rubber gloves, narrow masking tape, brass frame charm, color photocopy of photo, white glue, adhesive caulk, organza ribbon

Directions

1. When you get your metal squares, don't even THINK of doing this first step your-self—you'll get hurt! Give all squares to a handyman to file the sharp points off the corners and drill two holes along one edge for binding (using either a drill press or clamping metals between pieces of wood for safety and to keep metal from being warped when the holes are drilled).
2. Rub all squares with Scotchbrite pads in circular motion to create a frosted finish and get rid of scratches.

Rusted Iron Book

1. For each book, lay *one square only* on newspaper. Sponge on rust patina (rust forms as piece dries). Note: Do this only on front because rust will tend to rub off; if you want to make it more durable, spray rusted pieces with sealer. This will darken the color significantly. If not sealed, be sure to give out in cellophane bags with a note to handle gently to protect clothes.
2. Glue charm on with adhesive caulk. Thread two pieces of lacing through the two holes and tie. Rubber-cement a sticky notepad inside.

Copper Initial Book

1. Observe the heart photo—these show how copper, when heated, changes in color from orange/magenta to blue to gold. I colored the cop-per by holding with tongs over the flame of a gas stove. You can also bake, but you'll have to experiment to see time and temperature to get the color you want in your oven.
2. When cool, use tape to mask areas where you want copper to show through. I made the initial letter out of contact paper by squeezing Sizzix die and paper in a vise (if you don't have a vise, ask handyman to do this as well or—simpler—get a paper punch that will easily punch out large heart, star, or other shape). Peel and stick your letter or shape in middle of book front. Spray with gold paint. Remove tape and contact paper.
3. Rubber-cement a large notepad inside. Assemble book, threading leather lace through holes and tying loosely. Hot-glue beads onto tie ends.

Brass Stripe Book

1. Use tape to mask off stripes. Squeeze Rub 'n Buff onto your gloved finger and rub on metal until you're happy with how it looks. (You will never get it perfectly even—that's the beauty of this product. If you want even color coverage, spray-paint a contrasting color like silver at this point.)
2. Glue photo with white glue into little frame, then glue the whole unit to the book front with caulk adhesive.
3. Rubber-cement a large notepad inside. Assemble book, threading ribbon through holes and tying loosely.

Decorating with Fruit

This is not a centerpiece but rather decor elements you can make with fruit. Use the carved oranges in centerpieces or even submerge them in a clear vase or pitcher with simple flowers on top!

Materials

Grape Topiary

Plaster pedestal
12" green Styrofoam cone
Caulk adhesive

Grapes
U-pins
Toothpicks or wooden skewers

Apple Candleholders

Apples
Candles

Knife

Carved Oranges

Oranges
Permanent marker

Large U-shaped linoleum
gouge

Directions

Grape Topiary

1. Glue cone to pedestal with caulk adhesive. Let it cure for several days.
2. Take a bunch of grapes, strip one side of fruit and—starting at bottom—wrap flat side of bunch around the cone, securing with U-pins. Continue until cone is covered. Fill in gaps with small grape clusters secured with toothpicks. Or add kumquats, halved star fruit, or other novelties.

Apple Candleholders

1. Use apples that will stay upright. Insert the knife blade in the center of the apple top to about a 2" depth and turn it to create a cylindrical hole. Use trial and error to make the hole just big enough for the candle to fit snugly.

Carved Oranges

1. Draw design you want to cut onto the orange with permanent marker.
2. Following your lines, hold the gouge fairly flat against the orange and push it through just the orange layer to expose the white pith underneath. Be very careful not to cut toward the hand holding the orange, as the gouge is sharp.

Seashell Candles

Materials

Large (4"–5" across) deep seashells
Gold or silver Sculpey
Caulk adhesive
Wicks
Wax coloring
Fragrance (if desired)
Microwax and heatproof container for melting it

Directions

1. Set shell on a flat surface and look at it from the side to judge how "level" it is. Roll 3–4 small balls of Sculpey and press them on the underside of the shell to serve as "feet." Bake shell with Sculpey attached. When cool, turn shell over, pull feet off, and glue them back on with caulk adhesive. Note: If you plan to put candles on table in a box of sand, you won't need to do this, as you can level them in sand.
2. Fill each shell with water to check for leaks. If you find any, fill them on shell inside with caulk and let dry. Glue metal base of wick to lowest point inside shell.
3. Melt wax in microwave according to directions; stir in color and fragrance if you wish. Fill shell with wax. When cool, trim wick to just over ¼". Burn one at home to make sure shells will last as long as your party. If not, you need bigger shells.

Hand-Colored Tallit

You can download this artwork from my website or use simple clip art or even art from a Bible coloring book (ask at your synagogue's religious school). If you're letting guests make tallitot, have a seamstress make a reinforced hole in each corner (3–4 finger widths from edges) ahead of time and have fringes and an instructor there with big rope demonstrator model to show how to tie them.

Materials
Artwork printed out on paper (if using it more than once, have it laminated)
Masking tape
Graphite paper
Pen
Silk blank (can be virtually any size, mine is 22" x 72")
Marvy Uchida DecoFabric pen in gold for outlining and Fabric Brush Markers for
    filling in

Directions
1. Position artwork where you want it and secure it with masking tape on three of the four corners of the paper. Slide a piece of graphite paper (shiny side against fabric) under artwork paper and tape fourth corner to fabric. Draw over lines of artwork with pen. Undo one corner and peek at fabric to make sure lines transferred.
2. Remove all paper. Place silk on a solid, fabric-covered surface that you don't mind getting marred by markers bleeding through. Go over all lines with the gold outlining pen, moving the pen steadily along so it doesn't bleed excessively in any one spot. You may want to try it out on scrap fabric first to get the hang of it.
3. Fill in outlined areas with other markers, staying away from outlines and letting markers bleed toward lines. Fill in lightly where gaps remain.
4. Go over outlines again with gold pen to correct spots where other colors have bled into them. Let whole thing dry.

Rope Kippah

This craft is so simple, elementary-age kids can do it. Use fluffy chenille, angora, or any yarn and, to make it more festive, you can even change colors when you add yarn.

Materials
3 yards ⁵⁄₃₂" cotton piping cord
Yarns, any color or thickness
Hot-glue gun and gluestick
Decorative studs, if desired

Directions
1. Cut a piece of yarn about 2 yards long. Wrap yarn around one end of cording in even rows; be sure to wrap over the end of the yarn to secure it and keep it from unraveling. When you've covered about 2" of the cording, bend covered cord into a tight little spiral and use the yarn to lash the cording together so it keeps that shape.
2. Continue wrapping the cording with yarn. After every ten wraps, bend the cord so it lays along the inner row of cord and lash the outer row to the inner row with one yarn wrap around both rows.
3. Keep wrapping the cord and lashing it every inch or so to the neighboring row until the kippah is the size you want. To add yarn, just tie the new piece to the existing piece and wrap over the knot to hide it. Finish by securing cord and yarn end to kippah with a spot of hot glue. Glue on decorative studs if you wish.

fourteen MitzvahChic on a Budget

I hope it's clear throughout this book that "chic" and "style" do not mean "expensive." Good taste and style—these are timeless and transcend matters of price. The simplest table decoration, if it's rendered with sincerity, *panache*, and aesthetic charm, is as authentic an expression of "chic" as the most expensive Paris couture.

So this chapter should really be called "How to Cut Corners and Still Give Everyone a Wonderful Experience." Since I totally believe you don't have to compromise quality to save money, I'm not going to give any silly suggestions like have the bar mitzvah on a Monday and you'll get a slightly better price from the caterer. That's true. In fact you'll save a fortune because no one will be able to come! How expensive could it be to feed six people?

Here are my favorite ideas for saving money. Remember, you can always offer to barter in lieu of some cash. Have no professional skills to swap? Offer to do some work for the vendor; ask for a discount off your bill for whatever friends you send his way who actually hire him; give him time in your vacation home. On second thought, if you have a vacation home, why are you reading this chapter?

Overall

- If you're faced with having two parties because your child wants one of his own with his friends—and what child doesn't?—have the adult party during the bar mitzvah weekend but wait and cohost a joint kid party with one or more of your son's good friends who are also becoming bar mitzvah.

Invitations

- Abandon the notion that the only good invitation is the ultra-deluxe store-bought kind. Unique homemade cards will trump those every time because they've got heart.
- They can also be the most beautiful with the wealth out there of wonderful papers and envelopes, ways of incorporating photographs, brass charms, ribbons—you name it. Some websites have designed "print your own" bar/bat mitzvah invitation blanks. Even Staples and Office-Max stock sheets of ready-to-print full-size and enclosure cards with envelopes.
- Making the invitation can also become a sort of meditation. Repetitive work, as long as it flows smoothly, is very relaxing. The trick is to do something simple, quick, and beautiful enough that you'll feel satisfied at the end, not worn out. Check out the ideas in "Crafts for Style and Therapy."
- Don't hire a calligrapher. Many envelopes can go through a computer printer, and the typefaces available are gorgeous! Just be sure the paper surface isn't too smooth or the ink can rub off. If you don't know how to print your own envelopes, ask a computer-savvy friend to help you. Give them plenty of time—computer-savvy friends aren't always sitting around with nothing to do, you know! (Sorry, just letting off some steam.)

The Party Space/Catering

- The cheapest place you can entertain your guests is at home—as long as home doesn't require major renovations to be presentable. And you don't have to put your furniture in storage . . . or rent a tent (see Chapter 4). Most of us don't have big enough houses, though, but perhaps a close friend does. The drawback here is that unless it's an old Victorian house with a huge ballroom, it's likely your guests will be cramped. And cramping is a major threat to a good mood.
- The next cheapest option may be a local fire hall, community hall or,

dare I say it, church basement. Don't worry that it's an inelegant space. Dress the tables in a pretty way and put all your favorite people in the room, and it will be heaven on earth. One real beauty of these rooms is, unlike many synagogues that require you to use a particular caterer, you can usually bring in your own food and save a fortune.

- In some synagogues, the auditoriums are as cheap to use as renting a fire hall. This is true only if they will let you bring in your own food or the list of approved caterers includes one that's really inexpensive. Such synagogues are hard to come by in my neighborhood.
  - Synagogues have approved caterers because of insurance concerns, kosher requirements, or possibly because the caterers pay a fee for the exclusive rights. If the roster doesn't include a low-priced option, though, this keeps people of modest means from being able to use their own synagogue!
  - Such a policy should be opposed (by you and like-minded mitzvah parents). Storm the Bastille! Petition the synagogue administration or catering committee early on in your planning and tell them you don't want to hold a bat mitzvah party in a church basement—you want to be able to use your own synagogue!
- Any place that lets you bring in your own food is an incredible cost-saving find.
  - If you decide to handle the food yourself, hire some college kids and local moms to take care of heating and serving the food. Order trays from all the best places around: sushi, Chinese, gourmet pizza, etc. Make some simple dishes yourself.
  - China and utensils will be a problem, as the caterer usually supplies them. You can create a "co-op," though, with other parents whose children are becoming b'nai mitzvah. From a restaurant supplier, purchase place settings, utensils, water glasses and wineglasses, plus inexpensive serving pieces. Then take turns using the equipment at all your parties. If you don't have a restaurant supplier in your area, search online under "catering supplies." Buy extra—there's going to be some breakage along the way.
- If all this fails, remember that it's generally cheaper to have a party in a restaurant than to have a caterer serve similar food in a party hall somewhere. That's because the restaurant has already established its prices on the menu and can't charge you more.

- The absolutely most expensive thing you can do—other than picking the local five-star restaurant—is to pick a locale that is not a restaurant (or a fire hall, community room, or other space used often for parties) and turn it into a party space just for the day. On top of all the normal expenses, you'll have to rent every chair and table and it's likely your vendors will charge you a premium for the extra aggravation involved.
- For best value, have a lunch instead of a dinner.
- Have a wine, juice, and soda bar instead of mixed drinks. Better yet, buy the wine and other drinks yourself and hire your own servers.
  - See if the wine vendor delivers, if he includes the use of wineglasses, and if he will allow you to return unopened bottles for a refund.
- Keep the menu simple. Have some meatless dishes (you should do this for your vegetarian friends even if you're not trying to save money).
- Have a different (less expensive but still quality) menu for the kids.
- Serve inexpensive and unusual ethnic foods. It will be a culinary adventure and no one will be able to determine if the food is cheap or not.
- Serve buffet style. It not only cuts down on the number of staff needed but also gives guests more freedom to roam and eat at their own pace. Sit-down dinners often roll out very slowly, holding guests hostage at the table while the food and activities of the party attempt to get in sync.
- Shop for a cake at your neighborhood bakeries, not the local "bakers to the stars." They may have very nice designs but no budget to advertise them.
  - If you're buying a cake, tell the caterer you don't want dessert—it's often served before the cake and the cake then goes uneaten.
  - Best idea of all: Buy individual cakes and use them as the centerpieces—the culinary equivalent of multitasking.

Music and Entertainment

- This is tough because the music is so key to the success of an event. Inexpensive food can still be beautiful and delicious, but how do you economize on music? Personally, this is not where I would cut costs. Still, you could get lucky and find a great band or DJ that's just getting started.
- You can have a string quartet instead of a dance band, but know up

front that your party will then, by definition, not rock. It will have a serene, mannered feel. Even if they play the *1812 Overture*.

- Remember, you're shopping for the leader/DJ's personality (see Chapter 4), not necessarily years and years of experience. So look around and be sure to see each candidate working an actual party (in person or on a videotape the DJ supplies).

- If you really like someone but he's relatively new to the business, don't be afraid to hire him. Most DJs learn by working for established people, so even if he hasn't been the head honcho at many parties, he may be fine as a leader. Just get a tape or go see him perform at a party to verify that.

- Price-shop. You may be surprised at the price range within your own community. If there are more DJs than the market can really support, you may be able to negotiate a lower price.

- Read Chapter 4 for a sense of the minimum package needed to have a good time. Don't go for pricey extras unless you're sure you have to have them.

- If you want to hire additional entertainment—and if you're on a tight budget, there's certainly no need to—hire someone who will create a giveaway, thereby eliminating the need for a separate party favor.

Decorations/Party Favors

- Make decorations yourself. See "Eight Complete Parties that Will Leave You *Farklempt*!" and "Crafts for Style and Therapy."

- Choose projects that are simple enough for novices (I've tried to make most ideas in this book that simple) and hire college students, local moms, or even conscientious high-schoolers to work on them.
  - Farm out some jobs to specialists. If you need holes drilled in a sheet of metal, ask the retired handyman in the neighborhood.

- Ask your friends to help you. It's fun to get together and play! As long as you're not starting a major project the week before the bat mitzvah.

- If you have a good eye, buy flowers in bulk and make the arrangements yourself.
  - If you don't have a good eye, get potted flowering plants or large bunches of one type of beautiful flower and place them in simple pots. Make simple topiaries by bunching one kind of long-stemmed

flowers together and trying raffia around the "trunk" of stalks if needed to keep them upright. Stick the trunk in a jar of water in a pot (surround jar with crumpled paper to keep in place) or stick the trunk in wet floral foam and cover the top with moss.

- Party favors are the focus of considerable angst. The later in the school year your child's party is, the more likely that the young guests will have already maxed out on T-shirts and the usual trinkets. One trip to the thrift store is enough to see how treasured the T-shirts are long-term.
  - If you're giving a T-shirt, it will have to be quite cool to have any staying power and may not be the best use of limited funds.
  - Again, being innovative can save you a lot of money. A moderate-quality T-shirt printed one color will cost about $5–$6. A desktop herb garden or "lawn" ready-to-grow in a four-inch round tin is something you can easily make yourself for less than $2. See "Beginnings" party to see this item, Appendix 2 to find materials vendor, and www.MitzvahChic.com links for downloadable label art.
  - Don't assume that the simplest ideas are passé. Candy wrapped in tulle with a ribbon can be just the thing at the end of a hard night of partying.
  - In fact, definitely look for candy favors for the kids before investigating the pricier options. Look online or at the local candy store.
- Attach place cards to the party favors. That way, you need to give only one party favor to each couple and you don't need to work out a separate presentation for the place cards.

Photography

- Ask friends who like to take photos (and are good at it) to take pictures at the party. Then you may be able to limit the professional photographer's participation to portraits at the synagogue.
- If there's an art college or any college with a photography major nearby, call the department and ask if any students there do special events.
- Call local photographers to see if they have apprentices who might be willing to do the job. Apologize for being too impoverished to hire the master photographer and say you wouldn't dream of asking him or her to do it for what you have to spend. You never know. If business is slow, he or she might be willing to take the job for less than the usual rate.

- Ask the photographer if he or she would be willing just to take the photos and hand the film (or a disk of digital images) over after the party. That way, you control the cost of prints and enlargements.
- Put a disposable camera on each table and encourage the guests to snap away. This has been a popular idea for some time, but there are a couple of drawbacks:
  - First, the cameras don't always produce good-quality photos, though the cameras have gotten better since they were first introduced.
  - Second, guests who need a camera like that for a rafting vacation or whatever are tempted to steal them.
  - This is an okay idea to supplement someone taking real photos, but if you love having great pictures, don't leave it entirely up to the guests.

fifteen The Kids Have the Last Word

This chapter presents actual views from real live teenagers. Parents of teenagers will nod knowingly, though, when I say that they all talked at once so there is no sifting out who said what or any way to statistically analyze which teenager is most like your own child. Nor is there any way to test if this particular batch of teenagers speaks for those you know.

I doubt that it matters, though. The biggest surprise of this chapter was how few surprises there actually were. Every assumption I had made about what teenagers would want turned out to be right on the money. With such a perceptive mother, no wonder my teenager is such a contented boy! Actually, there's no sensitivity or psychic ability required; if you've been a teenager and you live with a preteen now, it's pretty easy to know how they think.

The message of this chapter is not that you should indulge their every whim when planning their *simcha*. Kids this age don't have the experience to know the proper course when navigating the social landscape. Also, some are driven so crazy by the pressure of their situation that literally nothing you can plan or do will be okay with them. Yet, if you throw up your hands and actually do *nothing,* waiting for their permission to act, they won't be happy with the outcome either.

This is a little window into the teenage mind. It may surprise you, confirm that you're on the right track, or let you cross things they've identified as low priority off your to-do list. Use this chapter to talk to your child and—if you really disagree—at least to appreciate how universal his or her feelings are.

One interesting discovery along the way is that although adults think of teenagers as very different from them, the kids actually have similar perceptions about what creates party magic. Many showed an adultlike intolerance for crowding and other discomforts. On the other hand, they were quick to jump into any activity that looked even mildly entertaining and they were very appreciative of any attempt to amuse them. It's easy to see why. I interviewed several kids who were finishing seventh grade, and a school year's worth of attending at least one four-hour party virtually every weekend had clearly taken its toll. The excitement they had felt throughout the fall about dressing up and dancing the night away had, by February or March, given way to mind-numbing boredom. All agreed that a party held in the spring had to be ten times as much fun as a September party to be considered half as good.

This is very good news if you're hoping to try out some fun-sounding new party ideas. Don't be discouraged if your child initially doesn't want to consider deviating from the familiar formulas. As bored as they may be with the old routine, many kids don't want to be the first to try an untraditional idea, lest it be a humiliating failure. Champion your good ideas and keep talking them up. As the more experienced people, we know what works—especially if we've read the first several chapters of this book. To win your child over, appeal to that adventure-loving outlaw that lives—alongside the play-it-safe wallflower—within every teen. If you simply want to do what makes him or her happy, heed these words . . .

Should You Include Them in the Planning?

Yes! All our teens recognized the irony of being treated like know-nothing kids when planning the event meant to validate them as adults. Some kids fondly remembered the planning days as an enjoyable time of sharing that gave them insight into their parent's styles and attitudes as well as into adult values in general. A few admitted that they felt extremely stressed out whenever the mitzvah subject came up, and they warn parents not to buy into it if their frazzled child rejects perfectly good party plans. "Planning it should be fun," one teen noted. To achieve that, let your child choose among options that are all acceptable to you, the parents. Where there's a split decision, the parents win. This will help drive home the point that it's good to be an adult!

What Kind of Party Should It Be?

There was no ambiguity here. Kids want a kids-only party, with a great DJ, at night. Having one big lunchtime party is a popular concept with parents because it's time-efficient having the party right after the service and costs across the board are generally cheaper for a daytime affair. But one recent bat mitzvah complained that at her combo adult-child lunch party, she had to spend virtually the whole time talking to people she barely knew rather than enjoying herself with friends. Kids who are guests at such parties also feel somewhat "under surveillance" by the adults in the room. Overall, the kids recognize the need to receive the adults—they'd just prefer to do it away from "their" party.

How Grand Does the Party Need to Be?

What mattered most to the kids was having the party their way—their friends, their music, a chance to hang together in a relaxed atmosphere. They enjoy the novelty of an interesting venue or handsome decorating, but these were clearly lower priorities.

Why Do They Prefer Night?

One teen remarked, "It just feels more cool and special," and there were nods all around. Most felt that having the party at night helped to create a sort of "club" atmosphere that was very appealing. Other kids, being practical, appreciated that having a separation between the service and the party allowed them to go home and change into more comfortable clothes. The kids did not like, however, nighttime parties where everything happened late—no one thought it was a good idea, for example, to serve dinner at 10 P.M.

Change Clothes—Don't Kids Like to Dress Up?

Most said that the first several "black tie" parties they attended were fun and special. Sample comment: "It was fun to feel pretty and see everyone looking pretty." Soon, though, the realization set in that "the clothes are uncomfortable" and "it's hard to dance in a big dress." Boys tend to wear suits and girls wear dresses to services. All would prefer to be in their normal casual clothes when it's party time.

What's Wrong with Eating at 10 P.M.?

Teenagers are hungry almost all the time. The classic format of a party that starts with a cocktail hour followed by a long foodless pause, then food, then nothing doesn't suit their needs at all. First, they're bored to death during the cocktail hour (so plan an activity for them!). Then, once the party is rolling and they're engaged with their friends, they may miss the food service completely. The best situation for teenagers is food that's available most of the evening: either a low-maintenance buffet, or food on request off pushcarts or a snack bar.

And Another Thing about Food . . .

The kids all complained—nicely—about the double standard in food. While the adults dine sumptuously, the kids usually have their own menu: food that, according to my focus group, suggests they're large-size toddlers. With burned chicken fingers, soggy fries, and bland overcooked pasta as the standards, the food is dismal and, as Woody Allen quipped, the portions are too small. A friend of mine considers this a rare but not unheard of ploy by disreputable caterers, though I hope it's *very* uncommon. The caterer offers a kids' menu at a discount (though not always a big discount) from the adult price, and financially burdened hosts gratefully accept. The caterer then actually serves to the kids food that is shockingly bad. He doesn't even have to bring enough for everyone because he knows they're not going to eat it anyway. Meanwhile, the hosts, busy entertaining their adult friends, aren't aware the kids are going hungry. Intentional or not, the point is not lost on the kids. They've gone to as much bother and shown as much commitment as the adults in coming to this event, but they are not equally valued. You don't need to serve the kids expensive food, but make sure they get something really good. And also be aware that even at this young age, some kids are vegetarians, so be sure to offer some variety.

How to Pick the Place . . .

Our teenagers sounded like adults on the subject of party halls. They enjoy going to interesting places—one fondly remembered a party held in a famous science museum—but mainly a party space should just be comfortable and appropriate. As long as there's enough room for everyone to hang out together by a dance floor and DJ, they're basically happy. Rooms that are too big or too ugly were considered mistakes largely because of the expense hosts then incur trying to make them look better. A better alternative to extreme decorating, the kids suggested, is simply to turn down the house lights and use candles and the DJ-supplied disco lights. "The darker, the better," one concluded.

. . . and the All-Important DJ

Here again many voices spoke as one: no overweight guys in their fifties bursting out of their funky glitter party vests and shouting for everyone to *Do the macarena!* The kids want cool DJs who know their music and probably listen to it themselves. Don't pick a master of shtick—someone who considers himself the show—unless that's your taste or you're filming the sequel to *Dirty Dancing*.

Should We Play Games?

The kids well understood the power of games in breaking the ice and revving up the party's energy, and gave them a big thumbs-up. As one said, they make "things get fun sooner." Surprisingly, these young sophisticates were very fond of the goofy prizes they got for playing. One particularly chic young woman happily reported that she had six pairs of inflatable shoes in her closet at that very moment. That same girl also noted that her DJ had asked the family to supply him with some really good prizes (gift cards to the local video rental store) to keep the interest level up as the evening progressed.

What About Other Entertainment?

These kids could have written my chapter "The Major Party Decisions You Have to Make First." They really appreciated having something fun to do beyond dancing. Particularly as the school year wears on and the tedium sets in, you almost *have* to have something more going on. The kids didn't particularly like passive ideas—such as sitting for a caricature portrait—that took them out of the party. They much preferred entertainments like karaoke that let friends play and party together. Even a photo booth where digital photos are made into key chains, ID cards, and magazine covers was a good opportunity to have fun with friends by posing together. Having beautiful "masks" painted on their faces by airbrush, although it's passive, was also a hit because the kids returned to the action looking really good.

Do You Need to Give Out Party Favors?

Strictly speaking, no. But some teens shyly admitted that the promise of a good giveaway was almost the only thing that could motivate them to attend the last several parties of the year. What items make good giveaways? Here there were some real surprises—the kids liked practical everyday things: sweatshirts, flannel pants, flip-flops, decks of cards, flashlights, towels, gym bags, and socks. They have to be good quality, though. No one wanted a beach towel that's so thin you could fold it up and put it in your pocket. Also, no one wanted another T-shirt or scrub-suit . . . ever. Parents should also, I'm told, resist the urge to imprint something clever on the item. If you must imprint, your child's name alone will do. Everyone also agreed that they would cherish, as a giveaway, any "cool" thing. I leave it to you and the psychic hotline to divine what that would be. Visit www .MitzvahChic.com for some ideas.

Should There be a Theme?

This is (I hope) not a $100,000 question, but it certainly adds potential big bucks to your budget depending on the scale of your party. The teenagers, like most adults, enjoyed the thrill of a big idea carried through the decorations, party favors, and activities. They also agreed, though, that a theme wasn't really necessary and that small ideas or themes with no passion behind them were hardly worth the effort. "You shouldn't have a color as the theme," one commented, "and don't say the theme is 'the beach' and then just put a bucket of sand in the middle of the table."

A Last Detail: Sign-in Boards

This is a puzzle—what to use that you'll want to keep over the years? The simplest idea is a poster-size enlargement of the invitation mounted on foamcore, but will it become something you want to display forever? The teenagers thought this was one place where you could really get creative and they remembered one friend who had a chair for everyone to sign, and another who brought her actual bedroom door! Finally they decided, though, that for parents who don't want to figure out how to bring a door to a party, "a book is good."

Another intriguing possibility: Get an Andy Warhol–style pop art portrait of your child (or just a nice 8 x 8 headshot), put a very very wide white mat around it, put it on an easel, and let people sign the mat. After the event, just take it to the frame shop.

Final Thoughts

You may by now be feeling some indignation . . . *Oh, soggy fries aren't good enough, huh? At their age, we dipped our fingers in ketchup and pretended they were soggy fries!* Well, before you dismiss this current generation as jaded teens, I need to say that I was extremely impressed by the sincerity and goodwill of the kids I spoke to. They intuitively understood at a young age how important it was to put themselves aside to be present, emotionally supporting each of their friends through a stressful experience. They had tried consistently, under sometimes difficult conditions, to be good guests. They were, in short, the emerging adults their bar and bat mitzvah ceremonies said they had become. We should all recognize the enormity and grace of that achievement. I thank them for their honesty and I hope by writing this chapter I have brightened their chances of being understood, respected, and wowed by every party from this moment on.

sixteen Time Line and Checklists

Master Time Line

DATE FINISHED	TWO+ YEARS–18 MONTHS AHEAD (or whenever you start)

- Get the date (you may already have had it for a year or more).
- Sign up on the MitzvahChic.com Event Calendar for free gorgeous emailed planning reminders with checklists so you won't miss a thing!
- Check "The Torah for the *Farchadat* (confused)" to see which portions your child will have. Confirm portions with the rabbi. Read the portion and check the MitzvahChic Torah chapter for additional reading/viewing suggestions. Go to www.MitzvahChic.com links to find book and video order information.
- Make it a routine that once a week over dinner the family will discuss one idea from the Torah portion. Then your child will be very prepared to write the *dvar Torah* when it's time.
- Talk with your child about mitzvah projects related to the portion (see "Party Ideas for Each Torah Portion") or of special personal interest.
- Consult "Questions to Ask the Rabbi/Cantor" that follows this time line to see if you need any answered now.
  - At this point, you want to decide if you need to book the synagogue auditorium for kiddush or an evening party.
  - You also want to make the rabbi aware if your child has a learning issue that could dictate a longer course of study.
- Draft a preliminary guest list and discuss as a family the kind of celebration you have in mind—you need this to know what kind of reception space you're looking for.

- Decide roughly how many kids your child may invite; expect the final choice to be in flux up until the invitations go out.
- Check MitzvahChic.com vendor directory for your region for all vendors and ask experienced parents for their reaction to the venues, caterers, bands/DJs, and photographers listed in there. Start going around to hear bands/DJs. Solicit estimates from all vendors you're interested in.

DATE FINISHED	ONE YEAR AHEAD

- Based on vendor proposals, projected head count (and checklist at the end of this time line), work up a rough budget. If there are compromises to be made, discuss as a family where to make them.
  - Make sure everything you agree on is in writing in the contract and hire the . . .
    - Caterer
    - Band/DJ
    - Photographer and/or videographer
- Find out the actual date your child's tutoring will begin (should be at least nine months ahead, but add time if your child has any learning issues), how progress will be measured, and the synagogue's time line for completing the *dvar Torah,* mitzvah project, and other requirements.
- If you haven't yet delved into the Torah portion, check "The Torah for the *Farchadat* (confused)" for reading and viewing suggestions related to the Torah portion. Watch or read something together as a family and discuss your interpretation of its message.
- If you want to do your own invitation, start thinking about what it might look like (see samples in "Crafts for Style and Therapy").
  - Get ideas from MitzvahChic.com vendor directory, ideas sections, and discussion forum.
  - Review also "Party Ideas for Each Torah Portion" and "Eight Complete Parties That Will Leave You *Farklempt!*"
- Pick a theme if you wish and decide which ideas to use.
- Identify and hire people to do the work—party planner, art student, Kinko's, friends, you.
- If you have out-of-town guests coming, find a local hotel that will reserve a block of rooms or, for guests who need to walk to shul, local people who will put them up for the night.
- Inform close friends and family of the date and ask them to hold it.
- If you don't regularly attend services, make a point of attending often when there is a bar/bat mitzvah so you will be familiar with your synagogue's approach. Make notes on anything you want to ask the rabbi/cantor at your initial meeting in several weeks.

DATE FINISHED	NINE–TEN MONTHS AHEAD

- Your child begins tutoring. Often the process formally begins with a family meeting with the rabbi and/or cantor. Ask general questions here (see list at end of this chapter). If there's a sensitive issue to discuss—divorced parents or how a non-Jewish parent will participate, for example—parents should set up another meeting and come without their child.

- Find out exactly what your child will do in the service and in the months leading up to it. How will you know if he or she is making acceptable progress? What is the schedule of tutoring appointments?
- How does the synagogue want the parents to be involved?
- Are there any printed guidelines that answer all the usual questions parents have about synagogue policy? If not, whom should you ask when you have questions? Is it possible to be matched with a family that has recently gone through the process as mentors?
- Tell the rabbi/cantor what you are doing as a family to become familiar with the portion and to prepare for the ceremony. Solicit his or her suggestions.
- Finalize guest list with complete addresses.
- Make—or shop for and order—the invitations (more than you think you need), several extra envelopes, plus thank-you notes for your child to use afterward.
  - For wording discussion, see "The Little Party Details That Really Matter."
  - If you're making your invitation, keep in mind you'll need various enclosure cards plus a reply card and envelope. Plain white or cream-colored versions of these are available at office supply stores like Staples, but for unusual papers, you will need to buy extra paper and cut it down.
- While invitations are being printed, find any maps you'll include in the mailing and make photocopies. Also be sure to enclose a card alerting guests if the festivities start the evening or day before the service so they can make appropriate travel arrangements.
- Put a party end time so parents will know when to pick up their kids.
- If you want to buy, from a charity, a tallit for the bar mitzvah or handmade kippot for family members, order them now. See www.MitzvahChic.com links for charitable sources.
- Discuss decorating and party ideas with your child and/or introduce him or her to the party planner if you're using one.

DATE FINISHED	SIX MONTHS AHEAD

- Check in with the tutor to see how your child is doing.
- Child begins drafting the *dvar Torah*.
- If your son is laying tefillin, get them now and have his father, grandfather, or a clergy member teach the proper method.
- Decide if you will print the envelopes on the computer with a calligraphy typeface or have a calligrapher address them.
- If you're making your own centerpieces or party favors, get started buying the materials, crafting them, or assigning jobs to helpers. If you're using a party planner, finalize the concept.
- Order any imprinted items: kippot, party favors. (See MitzvahChic.com vendor directory and ideas sections.)

- Check in with the tutor to see how your child is doing.
- Discuss with rabbi and cantor any music or readings you would like to add to the service.
- Plan menu; make sure to include meatless options for vegetarians.
- Shop for a cake.
- Start shopping for clothes. But, particularly if your child is a boy, don't have anything altered until a few weeks before the big day.

DATE FINISHED	THREE MONTHS AHEAD

- Parents start talking about their speech and writing a first draft. (See "Writing a Great Speech and Finding the Courage to Give It.") Ask your rabbi for special poems or readings to incorporate. These can be read instead of a speech, if you wish.
- Give envelopes to calligrapher or address them yourself.
- Weigh a complete invitation at post office and buy stamps. When it's time to stuff the envelopes, write numbers lightly on the back of your response cards and record which number goes to which guest next to the names on your list. Then if you get a reply card with no name, you can just look it up.

DATE FINISHED	TWO MONTHS AHEAD

- Check in with the tutor to see how your child is doing. If he or she is really struggling, ask to adjust the size of the reading to allow him or her to do less with greater confidence.
- Prepare list of aliyot. Let everyone on the list know of the honor so they can review and practice the Hebrew readings.
- Mail invitations (you can wait two weeks to mail local invitations).
- If you're going to be dressing the tables yourself, find out from the reception hall when you can get in to set up. Remember, if your child is having a Saturday morning service followed by a lunch or dinner reception, you'll be occupied and unable to do anything yourself after Friday afternoon. Find out what the reception hall staff is willing to do; hire helpers to do the rest.
- If it's a dance party and your child is insecure about his or her dancing, ask the DJ to schedule a dancer to give a few lessons.
- Whatever relaxes you—massage, lunch with a friend, etc.—make an appointment to do it on the day before the bar mitzvah service.
- Figure out what relaxes your child and plan to do that also on the day before the bat mitzvah service.
  - Some kids feel more relaxed just going to school and being with their friends following their normal routine, but if your child would like to spend some special relaxed time with you or alone, reading, watching a video, etc., try your best to make it happen.

DATE FINISHED	SIX WEEKS AHEAD

- Have your child meet with the DJ/band to pick songs and games.
- Help your child polish the *dvar Torah* and write a "thank you" speech if one is planned.
- Parents finalize their speech.
- Have in-depth discussions with all your vendors to make sure you've made all necessary decisions and given clear direction. At this point, for example, the photographer should know the exact arrangements for taking pictures before the service. Is it the day before? The hour before?
- Assemble any maps or local information for out-of-town guests, including time and location of all events. Identify who can deliver eventual welcome baskets to hotel(s).
- Where transportation options are limited, ask local friends to pick up out-of-towners and drive them. If there are several people without transportation who need to go from Point A to Point B, consider hiring a van or small bus to take them.

DATE FINISHED	THREE WEEKS AHEAD

- Call anyone you haven't heard from and give caterer the final head count.
- Figure out seating arrangements and write place cards. Or give list to your party planner.
- If you've asked people to write notes to your child, place the ones that can be shared into an album to take to the reception.
- Get your son's suit altered. Make sure his dress shoes fit.
- Buy items to make up welcome baskets to deliver to out-of-town guests. Or order filled baskets from a supplier, giving recipients' names and hotel addresses.
- Make up toiletry baskets for the restrooms at your event, including such items as safety pins, Band-Aids, mild antacid tablets, etc. (Make sure any medication is in a childproof bottle and the baskets are out of reach of young children who might mistake medication for candy.)
- Ask friends to plan on transporting kids to the reception if it's not in the synagogue.

DATE FINISHED	THE WEEK BEFORE

- Have a rehearsal in the synagogue with as many of the participants as possible.
- Give aliyah list to the rabbi/cantor.
- Touch base with all your vendors for any last-minute instructions or questions.
- Take posed photos in the sanctuary if possible.
- Prepare welcome baskets for out-of-town guests. Tuck maps and local information inside. Give with addresses to delivery person.

- *BREATHE!*
- Go to your prearranged relaxation appointment.
- Give your child his or her relaxation time.
- Be sure in midst of all the chaos to take the time to let your child know that no matter what happens up on the bimah, you are so proud and that everyone who's coming loves and supports him or her. The day is really not about the "performance" but the sanctity of everything he or she did to reach this day.

Figuring Out the Budget

_____ Reading material and videos

_____ Invitations and postage

_____ Reception hall

_____ Table/chair/linen/china rental

_____ Caterer/food
- *Oneg(s)*
- Kiddush
- Party

_____ Wine & soda bar/mixed drinks

_____ Band or DJ

_____ Photographer & videographer

_____ Table and room decorations

_____ Party favors

_____ Hired transportation

_____ Hired help

_____ Additional entertainment

_____ Fees to the synagogue

_____ Donation to the rabbi/cantor

_____ Tzedakah

_____ Gift for child

_____ **TOTAL**

Questions to Ask the Rabbi/Cantor

Please use discretion in deciding which ones to ask in front of your child.

How well do the clergy know my child?

How can they become more personally acquainted before the big day?

Exactly what is our child going to be doing in the service?

How often will our child meet with the tutor? Will the tutor call us if there's a problem?

We attended the bar/bat mitzvah service of _____ (name). Can we expect our child's service to be the same?

What ideally do you want the parents and extended family to do in preparation?

We've been reading/viewing/doing _____ to become more familiar with the Torah portion and its messages. Can you recommend other materials we could use?

When should our child start his mitzvah project/*dvar Torah*/other requirements? Will you be working directly with him on these, or are they solely our responsibility?

Is there any printed information on the synagogue's policies and rules on bar/bat mitzvah preparation and on events held here? Do you have a time line that answers the basic questions? If not, whom should we talk to when we have questions?

Can you recommend a family who's recently been through the process at this synagogue and might be willing to mentor us?

What services and events will we be attending or hosting on the bar mitzvah weekend? Friday night service, Friday night *oneg Shabbat,* Saturday morning *oneg?*

How many aliyot and other honors are there in the service? Who may have one?

How may non-Jewish family members participate?

May we request special musical selections or readings, or a special mention for deceased family members?

Are parents allowed/expected to make a brief speech during the service? Are the b'nai mitzvah expected to give a "thank you" speech in addition to the *dvar Torah?*

Is there a dress code on the bimah? For guests in the sanctuary?

Do you have any guidelines we should share with guests?

Do you have copies of any booklets explaining the service that other families have created for their guests?

Is photography or videotaping allowed? How do we arrange it with the synagogue?

Does our bar/bat mitzvah fee cover all expenses, or are some not included—for the *oneg,* flowers for the bimah, etc.?

What have we forgotten to ask?

Insider Tips on Hiring Great Vendors

The MitzvahChic staff gathered some of the top vendors involved with our website to share their tips and tactics on how to find, interview, and hire the best possible suppliers to accomplish your dream event. Our roundtable—photographers Teri Bloom (teribloom.com) and Lorry Mulhern (lotusphotog raphers.com); event designer Michelle Gillette (dramaticeventdesign.com); and others—contributed to this list and the vendor interview questions that follow.

- Follow your intuition. Never talk yourself into hiring someone who sets off your alarm bells or doesn't feel like a good fit for you just because he or she is the hot vendor of the moment.
- Always do research ahead of interviewing a vendor to get a feel for his or her approach/philosophy and the quality of his or her work.
- Look for a high-quality website. It's a good indicator of their attention to detail as well as a wonderful place to prequalify vendors based on philosophy, style, quality of work, etc.
- Referrals from other vendors may mean there's a commission involved.
- Always look at the work. Referrals from friends may be more reflective of the vendor's chemistry with people than actual skill.
- Avoid vendors for whom a bar/bat mitzvah has become very routine. You should feel like the vendor is excited to be working for you and approaches each client with a genuine interest and curiosity about you and what you want to achieve.
- Vendors should be accessible and willing to talk along the way—as long as you're not taking up excessive time with unimportant matters.
- Meet face-to-face when the event is near. Make sure everyone's on the same page and that they know how to contact you with questions. Supply everyone with typed notes about what you want.
- Do your homework, be a good team leader and you'll have an amazing time!

QUESTIONS TO ASK ABOUT A VENUE	NAME OF THE VENUE		
How many rooms do you have and what is their capacity?			
Do you have floor plans that show how to set up tables to fit that number of people in?			
If you have more than one room, do you book all the rooms for parties at the same time? If so, will we be able to hear their music in our room? Will there be adequate parking and other shared facilities for everyone?			
Do you have outdoor space we could use?			
Do you have a specialty you're known for?			
How do you price your services?			
Can you give us (fax, email) a complete price list? When can we get that?			
Do you offer both buffet and waiter service?			
Do waiters give white glove service?			
What is included as standard with the meal?			
What is priced separately? • Room rental? • Linens? • Other equipment? • Anything else?			
Can we see linen options? Are any upgrades available?			
Are all staffing fees included in the contract price? Are all gratuities included?			
Are prices based on a certain number of hours? How many?			
Can additional time be purchased? When would you need to know?			
Do you have package prices? What is and is not included?			

QUESTIONS TO ASK ABOUT A VENUE	NAME OF THE VENUE		
Do you maintain a list of preferred professionals you refer clients to for other services like event planning, decorating, photography, etc.?			
Do any of these offer special deals to customers using your venue?			
Understanding that no site is perfect for every event, are there pros and cons to be aware of in planning a bar/bat mitzvah in this room?			
Are there any technical problems the DJ, caterer, or other vendors will have to deal with?			
Do you have any photos of the room set up for a party?			
Is there a kitchen on the premises?			
Are we required to use the in-house caterer and beverage service?			
What other guest services do you offer? Valet parking? Coat check? Babysitting?			
How are those services priced?			
Is there free parking on site?			
What are your payment terms?			
What is your cancellation policy?			
Do you accept credit cards?			
How much of your business comes from referrals?			
May we have references we can speak to?			
Notes, thoughts, follow-up plans			

QUESTIONS TO ASK A CATERER	NAME OF THE CATERER		
How would you complete this thought: *The best bar/bat mitzvah caterer does these things _____ and delivers these results _____?*			
Do you have a specialty you're known for?			
Do you normally do tastings? Is there a charge for them?			
What are your suggested menus for the time of day of our event?			
Can we have a complete price list?			
Do you include all staffing charges in your proposal?			
What will the staff-to-guest ratio be?			
Do your prices include gratuities?			
What is included and not included in your quote?			
If we have a cake, is there a cake-cutting fee?			
For liquor, is it a straight per-person charge or per bottle consumed?			
Can we supply our own liquor and bartender?			
If you supply the liquor, do you have the proper license and insurance in case of any accidents arising from the guests drinking?			
Which special diets and food allergies are you experienced in accommodating?			
Do you offer a kids' menu for bar/bat mitzvah–age kids?			
What are the options and pricing for that?			
What can you supply or coordinate in addition to food? Linens, other rentals, valet parking, other services?			
How do you price those items?			

	NAME OF THE CATERER		
QUESTIONS TO ASK A CATERER			
What is your process in working with a family?			
What is the pacing of the meal at a four-hour event?			
What are your payment terms?			
Do you accept credit cards?			
What is your cancellation policy?			
How long have you been in this business?			
How much of your business comes from referrals?			
May we have references we can speak to?			
Notes, thoughts, follow-up plans			

_____

_____

_____

_____

_____

	NAME OF THE PARTY PLANNER		
QUESTIONS TO ASK A PARTY PLANNER			
How would you complete this thought: *The best bar/bat mitzvah party planner does these things _____ and delivers these results _____?*			
How do you like to work with a family?			
What should we expect the process to be? How often would we meet? Starting how far in advance of the party?			
How do you determine what to charge?			
Are you known for a particular specialty or for planning parties with a certain flavor?			
Is your approach or service unique in any way from other vendors I might talk to?			

QUESTIONS TO ASK A PARTY PLANNER	NAME OF THE PARTY PLANNER		
Do you like to put the whole party together—hire all the other vendors? Do you always work with the same subcontractors?			
Do you mind clients calling you with questions or suggestions? How do you prefer to be contacted?			
How many bar/bat mitzvahs have you done?			
What do you consider most key to a successful one?			
How would you make ours unique?			
Do you like working with clients who have a lot of their own ideas? What if we don't have *any* idea of what we want?			
What would you want to know about us before you took this assignment?			
What would you need from us to get started?			
What should we do to help you do your best work?			
What are your payment terms?			
Do you accept credit cards?			
What is your cancellation policy?			
How long have you been in this business?			
How much of your business comes from referrals?			
May we have references we can speak to?			
Notes, thoughts, follow-up plans			

QUESTIONS TO ASK A PHOTOGRAPHER	NAME OF THE PHOTOGRAPHER		
How would you complete this thought: *The best bar/bat mitzvah photographer does these things* _____ *and delivers these results* _____?			
How do you price a job?			
Do you have package prices? What is and is not included?			
How long would you expect to shoot? Roughly how many photos do you deliver?			
Do you shoot digital or film? What do you think are the important differences?			
I've heard digital produces skin tones that need correcting—are you skilled with the software to do that? Or does the studio have someone who specializes in that?			
Can I have the negatives or photos on disk if I want them?			
If you have multiple photographers at your studio, who specifically would be doing our photography? Why would you assign him or her?			
What will happen if that person is sick or can't come at the last minute?			
Can I see samples of that photographer's work?			
How many bar/bat mitzvahs has he or she shot?			
Does the photographer mainly do photojournalism style photography or portrait work? (If you particularly want great candids, it's best to choose a photojournalism approach.)			
Will he or she set up any special lighting or use a flash? Don't dark hair and clothing just fuse into the background if there's no lighting behind them?			
How will I communicate with you about which people and shots are important to get?			

QUESTIONS TO ASK A PHOTOGRAPHER	NAME OF THE PHOTOGRAPHER		
If we want formal portraits, when should we plan on having them taken?			
Have you shot portraits at our synagogue before so you're aware of their policies and requirements?			
How do you work with the other professionals at the party?			
Is your approach or service unique in any way from other vendors I might talk to?			
How long after the party will we see proofs? When will the albums be delivered? (Give photographer a couple weeks' leeway on this.)			
What are your payment terms?			
Do you accept credit cards?			
What is your cancellation policy?			
How long have you been in this business?			
How much of your business comes from referrals?			
May we have references we can speak to?			
Notes, thoughts, follow-up plans			

QUESTIONS TO ASK A DJ/BAND	NAME OF THE DJ/BAND		
How would you complete this thought: *The best bar/bat mitzvah entertainer does these things _____ and delivers these results _____?*			
How many people do you normally send to work a party our size?			
What is the fee for that package?			
Can you give us a complete price list that shows all our options?			
Are all the extras—other equipment, games, etc.—that you can bring in on the price list?			
How many hours would you expect to play?			
How many breaks do you take during the party?			
How far ahead do you come in to set up? Do you handle all the communication with the site about setup time, or do we?			
We're thinking of having our party at [name of place]. Have you done parties there?			
Are there any pros or cons to using that room?			
How will you address the cons?			
Who would you assign to run our party? Why would you choose him or her?			
What happens if that person is sick or can't come at the last minute?			
How many bar/bat mitzvahs has that person done?			
How do you like to run a bar/bat mitzvah?			
What do you think sets you apart from other DJs or bands?			
Do you have video of our host doing a bar/bat mitzvah that we could see?			

QUESTIONS TO ASK A DJ/BAND	NAME OF THE DJ/BAND		
Do you have a CD of the band playing?			
What do you do to keep the kids behaving?			
What activities do you find are the most popular with kids? With adults?			
How would you do your own party?			
How can you tell if the music is too loud?			
How many times would we meet? Starting how far before the party?			
Do you have a suggested playlist we should look at?			
What happens if we don't know what we want?			
If my child wants some dance lessons, can you provide them?			
What are your payment terms?			
Do you accept credit cards?			
What is your cancellation policy?			
How long have you been in this business?			
How much of your business comes from referrals?			
May we have references we can speak to?			
Notes, thoughts, follow-up plans			

QUESTIONS TO ASK A TENT RENTAL COMPANY	NAME OF THE COMPANY		
We're having a party with [number of guests] at [location]. How big a tent do we need or can we fit?			
Would we have a designer working with us to iron out all the details?			
Have you put up tents in that space before so you know their policies and know exactly what will fit?			
If not, could you go to the location to measure? Would that cost extra?			
Do you have different levels of quality in tents? What are the ballpark prices for the different ones?			
What type do you recommend for this event?			
How comfortable will it be if there's extreme weather (rain, heat, cold)?			
We've all been at tented events where the ground was wet and everything sank. Can we prevent that if rain is predicted for the week of our event?			
What configuration of tables, dance floor, etc., would you suggest for the size tent you're recommending?			
Can we have a complete price list showing everything you can provide?			
In addition to tents, tables, and chairs, do you rent all the dishes, glassware, linens, and other tabletop stuff?			
Do you have tablecloth swatches?			
What are our options in chair styles?			
What are our lighting options?			
What are some of the more interesting things you rent that no one thinks to ask about?			

	NAME OF THE COMPANY		
QUESTIONS TO ASK A TENT RENTAL COMPANY			
How long before the event do you put up the tent? If we need more time for setup, can you put it up earlier? Is there additional cost?			
How far ahead of the event would you be able to tell us exactly when the tent will be put up? Do you use GPS to track where the tent is when it's en route?			
Do you know all the permit and environmental issues about putting up a tent in the locale we're discussing?			
What's your policy about linen stains, breakage, or damage to your equipment?			
Do you offer or coordinate any other services, like spraying for bugs and renting portable restrooms?			
How would you say you're different from your competitors?			
How long have you been in this business?			
What are your payment terms?			
Do you accept credit cards?			
What is your cancellation policy?			
How much of your business comes from referrals?			
May we have references we can speak to?			
Notes, thoughts, follow-up plans			

TRACKING THE GUESTS

A = Adults
C = Children

NUMBER WHO ARE COMING

Name & Address	Friday EVE		Sat. AM		Sat. LUNCH		Sat. EVE		Sun. BRUNCH		Invitation Sent	RSVP Received	Gift	Thank You Sent	NOTES
	A	C	A	C	A	C	A	C	A	C					

NUMBER WHO ARE COMING

A = Adults
C = Children

Name & Address	Friday EVE		Sat. AM		Sat. LUNCH		Sat. EVE		Sun. BRUNCH		Invitation Sent	RSVP Received	Gift	Thank You Sent	NOTES
	A	C	A	C	A	C	A	C	A	C					

Instructions on Making a Jacob's Ladder Toy

To download, go to www.woodcraftarts.com/jacob.htm or to www.familyfun.com and enter "jacob's ladder" in the search box. Look for a result called "Jacob's Ladder Toy." Remember, hiring a retiree to prepare the wood blocks will make your event more of a mitzvah while lightening your load!

Parent's Blessing of Children

For Sons
Y'simcha Elohim k'efra-yim ve'chi-mena-sheh
May God make you like Ephraim and Manasseh

For Daughters
Y'simeych Elohim K'sara, rivka, rachel, v'leya
May God make you like Sarah, Rebecca, Rachel, and Leah

The Three-Fold Blessing
(Said after blessing all the children)

Y'va-reh'ha Adonai v'yish-m'reha.
Ya-eyr Adonai panav eyle-ha vihu-neka.
Yoda Adonai panav eyle-ha v'ya-seym l'shalom.

May Adonai bless you and protect you.
May Adonai show you kindness and be gracious unto you.
May Adonai bestow favor upon you and grant you peace.

Family Flag Making

Create full-page-sized versions of one or both of these shapes (or download them from www.MitzvahChic.com) and ask guests to fill them in as follows:

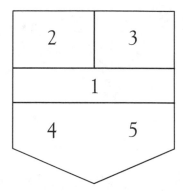
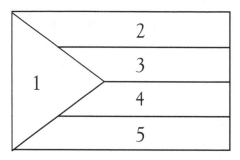

1. Write family name and words that express a key value you live by.
2. Draw picture or symbol of where your family comes from.
3. Draw picture or symbol of high point in your family life.
4. Draw picture or symbol of something your family excels at.
5. Draw picture or symbol of a hidden quality of your family.

Freedom CD/Tape Playlist

Richie Havens, "Freedom"
Alicia Keys, "Someday We'll Be Free"
Dave Matthews Band, "Cry Freedom"
Gladiator soundtrack, "And Now We Are Free"
Bob Marley, "Exodus"
Lauryn Hill, "Freedom Time"
Crosby, Stills, Nash & Young, "Find the Cost of Freedom"
Creed, "Freedom"
Pink Floyd, "A Great Day for Freedom"
Lynyrd Skynyrd, "Freebird"
Wyclef Jean, "Redemption Song"
Braveheart, "Freedom Theme"
The Who, "I'm Free" (from the rock opera *Tommy*)
Paul McCartney, "Freedom"

Uriah Heep, "Spirit of Freedom"
Indigo Girls (or Charlotte Church), "The Water Is Wide"

Manna Recipe

This recipe comes from Daniel Rogov, an Israeli writer who covers food, wine, and restaurants. Visit his wonderful website's manna discussion at www.stratsplace .com/rogov/israel/manna_breakfast.html not just to print out this recipe but also to find a fascinating history and discussion of manna.

8 ounces cake-quality matzo flour, sifted

2 teaspoons dried coriander leaves, ground extremely fine

½ cup boiling water

1 tablespoon sesame oil

2 tablespoons honey (or to taste)

1. Sift flour with coriander. Place flour mixture in a bowl and in the center make a well. Into this, pour the water and oil. Mix into a dough and knead on a well-floured board until smooth and elastic. Divide the dough into twelve equal portions.
2. Roll out a portion of the dough into a 4" circle and brush with more sesame oil. Roll out another dough circle and stack on top of first. Roll the combined circles to make a 6" pancake sandwich. Repeat until you have six pancake sandwiches.
3. Heat a heavy skillet over moderate flame, without oil, and fry pancake sandwiches one at a time, turning once so both sides are cooked. Keep skillet moving to prevent pancakes from sticking.
4. When all are done, separate the sandwiched pancakes. Spread one side of each lightly with honey and fold each single pancake in half and half again. Serve at once or cover with dampened cloth and set aside. Keep warm until ready to serve.

Tent-Building Instructions

Buy 10½ yards of 60-inch-wide fabric. Cut so you have one piece that is 60 inches x 4½ yards (this is the top and back) and two pieces that are 60 inches x 3 yards (these are the sides). Put a hole in (or sew tapes onto) the two corners on one short end of long piece and a hole on each long edge about 58 inches down the length of the fabric (this section is top); put a hole in each corner on one short end of the smaller fabric pieces. To assemble, get four 7-foot poles and weighted bases they will fit into. Screw long screws partway into the top of the poles (to act as fabric "stops"). Secure poles in bases and set them up in a square a little less than 5 feet apart. Hang the side fabric pieces first and then the top and back. There should be extra fabric dragging on the ground—pull it out and weight it in place with stones to give tent more width. "Furnish" with a rug and big pillows.

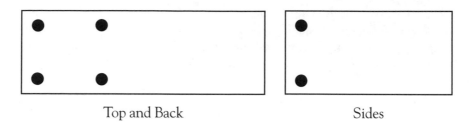

Top and Back   Sides

Appendix 2: Party Resources

Here is the contact information for items shown in Chapter 12. Web information is not included in most cases because things change so quickly in the cyberworld. For more ideas than appear here and in the party chapter, go to www.Mitzvah Chic.com. If you use this list and find a phone number is no longer valid, please let us know.

Beginnings

Tablecloth: BBJ Linen, 800-789-2729. Ask for Coral Lamour

Tuscan Pot With Baby Footprints: See "Crafts for Style and Therapy"

Tree: Ask a tree-trimmer to get branches that look like small trees for you

Battery Twinkle Lights: Barnard, Ltd., 888-5-THEMES (888-584-3637). Ask about Item 15149. Save-on-Crafts, 831-475-2954 or 831-475-1801

Pastel Favor Leaves: Beaucoup, 877-988-BEAU (2328), www.beau-coup.com

16-ounce Tins for Garden: House of Cans, 847-677-2100. Ask for Item 20-16 (4" diameter x 2⅜"). SKS Bottle, 518-899-7488. Ask for Item 5563-07

Label Artwork: Download at www.MitzvahChic.com links

Blank Round Labels for Tins Do-It-Yourself: Desktop Supplies, 800-443-3645. Make your own design on one sheet and then run the label sheets through a copier (be sure to get copier-compatible, 3⅓" round)

Printed for You 3" Round Label: U.S. Box, 800-221-0999

Low-Effort Alternative: Beaucoup, 877-988-2328. Seeds for a garden of edible flowers packaged in a tin with flower bed markers and instructions. No custom label. (See www.MitzvahChic.com links and "Eight Complete Parties That Will Leave You *Farklempt!*" for more ready-to-order alternatives)

Plant a Tree in Israel: Jewish National Fund, 800-542-TREE (8733), www.jnf.org

Bird's Nest & Eggs: Barnard, Ltd., 888-5-THEMES (888-584-3637)

Wire Baby Bassinet: Found locally, but a similar item is a baby buggy at Favor Online, 508-783-8585

Some More Good Ideas: Put on tables anything that means "new": fresh crayons, eggs, little rolled diplomas, baby bottles, seeds

Song

Square Candle: Actually two block candles hot-glued together and wrapped with sheet music. Found locally at Michael's Crafts; you could also use round candles

Singing Table Ribbons: See "Crafts for Style and Therapy"

Blank Lyric Diamond Art: www.MitzvahChic.com links for downloads

Kalimbas: Music Treasures, 800-666-7565. Ask for 8-key kalimba.

Place Cards with Musical Note Dots: www.MitzvahChic.com links for downloads

Place Cards with Audience Heads: www.MitzvahChic.com links for downloads

Drumsticks (imprinted): Erickson Promotions, 856-751-9870

Flowers: Nancy Rackow, Blooms & Baskets, 215-782-8820 (Philadelphia area)

Tablecloth: Kirby Tent, 800-446-1011. Ask for Black and White Stripe

Some More Good Ideas: Irish Tin Whistles (as party favors) from Music Treasures, 800-666-7565. Wooden Drums (as grand prizes or table decor) from High Falutin' Drums, 732-583-2139

Saving Grace

Tablecloth & Napkins: www.weddinglinens.com, or call Cloth Connection at 845-426-3300 and ask for Gold Leaves Organza (I show it over Copper Tissue Lamé)

Ribbon Candles: Internet source only, see www.MitzvahChic.com

Pillar Candles: Bought locally (A. C. Moore)

Frame Charms on Candles: Impress, 206-901-9101. Ask for Frame Charms (I spray-painted them copper)

Books on Rescuers: Museum of Tolerance, 800-900-9036. Ask for *Rescuers: Portraits of Moral Courage in the Holocaust* by Gay Block and Malka Drucker. United States Holocaust Memorial Museum, 800-259-9998. Ask Museum Shop about Block and Drucker book and other books on rescuers

Courage Stones: See Dream Stones or Gem Photo Magnets in "Crafts for Style and Therapy"

Some More Good Ideas: Order invitations from the Jewish Foundation for the Righteous and give support to Gentiles who rescued Jews in the Holocaust, 212-727-9955

Gifts

Cake: Weinrich's Bakery, Willow Grove, PA, 215-659-7062, www.weinrichbakery.com
Treasure Chests & Keys: www.rainbowkeys.com
Cake Charms: Internet source only, see www.MitzvahChic.com
"What Charms Mean" Artwork: www.MitzvahChic.com links for download
Ball Chain Necklace: Jewels Express, PO Box 1753, Spokane, WA 99210-1753
Square Votive Holders: Save-on-Crafts, 831-475-2954 or 831-475-1801
Invitation: See "Crafts for Style and Therapy"

Tips for "Gifts"

Place the ribbons and their treasure between the cardboard cake board and the dish so the charms won't get covered with cake and you don't have to worry about sterilizing them ahead of time.

When trying keys, make sure tooth side is pointing toward the number on lock bottom. Otherwise, even the working keys may not work!

Shine

Tablecloth: www.weddinglinens.com, or call Cloth Connection at 845-426-3300 and ask for Copper Tissue Lamé
Punchbowls: Hubert, 800-543-7374. Ask for Punch Bowl/Cake Set, Item 17720
Shining Castle: See "Crafts for Style and Therapy"
Chair Place Card Holders: Wilton, 800-794-5866. Ask for Chair Place card Holders
Gold Notecards: Paper Direct, 800-A-PAPERS. Ask for Gallery Reception Cards
Ready-to-Print Prayers on Card: www.MitzvahChic.com links for downloads
Copper Luminaria: See "Crafts for Style and Therapy"
Candle Favors: Red Envelope, 877-733-3683. Beaucoup, 877-988-BEAU (2328)
Organza Bags: U.S. Box, 800-221-0999. Save-On-Crafts, 831-475-2954 or 831-475-1801 Favor Online, 508-783-8585
Flowers: Nancy Rackow, Blooms & Baskets, 215-782-8820 (Philadelphia area)

Heart

Tablecloth & Napkins: www.weddinglinens.com, or call Cloth Connection at 845-426-3300 and ask for Celadon and Gold Swirl Damask
Heart-Shaped Balloon: www.MitzvahChic.com to find link
Balloomination Inside-Balloon Light: wowcoolstuff.com, 800-381-6433. Or for lights that go inside balloon with no stick, try balloominator.com, 877-504-3550
Pot: Spray-painted terra-cotta pot with a large calligraphed letter
Streamers: Wide gold ribbon found locally, attached to balloon with double-sided tape

Words on Your Heart Votives: See "Crafts for Style and Therapy"

Clear Heart-Shaped Box: U.S. Box, 800-221-0999. Ask for the large PVC heart box, Item NO2. Fill with Ferraro-Rocher or other gold candy. Go to www.MitzvahChic.com for candy link

Heart-Shaped Place Card Holders: Favor Online, 508-783-8585. Ask for heart place card holders. Wrap With Us, 800-962-0891

Fancy Notecards: Paper Direct, 800-A-PAPERS. Ask for Glitz postcards.

Pochettes for Seed Hearts: Paper Direct, 800-A-PAPERS. Ask for Invitation Pochettes. Go to www.MitzvahChic.com to download inside artwork

Seed Hearts: Andover Accents, 888-783-8518

Heart Stickers: Found locally at crafts store

Glass Tubes Heart-Shaped Tea and Sugar: Beaucoup, 877-988-2328, www.beau-coup.com

Some More Good Ideas: *Music.* Make it a special moment to play/sing at the party Debbie Friedman's rendition of the *Ve'ahavta* (on CD titled *Sing Unto God*). Go to www.MitzvahChic.com links for downloadable song sheet and CD order info
Other Heart-Shaped Stuff. See internet-only ideas at www.MitzvahChic.com
For stationery, postcards, stickers, favor boxes, get catalog from Paper Direct, 800-A-PAPERS
Heart-shaped party favor boxes in white, gold, or silver from local crafts stores
Silky organza bags with chocolate hearts at Favor Online, 508-783-8585
Heart-shaped boxes and organza bags at Papermart, 800-745-8800

Dreams

Tablecloth & Napkins: www.weddinglinens.com, or call Cloth Connection at 845-426-3300 and ask for Brown Velvet Tablecloth and Butter Yellow Napkins

Crystal Ball Centerpiece: See "Crafts for Style and Therapy"

"What Do You Dream Of?" Cards: www.MitzvahChic.com links for download

Envelopes: Staples, 800-3STAPLE (1-800-378-2753). Ask for Columbian Invitation Pastel Envelope Assortment

Dream Stones: See "Crafts for Style and Therapy"

Lucky Stones Etched With "Dream": Carriage House Glass, 866-229-1391 (20 colors, very deeply etched glass)

Organza Bags: Save-on-Crafts, 831-475-2954 or 831-475-1801. U.S. Box, 800-221-0999. Favor Online, 508-783-8585

Wooden Doll: Armoires & "Dream Box" Chest: Found locally at Michael's Crafts and decoupaged with cloud paper and (armoires) "dream" artwork on front, peel-and-stick lettering on top. See www.MitzvahChic.com for links to cloud paper and lettering

Cloud Stationery: Designer Papers, 800-695-3939 x 11. Save-on-Crafts, 831-475-2954 or 831-475-1801

Fortune Cookie Place Card Holder: Asian Ideas, 888-384-3327. Wedding Things, 888-338-8818

Custom Fortune Cookies: WowCoolStuff.com, 800-381-6433. Wonton Food, 800-776-8889

Some More Good Ideas: Check out the Salvador Dalí Museum store for dreamware for party favors, 727-823-3767

"Dream" Quotes

Go to www.MitzvahChic.com and download ready-to-print cards with dream quotes or type in some of these.

Reality is wrong. Dreams are for real.

—TUPAC SHAKUR

He felt that his whole life was some kind of dream and he sometimes wondered whose it was and whether they were enjoying it.

—DOUGLAS ADAMS, *THE HITCHHIKER'S GUIDE TO THE GALAXY*

Those who dream by day are cognizant of many things which escape those who dream only by night.

—EDGAR ALLAN POE, "ELEONORA"

Last night I dreamed I ate a ten-pound marshmallow, and when I woke up the pillow was gone.

—TOMMY COOPER

We need men who can dream of things that never were.

—JOHN F. KENNEDY

To accomplish great things, we must dream as well as act.

—ANATOLE FRANCE

Go confidently in the direction of your dreams. Live the life you have imagined.

—HENRY DAVID THOREAU

Everything you can imagine is real.

—PABLO PICASSO

Hope is a waking dream.

—ARISTOTLE

I have a dream that one day this nation will rise up and live out the true meaning of its creed: "We hold these truths to be self-evident, that all men are created equal."

—MARTIN LUTHER KING JR.

There are more things in heaven and earth, Horatio, than are dreamt of in your philosophy.

—WILLIAM SHAKESPEARE, *HAMLET*

Nothing happens unless first a dream.

—CARL SANDBURG

It may be that those who do most, dream most.

—STEPHEN LEACOCK

If you can imagine it, you can achieve it. If you can dream it, you can become it.

—WILLIAM ARTHUR WARD

Hold fast to dreams, for if dreams die, life is a broken-winged bird that cannot fly.

—LANGSTON HUGHES

A dreamer lives for eternity.

—ANONYMOUS

Reach high, for the stars lie hidden in your soul. Dream deep, for every dream precedes the goal.

—PAMELA VAULL STARR

Whatever you can do or dream you can, begin it. Boldness has genius, power, and magic in it.

—JOHANN WOLFGANG VON GOETHE

Good planning helps to make elusive dreams come true.

—LESTER R. BITTEL

Glory gives herself only to those who have always dreamed of her.

—CHARLES DE GAULLE

To accomplish great things, we must not only act, but also dream; not only plan, but also believe.

—ANATOLE FRANCE

There are powers inside of you, if you could discover and use, would make of you everything you ever dreamed or imagined you could become.

— ORISON SWETT MARDEN

We have got to have a dream if we are going to make a dream come true.

—DENIS WAITLEY

Tzedakah

Jewel-Color Napkins: www.weddinglinens.com, or call Cloth Connection at 845-426-3300 and ask for Lime and Teal Satin Napkins

French Jeweled Toy Box: See "Crafts for Style and Therapy"

Tallit Bags, Mezuzot, Kippot, Spice Sachets: Bought from Lifeline for the Old, a charity of elderly artisans in Israel, www.lifeline.org.il

Products That Support Breast Cancer Research: www.MitzvahChic.com for links

Candy Bar Party Favors That Help Endangered Species: Endangered Species Chocolate Company, 541-535-2170 (Oregon)

Some More Good Ideas: Order invitations from the Jewish Foundation for the Righteous and give support to Gentiles who rescued Jews in the Holocaust, 212-727-9955

Also see "Making Your Event More of a Mitzvah" and www.MitzvahChic.com links for more charity and product ideas.

Appendix 3: Craft Resources

Here is the contact information for items shown in Chapter 13. Web information is not included in most cases because things change so quickly in the cyberspace world. For more ideas than appear here and in the party chapter, go to www .MitzvahChic.com. If you use this list and find a phone number no longer valid or product no longer carried, please let us know.

Soap With a Purpose

Clear Melt & Pour Glycerin Soap Base: Sunshine Discount Crafts, 800-729-2878 (Item MS-DP-SP100)

Soap Fragrance: Sunshine Discount Crafts, 800-729-2878

Soap Molds: Sunshine Discount Crafts, 800-729-2878. Get the combo oval and round mold for individual soaps (Item M-152) or loaf mold (M-153)

Makeup "Prizes": Shop locally to find things small, colorful, and interesting enough. If you want to give soap to boys, put a Susan B. Anthony or Sacajawea dollar in it

Organza, Suede, or Burlap Bags: U.S. Box, 800-221-0999

Gem Photo Magnets

Giant Clear Gems: Save-on-Crafts, 831-475-2954 or 831-475-1801

Magnets: Sunshine Discount Crafts, 800-729-2878, round ¼" ceramic magnets

Word Gem Artwork: www.MitzvahChic.com links for download

Mod Podge: In Matte or Gloss at Dick Blick, 800-828-4548. Go to www.MitzvahChic.com for link

Foam Brush: Dick Blick, 800-828-4548. Go to www.MitzvahChic.com for link
Rusted Iron Sheets: Sunshine Discount Crafts, 800-729-2878. Ask for Rusted Sheets Small
Plain Iron Squares: Metalliferous, 888-944-0909. Ask for 4" Enameling Iron Squares
Cello Bags: U.S. Box, 800-221-0999. Ask for Stand Up Polypropylene Gusseted Bags in gold or silver stripe or iridescent

Party or Sleepover in a Can

Paint Cans: House of Cans, 847-677-2100. SKS Bottle, 518-899-7488. Also available at most home center or paint stores
Party Papers to Make Your Own Label: Designer Papers, 800-695-3939 x11. "Julia Sleep-Over" paper is Balloons and Confetti flat card. "Griffin's Party in a Can" is a Sonburn design found at OfficeMax. See Sonburn papers at The Royal Store, 800-NOW-ROYAL
Rubber Mallet: Dick Blick, 800-828-4548. Go to www.MitzvahChic.com for link
Full Sheet Labels: Desktop Supplies, 800-443-3645
Can Contents:
  Truth or Dare   Internet only, go to www.MitzvahChic.com
  Gel Jewelry/Makeup   Internet only, go to www.MitzvahChic.com
  Hackey Sacks, Sunglasses, Card Games   Internet only, go to www.MitzvahChic.com

Homemade Invitations That Look Custom

See ideas section at www.MitzvahChic.com for additional unique invitation ideas.
Ready-to-Print Invitations: Paper Direct, 800-A-PAPERS
Envelopes: Envelope Mall, 800-632-4242 (in Illinois, 312-666-1838)

Scratch-off Tickets

Scratch Sticket: Impress Rubber Stamps, 206-901-9101

Ribbon and Charm Invitations

Card Sets & Liner Paper: Paper Direct, 800-A-PAPERS, or Marco's Paper, 888-433-5239 (has prefolded square cards and many unusual papers)
Heart & Key Charms: Fancifuls, 607-849-6870. Key is Item 3646 and Heart is Item 1041, but smaller sizes are available
Jump Rings: Fancifuls, 607-849-6870, Item 9917-JR-4
Sealing Wax & Monograms Stamp: Nostalgic Impressions, PO Box 1309, Selden,

NY 11784-1309 (no phone ordering). They also have angel and musical note stamps to use for other theme parties

Organza Ribbon: Papermart, 800-745-8800. Save-on-Crafts, 831-475-2954 or 831-475-1801

Small White Envelopes: Marco's Paper, 888-433-5239. Ask for Coin Envelopes

Clear Box for Mailing Heart Invitation: Veripack, 800-388-4344. Has 8⅝" x 5⅝" size that will fit a normal sheet of paper folded in half; also has three larger sizes. Marco's Paper, 888-433-5239. Ask for Clear Folding Boxes for Cards and be sure to make invitation right size to fit (5" x 7" will fit their #7 box)

Singing Table Ribbons

Fabric: Shop locally for fabric for best sense of color and appearance. My sequined velour was purchased at Joann Fabric

Stitch Witchery: Local fabric store or Joann Fabric, 800-525-4951. Go to www.MitzvahChic.com for link

12" Square White Felt: Buy locally at craft or fabric store, or from Sunshine Discount Crafts, 800-729-2878

Cool-Peel Transfer Paper: Epson Cool-Peel Iron-On Transfer Paper at Staples, 800-3STAPLE

Lyric Diamonds: Download blanks at www.MitzvahChic.com and fill in your own lyrics

Gold Fabric Paint: Joann, 800-525-4951

Dick Blick, 800-828-4548. Go to www.MitzvahChic.com for link

Forest Rain Sticks

Cardboard Tube: Papermart, 800-745-8800. Ask for 2 x 18 or 2 x 24 mailing tubes with plastic end caps

Woodgrain Contact Paper: Tuffware, 800-729-2645. Aubuchon Hardware, 800-282-4393, ext. 2000

Shining Castle

Foamcore: Dick Blick, 800-828-4548. Go to www.MitzvahChic.com for link

Graphite Paper: Dick Blick, 800-828-4548. Go to www.MitzvahChic.com for link

White Sculpey: Dick Blick, 800-828-4548. Go to www.MitzvahChic.com for link

White Tacky Glue: Dick Blick, 800-828-4548. Go to www.MitzvahChic.com for link

Use this pattern or download it from www.MitzvahChic.com links. You need to enlarge this pattern so that each strip of five building facades is 30" wide and a bit less than 10" high. Some copy shops can create output that large; if yours can't, have them copy it in sections and you can tape them together with wide clear tape. The tape will actually keep the pattern from tearing after multiple tracings, so it's a good idea to tape over all lines anyway.

Make two copies of any parts with gray or patterned areas and cut these pieces out separately. The gray pieces are to be cut out of foamcore, the patterned out of white cardboard. If you don't wish to do that, feel free to simplify—the castle should still look nice. The dotted lines on the top edge indicate where I notched the edge to look more like a castle but, again, you don't need to.

Copper Luminaria

Copper: Dick Blick, 800-828-4548. Go to www.MitzvahChic.com for link.
Copper Canisters: A more elegant (and simpler!) alternative to covering soup cans. Kitchen Kapers, 800-455-5567, set of four with lids. Go to www.MitzvahChic.com for link
Artwork: Ask computer-savvy friend or child to create large-type name, or go to www.MitzvahChic.com links to download some clip art
Caulk Adhesive: Home Solutions Crystal Clear Glue, Aubuchon Hardware, 800-282-4393, ext. 2000

Dream Stones

See also Gem Photo Magnets for an alternative type of word stone.

Sculpey: Dick Blick, 800-828-4548. Go to www.MitzvahChic.com for link
Rubber Stamp "Dream": Rubber Stamp Champ, 800 4MY-STAMP. Ask for a hand stamp, "three lines" (.75" image area) size with the word "Dream" in "36-point Monotyp Corsiva"
Sun Face Charm: Fancifuls, 607-849-6870, Item 4453
Organza Bags: U.S. Box, 800-221-0999. Papermart, 800-745-8800. Save-On-Crafts, 831-475-2954 or 831-475-1801. Favor Online, 508-783-8585

Crystal Ball Centerpiece

10" Party Bowl: Save-on-Crafts, 831-475-2954 or 831-475-1801. Ask for Item 07891750071, 10" Bubble Ball Glass Vase
10 x 8 Reducer: Find in aluminum ductwork section of your local home superstore
Floral Pin Frog: Sunshine Discount Crafts, 800-729-2878
Light Source: Shop in local home superstore for Energizer Folding Fluorescent Lantern, or go to www.MitzvahChic.com for link

Toddler Sock Change Purses

Purse Frames: Sunshine Discount Crafts, 800-729-2878. Ask for 2" gold or silver
Socks: Toddler large or extra large; shop locally at Baby Gap; Gymboree; children's, shoe, and department stores. Or go to www.MitzvahChic.com and use links

Baby Albums

Chiyogami or Mulberry Paper: Flax, 888-FLAXART (352-9278)
Baby Shoe Charms: Fancifuls, 607-849-6870, Item 1491
Organza Ribbon: Papermart, 800-745-8800
Save-on-Crafts, 831-475-2954 or 831-475-1801
Brass Eyelets: Dritz Large Eyelet Set from local fabric or craft shop
Bainbridge Board: Local art supply store or Dick Blick, 800-828-4548
Copper: Dick Blick, 800-828-4548. Go to www.MitzvahChic.com for link
Copper Organza Ribbon: For this small quantity, shop locally at a craft or fabric shop
Deckling Scissors: Dick Blick, 800-828-4548. Go to www.MitzvahChic.com for link

Tuscan Pots

Pot: Plain terra-cotta flowerpot from any plant or craft store
Primer/Sealer: Buy Kilz brand spray or liquid paint locally or from DoItBest, 260-748-7175 (if that area code doesn't work, try 219)
Marine Sand: Shop in local aquarium store, as it's expensive to ship. If you can't find it, call Aquarium Pros, 847-328-2233
White Sculpey: Dick Blick, 800-828-4548. Go to www.MitzvahChic.com for link

Changing Masterpiece Frame

Frame: Have fun shopping for this locally in frame, craft, or antiques shops. If you have no luck, call PictureFrames.com at 800-221-0262
Fabric: Look for heavy polished white cotton at local fabric store

Words on Your Heart Votives

Candle Cups: Shop locally at housewares or craft store
Peel-and-Stick: Dick Blick, 800-828-4548. Go to www.MitzvahChic.com for Lettering link
Primer/Sealer: Buy Kilz brand spray paint locally or from DoItBest, 260-748-7175 (if that area code doesn't work, try 219)

Jeweled French Toy Box

Hatbox: Sold at such national chains as Ross and T.J. Maxx, but if you can't find locally, call Hatmonger at 214-828-0639. To make your own, cut a 22" cardboard circle by tying a pencil to a string, tying the string to a thumb tack (shorten string to 11"), and sticking the thumb tack into the center of a 23–24" square of cardboard. Hold pencil so string is taut and draw circle. Cut out. Shorten string 1" and draw a second circle 1" in from the outer edge. Make several cuts from outer edge to the inner line. Fold cut pieces up along line. Cut a piece of stiff cardboard 8" wide and 64" long. Put tacky glue on outside of folded-up pieces of base. Glue this long piece to the base, overlapping and gluing the short ends where they come together. Paint as instructed.

For custom-made to your specifications, contact Sarah's Hat Boxes, 603-547-3840, sales@sarahshatboxes.com
Plant Urn: Shop in your local nursery or home center store
Closet Pole Socket: Local home center store, or contact John Sterling Company, 800-367-5726, for names of retailers
Chandelier Crystals: The Kiefer Companies, 218-736-7000
Primer/Sealer: Buy Kilz brand spray paint locally or from DoItBest, 260-748-7175

Caulk Adhesive: Buy kitchen/bathroom caulk locally or get painter's caulk at Aubuchon Hardware, 800-282-4393, ext. 2000

Acrylic Paint: Dick Blick, 800-828-4548. Go to www.MitzvahChic.com for link

Metal Books

Metal Squares: At Metalliferous, 888-944-0909 or 212-944-0909:

4" iron squares (IR4721)

6" copper squares, 24 gauge (CU1881)

6" brass squares, 22 gauge (BR6039)

6" copper squares also from Dick Blick, 800-828-4548. Go to www.MitzvahChic.com for link

Rust Patina Solution: At Metalliferous, 888-944-0909 or 212-944-0909. Ask for 1 pint Jax Solution Antique Rust liquid (JX1021)

Prerusted Metal: 3" x 4" metal signs (Item 24-7106) at Sunshine Discount Crafts, 800-729-2878

Rub 'n Buff: Dick Blick, 800-828-4548. Go to www.MitzvahChic.com for link

Brass Head Charm: Fancifuls, 607-849-6870 (Item 4467, Large Garden Face)

Brass Frame Charm: Fancifuls, 607-849-6870 (Item 2363, Large Frame)

Caulk Adhesive: Buy kitchen/bathroom caulk locally or get painter's caulk at Aubuchon Hardware, 800-282-4393, ext. 2000

Sizzix Letter Die: Sizzix, 866-742-4447, Fun Serif Uppercase letter

Decorative Paper Punch: Dick Blick, 800-828-4548. Go to www.MitzvahChic.com for link

Contact Paper: Buy locally at hardware store, Target, Wal-Mart, or similar store

Organza Ribbon: Papermart, 800-745-8800. Save-on-Crafts, 831-475-2954 or 831-475-1801

Suede Lacing: Local craft store or Sunshine Discount Crafts, 800-729-2878

Scotch-Brite Pads: Local hardware store or call Aubuchon Hardware, 800-282-4393 ext. 2000 and ask for Scotch-Brite pads, SKU 612065

Sticky Notepads: In 3" x 3" for 4" books or 3" x 5" or 4" x 4" for 6" books, from Staples, 800-3STAPLE

Loose-Leaf Rings: Staples, 800-3STAPLE

Decorating with Fruit

Pedestal: Floracraft Cherub Plant Stand from The Craft Place, reachable online (www.thecraftplace.com) or by fax only (616-454-6827)

Green Styrofoam Cone: Buy locally or call Crafts, Etc., 800-888-0321, and ask for Item C-412Gpp for the 4" x 12" cone

Caulk Adhesive: Buy kitchen/bathroom caulk locally or get painter's caulk at Aubuchon Hardware, 800-282-4393, ext. 2000

U-Pins: Floral Pins from Sunshine Discount Crafts, 800-729-2878 (Item FL-FC-3232)

Lino Cutter for Oranges: Dick Blick, 800-828-4548. Go to www.MitzvahChic.com for link

Seashell Candles

Seashells: Sold at craft stores and shell shops. Must buy in person to make sure they're big enough (4"–5" across)

Gold or Silver Sculpey: Dick Blick, 800-828-4548. Go to www.MitzvahChic.com for link

Caulk Adhesive: Buy kitchen/bathroom caulk locally or get painter's caulk at Aubuchon Hardware, 800-282-4393, ext. 2000

Wicks, Wax Coloring, & Scent: Sunshine Discount Crafts, 800-729-2878. Wicks are Item MICRO-3. Ask also about candle dye and candle fragrance

Microwax: Microwaveable wax from Sunshine Discount Crafts, 800-729-2878, Item MS-CX-MICRO-5 (5 pound bag)

Hand-Colored Tallit

Silk Blanks: Silk Connection, 800-442-0455, 22" x 72" 12-mm crepe de chine (can buy smaller for children)

Graphite Paper: Dick Blick, 800-828-4548. Go to www.MitzvahChic.com for link

Fabric Markers: Dick Blick, 800-828-4548. Go to www.MitzvahChic.com for link

Rope Kippah

Cotton Piping: Joann Fabrics, 800-525-4951. Go to www.MitzvahChic.com for link

Yarn: Shop locally—it's too hard to determine color accurately online.

Decorative Studs: The Rhinestone Guy, 888-594-7999. Ask for nailheads for plain metal shapes or letters; also have crystals of all types

Index